HIGHPERFORMANCE MARKETING

Bringing Method to
the Madness of Marketing

NARAS EECHAMBADI

Dearborn™
Trade Publishing
A **Kaplan Professional** Company

This publication is designed to provide accurate and authoritative information in regard to the subject matter covered. It is sold with the understanding that the publisher is not engaged in rendering legal, accounting, or other professional service. If legal advice or other expert assistance is required, the services of a competent professional should be sought.

President, Dearborn Publishing: Roy Lipner
Vice President and Publisher: Cynthia A. Zigmund
Senior Acquisitions Editor: Michael Cunningham
Development Editor: Karen Murphy
Senior Project Editor: Trey Thoelcke
Interior Design: Lucy Jenkins
Typesetting: Janet Schroeder

© 2005 by Naras Eechambadi

Published by Dearborn Trade Publishing
A Kaplan Professional Company

Printed in the United States of America

05 06 07 10 9 8 7 6 5 4 3 2 1

Library of Congress Cataloging-in-Publication Data

Eechambadi, Naras.
   High performance marketing: bringing method to the madness of marketing / Eechambadi, Naras.
      p. cm.
   Includes bibliographical references and index.
   ISBN-13: 978-1-4195-0823-3
   1. Marketing   I. Title.
HF5415.E39   2005
658.83—dc22

                                                2005013536

This book is dedicated to
Amma and Appa, for their unwavering love and support
For Beena, Kishore, and Kavitha for putting up with me

C o n t e n t s

Accountants and financial executives in some companies have become famous, or rather infamous, for exhibiting misplaced creativity, but marketers have long been sought after, recognized, and celebrated for their creative abilities. Brilliant marketing can be a tremendous engine for corporate growth, increasing profits, and generating excitement among customers and employees. Apple Computers, Virgin, and Nike are examples of companies in diverse industries that have been extremely successful through brilliant and innovative marketing.

Not all marketers are brilliant, however, and not all marketing programs are successful. Marketing as a business function is being challenged as never before. Businesses are finding that the cost of communicating and dealing with increasingly choosy and fickle customers has ballooned in recent years. They are also aware of the increasing complexity of managing customers across multiple channels. The leaders of these businesses want answers and accountability. They are unwilling to treat marketing as a "black box" or an "art form" that defies measurement. Measurable performance results, rather than the politicized, often arbitrary, budgeting practices of the past, will guide future corporate investments in marketing.

As a result, marketing is being called on to rethink the way it operates, and to rigorously defend and validate its actions. Unfortunately, marketers are not well equipped to deal with these challenges. Comprehensive performance management requires an understanding of where money is being spent, for what purpose, and how these activities impact revenue, margins, or other financial measures. Assessing a marketing program's impact based on facts and figures rather than feelings and hunches requires an approach to marketing that is rigorous, repeatable, and predictable from the inside and transparent from the outside. Marketing needs a rational and understandable framework that enables assessment of its actions in an objective way, something that brings method to the madness of marketing.

High Performance Marketing makes it possible to develop such a framework within any organization. It emphasizes measurability and repeatability through well-defined, disciplined processes. It also promotes a learning culture that carefully tests and continually improves the performance of marketing campaigns. High Performance Marketing enables businesses to discard poorly performing campaigns and invest more on marketing efforts that achieve business objectives. It also embraces the use of analytics, customer and market information, and technology in ways that most marketers have failed to fully exploit in the past.

In this book, you will learn about how to leverage the right information assets and enable technologies to achieve strategic objectives and meet well-defined business goals within your own organization. You will also learn how to diagnose your company's performance along the dimensions of High Performance Marketing, and how to leverage these dimensions in a highly effective marketing approach. *High Performance Marketing: Bringing Method to the Madness of Marketing* won't spend much time discussing basics, such as the Four Ps of marketing. We assume that readers have a basic level of marketing knowledge, and we do not want to bore you with concepts you may have picked up in business school or early in your career. In fact, much of what you learn in this book is not taught in any business school today (although we certainly hope that will change in the future).

A PRACTICAL PERSPECTIVE, COUPLED WITH PRACTICAL TOOLS

In writing *High Performance Marketing*, I have drawn on the insights from my professional experiences as a senior marketing executive and consultant with a leading global strategy consulting firm, as well as my perspective as the founder and CEO of Quaero, a unique marketing services company with world-class clients. The case studies in this book are drawn directly from detailed executive interviews and reflect a powerful new shift in organizational strategy and marketing resource management. As these case studies demonstrate, executives can realize extraordinary payoffs if they invest their limited marketing resources in a rigorous and disciplined way. Those investments pay off not only in terms of marketing performance, but also by enabling huge gains in sales and service performance, as well as strengthening pricing power—leading to increased revenues and improved bottom line performance

High Performance Marketing provides a clear approach, actionable methods and tools, and an array of real-world practices to guide executives as they strive to maximize returns on marketing investments and ensure the steady growth of customer value. Working in this area for over 20 years, I have repeatedly seen that enhancing marketing results requires executive leaders to address several dimensions of performance. These performance dimensions allow us to engage in marketing initiatives, generate results, and continually improve over time. *High Performance Marketing* explains these performance dimensions and how to use them to improve performance in a sustainable way

Each performance dimension discussed in this book can be applied methodically and systematically to assess the effectiveness of existing marketing organizations. They also serve as accelerators for change, greatly enhancing a marketing organization's productivity over time. Through the process of more than 150 engagements with Fortune 500 companies across a range of industries, Quaero has developed a logical, useful system for applying these accelerators, called the Marketing Performance Accelerators framework. This book explains how marketing leaders can use this framework to close the Strategy-Execution Gap within their own organizations.

Applying the principles and practices of *High Performance Marketing* enables organizations to sustain high levels of performance despite turnover in management and skilled employees by institutionalizing processes and preserving institutional memory. This approach enables the effective linking of marketing to:

- Financial metrics and approaches
- Operational areas, such as call centers
- Sales and service
- Retail channels
- Sales partners

As a result, skilled marketers learn that understanding and applying this framework will help them frame marketing issues and present solutions effectively to CFOs, COOs, CEOs, and other senior leaders who run the organization. This book explains how companies can use this assessment to focus their efforts at improving marketing performance. Registered buyers of the book have access to the Web version of a tool that provides an interactive and detailed assessment, as well as the benefit of sharing experiences with other readers of the book.

HOW THIS BOOK IS ORGANIZED

High Performance Marketing is organized into three parts. Part One: Performance in Perspective, uses an array of anecdotes, stories and statistics, to lay out the key challenges and demands now facing the marketing organization. Further, it explains the debilitating Strategy-Execution Gap that most marketing organizations confront and provides insight into how to close that gap. Here is what you will find in each chapter.

- *Chapter 1: The Marketing Mystique.* Marketing organizations tend to rely on conventional marketing strategies and "gut-feel" decision making to meet their objectives. Unfortunately, these approaches typically lead to inconsistent performance and leave marketing executives incapable of justifying investments and building confidence. As the compelling case studies in this chapter demonstrate, enterprises can realize far more powerful returns by merely investing their resources in a more disciplined and measurable way. Here, we introduce a framework designed to help marketing executives and professionals construct a rigorous, disciplined, and comprehensive approach for marketing investment that ensures maximum returns and payoffs.
- *Chapter 2: The Strategy-Execution Cycle.* The first challenge associated with generating higher marketing performance lies in carefully assessing current capabilities and competencies relative to business objectives. Uneven, misaligned competencies in various dimensions of performance will undermine an organization's ability to meet its goals, therefore, organizations must assess current levels of performance in each dimension. This chapter provides a rationale for and explanation of this critical upfront analysis.

In Part Two: Dimensions of Marketing Performance, we lay out the key dimensions of our Marketing Performance Framework and provide an array of examples and case studies to validate key points. Our central thesis is that marketers can close the Strategy-Execution Gap, and generate superior marketing performance, through disciplined management of six dimensions or competencies. Here is what each chapter offers.

- *Chapter 3: Decisive Leadership, Actionable Strategies.* Marketing effectiveness demands decisive leadership. Central to these efforts will be the marketing organization's ability to translate high-level corporate strategies and objectives into actionable marketing strategies and specific plans. This plan must enable marketing leaders to identify objectives, invest resources, and leverage key capacities. In this chapter, you learn how to create actionable strategies and a resulting plan that sets clear goals and expectations.

- *Chapter 4: The Measure of Marketing.* Like other operational activities, the measures of marketing performance must be clear, definable, and *central,* not peripheral, to the development and management of a performance-driven marketing organization. This chapter explains the characteristics of successful measurements, and how to set up a measurement process that is credible to business leaders and stakeholders outside of marketing. This chapter also details the performance measurement model we have developed at Quaero, and describes how you can use this model to acquire and analyze data, issue initiatives, report findings, and drive decisions that can improve performance. The case studies here enable you to see the framework in action through the experiences of top clients who have put it to the test.

- *Chapter 5: Out of the Black Box.* Marketers have devised sophisticated ways of managing and measuring advertising, direct marketing, public relations, call centers, and retail channels. Too often, however, we have failed to achieve this discipline in a wider, integrated sense. The continual advancement of established organizations depends on the power and predictability of visible process. This chapter focuses on achieving this goal by developing process discipline. By using the principles and techniques described in this chapter, you learn to create marketing programs based on visible, predictable processes. By doing so, you set up a sustainable framework for continuing success within your organization.

- *Chapter 6: Orchestrating the Organization.* Organizational alignment is about improving the way in which organizational, human, and information capital are orchestrated to achieve the strategic intent of the organization. This alignment can determine whether the organization executes the marketing processes effectively, and it creates a unique value that few companies can replicate. Orchestrating that alignment deals not just with structure, but with skills, motivation, process, and shared objectives. In this chapter, we will discuss the critical actions and components necessary for bringing marketing into alignment with other parts of the organization—including sales, service, and finance—to realize key performance objectives.

- *Chapter 7: Capitalizing on Knowledge.* Effective marketing leaders must establish a disciplined approach toward the management of information assets. The next era of marketing depends on the ability to dynamically learn and adapt, anticipate, and act. This discipline will separate companies that clearly know their customers from those that do not. This chapter explains why customer intelligence will lie at the core of market leadership, and how to organize, integrate, analyze, and apply information as part of a rigorous process that is aligned with your strategic business objectives.

- *Chapter 8: The Architecture of Action.* Marketing technology has enabled companies to greatly enhance the precision of analysis, the productivity of campaigns, and the personalization of customer interactions. Big money has been invested in implementing marketing and customer-oriented technology, but the demands associated with rolling out the technology often have distracted from the larger, strategic mission. In this chapter, you learn how to incorporate technology at the core of a disciplined marketing approach. This chapter explains how your marketing and IT organizations can collaborate successfully to fully leverage the value of technology and turn it into a powerful enabling force.

The final section of the book, Part Three: Discipline and Dynamism, will bring the previous ideas on marketing performance together and discuss the steps that can be taken to drive new levels of performance. Here are some details about each of the chapters in this section of the book.

- *Chapter 9: The Performance Agenda.* The preceding chapters have focused on leading practices in each of the six dimensions of marketing performance. This chapter provides some practical advice on how to make progress within individual marketing dimensions. Case studies speak to the typical one-dimensional improvement projects that organizations must address and demonstrate how to make a business case for each. Specific examples reinforce an understanding of the connectedness that exists among the dimensions.

- *Chapter 10: Discipline and Dynamism.* Achieving high performance is not the end of the journey, it is just the beginning. Maintaining high performance requires sustained vigilance, flexibility, and a determination to continuously apply learning through a disciplined governance process across all performance dimensions. This chapter examines some of the core success factors associated with achieving executional excellence. Recognizing that strategic initiatives will always fall short without a rigorous commitment to execution, this chapter lays out some actionable ideas, checklists, and tools to ensure you are executing to plan.

- *Conclusion: Marketing Frontiers–The Future Is Now.* Companies are investing heavily in Balanced Scorecard, Six Sigma, and other performance-focused initiatives. As the final chapter points out, these efforts will continue to evolve—and eventually converge with performance-driven marketing initiatives. Marketing, however, cannot wait for corporate-wide standards of performance management and measurement. In this final chapter, we speculate about how the coming transformation of marketing will transform markets and economies.

HOW TO USE THIS BOOK

This book tells you how to diagnose your performance and put together a comprehensive system for continuously measuring and improving marketing performance. Included in the text are case studies and examples of how companies have used these techniques to improve their marketing performance in each dimension as well as how the dimensions, interact to reinforce each other and enhance your ability to improve overall performance.

We recommend that you read the chapters in sequence. Because the early chapters set the stage for understanding the dimensions of the high performance marketing model, the capabilities and techniques you learn in each chapter build upon each other. However, readers who have a particular interest in one or two dimensions may find it useful to go back and review specific chapters in detail.

For those of you who are interested in going beyond the concepts laid out in this book, I encourage you to register at the Web site for readers of this book http://www.high-performance-marketing.com. There, you will find more examples and in-depth examination of the concepts presented here and some useful tools to apply these concepts. The site also offers an opportunity to discuss your application of these concepts with your fellow marketing professionals and gain additional insight from the experiences of others. The application of these concepts is often situation specific, and you best learn how to get the most from these concepts by actually putting them into use. Reading this book is just the beginning of an exciting journey into a promising future for marketing and marketers.

FOCUS ON PERFORMANCE

While I was in the process of writing this book, a colleague asked me a question that confounded me for some time: Would the book appeal to aspiration or anxiety? It is an interesting question, one that is sometimes applied to marketing messages and advertisements. It is a question that certainly can be applied to leadership style, but it also defines the relationship between author and reader. Does one communicate most effectively through hope and optimism or threats and fears? Carrots or sticks?

Having reflected on the question, I realize this book is about neither hope nor fear. This is a book about performance, and performance is what you make of it. Some will embrace the opportunity to shine in the light of results and responsibility, while others will wither and wilt in that very same light. The bottom line? If a company is to thrive in the coming years, it must cultivate and build a performance culture. Nowhere is this more true and important than in the realm of marketing.

A work such as this is never the work of one person, despite what the cover might say. Over the years there have been many clients and colleagues who have taught me everything I know about the business of marketing. Fred Phillips at MRCA, Roland Rust at the University of Texas at Austin, and Debbie Starkman at BBDO were all early mentors who instilled a love of information and fact-driven marketing very early in my career. Andrew Parsons, Sandi Peterson, and Mark Leiter have been steadfast supporters since my early days at McKinsey, were crucial in my decision to launch Quaero, and have been there for me since then as well. Many clients have taught me a great deal and gave generously of their time during the writing of this book. Most of them are mentioned by name and quoted in the book, so I will not list them here. Others were prohibited by company policy from being identified, and since their stories are thinly disguised in the book, I don't want to get them into trouble by naming them here. They know who they are and I truly appreciate their help and guidance.

My colleagues at Quaero have taught me a great deal and many of them actively contributed to specific chapters. In particular, Paul Becker suggested the title, Steve Schultz helped write the measurement chapter, Niall Budds drafted the chapter on information assets, and Tangirala Sarma got me started on appropriate technologies, as did Bridgette Rippel on effective processes. Monique Sato helped get the project off the ground and kept it moving in the early days. Without Britton Manasco this book could not have been written. Britton did the secondary research, participated actively in all of the interviews, as well as the lively discussions that followed, and helped shape the early versions of all of the chapters. Sandra Daise worked diligently to ensure that we received permissions for the numerous references and quotes in the book and helped keep things organized.

The idea for the six dimensions of marketing effectiveness was developed by Ken Demma for a workshop we were doing in Monterey, California, for the Customer Think Summit. It later became the framework for organizing much of our thinking, shaping our work with clients, and serving as the organizing principle for this book. Scott Kaufman has done a great deal to make this framework practical and useful through his leadership on the development of MAST with support from Roman Lenzen. I also owe thanks to Bob Thompson of CRMGuru for providing a great forum to meet with fellow gurus from all over the world with a passion for customer relationship management and engage in some very lively discussions. In particular, I am grateful to Paul Greenberg, who has been generous with his support, encouragement, and experience sharing.

John Willig, my agent, educated me about the book publishing business and saved us a great deal of time. Thanks are also due Michael Cunningham at Dearborn for his early support for this project and for assigning Lorna Gentry to work with me on the book. Lorna made the editing process seem easy.

Finally, special thanks are due to my family, who had to live with me while I was working on the book. In particular, I have to thank my daughter, Kavitha, who not only gave up her claim on my time on many a weekend, but monitored my progress frequently. Her constant prodding was a great motivator and this book may never have been finished without that push.

1

THE MARKETING MYSTIQUE

From Discipline to Excellence

"Marketing is the distinguishing, the unique function of business. It is the whole business seen from the point of view of its final result, that is, from the customer's point of view. Concern and responsibility for marketing must therefore permeate all areas of the enterprise."

Peter Drucker, *The Practice of Management*, 1954

Marketing is in the midst of a far-reaching transformation. We as marketing executives are under intense pressure to meet demanding financial targets and establish new levels of accountability. But the sheer enormity of choice and complexity we now face is undermining our ability to meet these demands.

Profound new changes in the management of marketing performance lie ahead of us. The ability to create engaging, enduring and highly profitable customer relationships will separate tomorrow's vaunted success stories from case studies in missed opportunity. But marketing must take an active and assertive role to establish its rightful place on the frontier of customer value.

Tomorrow's marketing leaders will recognize their opportunity now to drive innovation and improvement on the "demand side" of business. They will seize this moment to demonstrate the unmet power and potential that marketing represents. They will then realize just how misallocated, misspent, and underutilized today's marketing capital and resources have been. The stakes, quite clearly, are enormous.

IS THE MARKETING MODEL BROKEN?

Corporations spend nearly $250 billion annually on marketing media in the United States alone.[1] This does not include the cost of non-media expenditures (such as promotions, rebates, sponsorships) and the significant staff and other overhead costs of implementing marketing programs (technology, analytics, data). Added together, the annual marketing costs of these expenditures climb to nearly $1 trillion.[2]

Marketing executives acknowledge that at least one-fifth of their spending is wasted, according to a recent study by the Marketing Leadership Council.[3] This is almost certainly a conservative estimate, one that fails to account for the potential returns to be derived from investing marketing resources more effectively. As a result, many executives themselves are questioning conventional approaches to marketing. In 2001, global ad spending plunged 7 percent to $440 billion (forcing ad agencies to lay off 40,000 employees—19 percent of their workforce).[4] "The traditional marketing model is broken," Jim Stengel, Procter & Gamble's top marketing officer told a room full of ad agency executives in early 2004.[5] Is the model truly broken?

Consider the "Big Three" American auto makers. Between 1995 and 2000, their marketing spending grew at a rate of 21 percent per year and the average cost of marketing per vehicle by 87 percent (to an average of $2,900 per car).[6] However, their combined market share dropped by more than four percentage points. Nevertheless, the car companies continue to be leading marketing spenders—and there is very little evidence that their marketing approaches will change any time soon.

Similar disappointments have played out in the high-growth, wireless communications sector. Despite heavy ad spending, the introduction of number portability resulted in 10 to 15 percent of wireless phone users with T-Mobile and AT&T Wireless switching services within a one-year span.[7] Nor did AT&T's multi-million dollar Super Bowl commercials and its extensive "mLife" campaign apparently do anything to prevent far-reaching corporate turbulence amidst massive customer turnover.

Such trends have contributed to widespread erosion in the credibility and esteem of marketers. Top executives cast a jaundiced eye on their marketing departments' claims, and constantly threaten to cut marketing budgets. According to a recent Accenture survey, 200 senior executives ranked marketing's contribution to their business much lower than those of other functions within the organization.[8] In fact, just 23 percent of executives said that marketing makes a very significant value contribution, compared with 61 percent for sales and 43 percent for customer service. One senior marketing executive we interviewed for this book, who controls more than $1 billion in marketing spending annually, said marketing line items are the "last in, first out" in the budgeting and budget cutting processes, respectively.

THE DIMINISHMENT OF THE MARKETING MYSTIQUE

In recent years, senior executives and boards have demanded greater *accountability* from marketing, which typically indicates some mistrust or lack of understanding of marketing's methods. As with the corporate scandals that rippled through the U.S. economy in the early years of the millennium, it is clear that trust in marketing has been frayed and confidence diminished. Now, corporate leaders are asking marketing leaders to more clearly demonstrate the impact and value of programs in return for vast marketing investments. This press for accountability is a drive for visibility and transparency in a sphere of business activity that is relatively opaque.

Rather defensively, marketing has responded to these demands by placing greater emphasis on ROI (return on investment) measurement. One study from Forrester Consulting involving senior executives from an array of industries found that the executives' most significant current objective is "measuring marketing effectiveness, or ROI."[9] But obtaining this measurement is hardly a panacea. While measurement is an essential dimension of overall marketing performance, marketers are liable to be disappointed by what they learn if and when they do measure ROI. Breakthrough thinking is necessary if we are to elevate marketing performance to new levels as opposed to merely measuring today's mediocre results.

The modern, networked economy lays out enormous challenges for today's marketing organization. The rapid commoditization of products and services has been widely reported and recognized. It is also clear that competition has intensified, often arising from unexpected places to "disrupt" established markets. Less appreciated and under-stood are the demands, priorities, and actions of customers and prospects. Among today's trends, we find:

- *Rising expectations.* The communications and computing revolutions have made it easier than ever for individuals and organizations to rethink their options. Consumers are enticed with offers and opportunities that encourage them to defect, compare, and leverage their bargaining power. Considering that 200 million Americans alone have Web access,[10] it is now common for consumers to use the Web to compare options and prices for automobiles, term life insurance, airline tickets, travel packages, telecommunications services, and almost any other commodity offered on the marketplace today. Sellers must make increasingly impressive offers to attain customer loyalty, as well as provide customers the convenience of being able to purchase "when, where, and how they want." Business buyers, in the meantime, are extracting ever more value from their deal-hungry vendors and are requiring them to run a complex gauntlet of demands.
- *Heightened resistance.* Research suggests that consumers have an extremely negative opinion of marketing and advertising. According to a recent survey from Yankelovich Partners, 60 percent of respondents state that their opinion of marketing and advertising has become much more negative in recent years and 70 percent say they "tune out" advertising more than they did a few years ago.[11] Technological advances such as TiVo (for the television) and "pop-up blockers" (for the Internet) make it easier than ever for consumers to resist marketing messages. Nearly half of respondents say that the amount of marketing to which they are exposed actually "detracts from their enjoyment of everyday life" and 36 percent say they find their shopping experiences "less enjoyable because of all the pressure to buy." Indeed, 60 percent of respondents state that they actively try to "resist or avoid being exposed to marketing and advertising."[12]
- *Unpredictable behavior.* Where once customers could be counted on to complete all of their browsing and buying within a single channel, they are now just as likely to "channel surf." As Paul Nunes and Frank Cepedes argue in *Harvard Business Review*, con-

sumers are "poaching value left and right...They routinely avail themselves of the services of high-touch channels, only to buy the product at the end point of another, cheaper channel."[13] This is leading to an extraordinary mismatch between corporate assets—stores, inventories, agents, and broker channels—and buyer activities. In many cases, these "stranded assets" reflect a costly failure to align corporate investments and customer behavior.

Many of these trends are unprecedented, particularly in their scale and scope. They have left corporate leaders bewildered and uncertain. The customer has become a mystery. Seeking counsel on the future of customer value and growth, corporate executives have naturally turned to their senior advisors in marketing. Unfortunately, they often have not been impressed by the caliber of insight they receive.

Instead of providing clarity on the trajectory of customer behavior, marketing retreats to the security of its organizational "black box." Marketers speak of "awareness" metrics and "share of voice," Web site "hit rates" and promotional "lifts." This is language that the typical Fortune 500 CEO, who these days rarely has a deep marketing background, simply does not value or understand. When marketers describe their programs and strategies, their explanations often obfuscate and confound rather than enlighten. The sad truth is that marketing, as the wizard behind the curtain, simply does not have the insights, perspectives, and strategic directions to offer.

Like academicians in search of tenure, many marketing professionals have sought refuge from change and uncertainty in narrow, specialized and obscure realms of activity. They've learned more and more about less and less. As a result, even as marketing continues to mystify the executive suite, the marketing mystique itself is rapidly fading.

MARKETING'S NEW IMPERATIVE

It wasn't always this way. Marketing and brand management were highly strategic roles for much of the twentieth century. Pioneers such as Procter & Gamble put powerful executives in charge of the brands in their portfolio. The marketing programs were thought of as the "hub of the wheel" and expected to capitalize on what Philip Kotler called the

"Four Ps" of product, price, promotion, and place.[14] In recent decades, marketing has been stripped of much of its authority over operations, and has been defined (or has defined itself) in increasingly tactical ways.[15] As a result, marketing insights, skill sets, and capabilities are no longer seen as strategic to corporate outcomes.

In the eyes of many executives, marketing has become synonymous with advertising or marketing communications. Promotional activities, which often amount to price-cutting efforts, seem to consume an inordinate amount of marketing time, resources, and energy. Consider how this approach has played out in the consumer product goods sector. When scanner data became available in the early 1980s, companies realized the true power of consumer and trade promotions to move product.[16] They ended up greatly increasing trade and consumer promotion budgets. To the detriment of their brands, they trained consumers to be extremely price sensitive. Billions of additional dollars ended up being spent on promotions that were disguised price cuts, corroding bottom lines for most marketers and enriching retailers, without there being any true, long lasting consumer benefit. It wasn't until the early 1990s when P&G introduced the concept of "everyday low prices" that this madness subsided.

As the marketing organization has fragmented, specialized and become more opaque, its relevance and influence has declined. Andrew Abela, former managing director of the Marketing Leadership Council and now Professor of Marketing at the Catholic University of America in Washington, D.C., observes a growing challenge to the notion of "optimizing the marketing mix."[17] While optimization "implies a static environment," marketers are performing in an increasingly dynamic, competitive, and unpredictable environment, he adds. This may be a key factor feeding the demand for change in the marketing profession.

Another factor may be sheer disappointment. In recent years, there has been tremendous corporate interest in "customer-centric" and "market-driven" initiatives. Rightly, companies have recognized that vast opportunities exist for driving customer value and profitability. Unfortunately, many of these initiatives, which typically involved vast investments in Customer Relationship Management (CRM) technology, have proven too large, unwieldy, and unfocused to deliver the results that many had expected.

One IBM study found that 85 percent of organizations, both large and small, have failed to realize expected benefits from their CRM projects.[18] McKinsey found that only 20 percent of U.S. retail banks–some of the most significant backers of CRM–have realized profitability gains as a result of their efforts.[19] Considering that a complex CRM installation can cost more than $100 million and take three years to complete, disappointments and unmet expectations have provoked an understandable backlash. Fortunately, emerging evidence suggests that CRM is starting to pay dividends in many companies that have studied the reasons for their initial failures and taken steps to deal with some of them.

A core problem with many customer initiatives is an absence of clear responsibility. When everyone is responsible for building customer relationships, then no one is. Weak leadership, unclear lines of authority, and widespread dispersal of resources have proven a significant liability in these initiatives. The failure and frustration associated with such "transformative" efforts has perhaps diminished marketing more than any other group within the organization.

While customer-focused leadership and responsibilities tend to be widely decentralized, marketing, by a significant margin, is more likely than any other function or division to have "ownership" of CRM technology projects, according to IBM's research.[20] Although marketers' unfamiliarity and discomfort with technology can contribute to poor performance, technology is not marketing's most important challenge. Instead, marketing's key problem is its inability to assert itself in an area where it is most strategically relevant: customer value. Ultimately, corporate success or failure revolves around the customer. With this in mind, CEOs, CFOs, and other senior executives are looking for strategic guidance on customer trends, expectations, opportunities, and risks. Front-line operational groups, from sales and service to logistics and fulfillment, are seeking customer insight and direction to ensure successful execution.

The question is, where will leadership come from with respect to customer strategy, execution, and value management? Marketing now has the opportunity to step into this critical role. It can regain lost relevance and reassert its leadership in the coming years.

PERFORMANCE-DRIVEN MARKETING

If the moment is seized, marketing can be a powerful force in customer-focused innovation and improvement. After all, marketing has the most strategic and analytical perspective on the customer. It has a unique position in the assessment, cultivation, and management of customer relationships–the organization's most critical assets. Marketing has the power to hear the voice of the customer and operationalize this insight to build new levels of customer value.

Recognizing marketing's vast potential, this book encourages marketing leaders to rise above the tactical silos and boxes within which they have allowed themselves to be positioned. It encourages leaders to envision a larger, more visible and more relevant role for marketing.

Breakthrough approaches to customer-focused growth are more necessary now than ever before. Unfortunately, while many companies have made great strides in the "supply-side" areas of product development, supply chains, and operational management, few companies have demonstrated the same types of innovations on the "demand side" of their business. This lag in innovation creates an opportunity for marketing to step forward and close the gap between strategy and execution that has opened up on this front (you learn more about this issue in Chapter 2, "The Strategy-Execution Cycle—From Assessment to Investment"). As we see it, the central role of marketing is to execute and enhance the growth strategies of the business. The marketing organization's primary objective, in other words, is to drive results by linking the strategy of the business to front-line, customer-focused execution. The realization of powerful business results, however, will depend on a renewed and reinvigorated focus on *marketing performance*. The elevation of marketing performance, in turn, depends on the rigorous assessment and measurement of marketing investments. It is those measures and results, not the politicized and emotionally charged budgeting practices of the past, which will guide the investment of corporate resources in marketing. By clearly identifying the linkages between investments and outcomes, the marketing organization will learn how to maximize returns. It will discover new ways to generate more from less.

Harrah's Entertainment defied the extravagant Las Vegas building boom of recent years, realizing a far greater return on its operational assets through precision marketing and personalized service. With $46 million in profit in 2003, Harrah's became the most profitable casino on the Las Vegas strip. The company's announcement in June 2004 that it would acquire Caesars for $5.2 billion in cash and stock also made it the world's largest casino entertainment company. Harrah's CEO Gary Loveman explains that the company has "come out on top in the casino wars" by carefully measuring the impact of its investments and "using the results to develop and implement finely tuned marketing and services strategies that keep our customers coming back."[21]

Marketing performance also is about transparency and accountability. By actively communicating and reporting results to the rest of the organization, marketing is likely to enhance its credibility in the executive suite. In addition, such openness will open up new conversations, within marketing and beyond it, that enable innovations, productivity gains, and smarter resource deployments throughout the enterprise.

Capital One offers a compelling example of a company that demands accountability from marketing. Indeed, it conducted 80,000 campaign tests in 2003, on everything from marketing copy to price points to credit lines. The company, which recently posted revenue of more than $9.8 billion and net income of more than $1.1 billion, relies on this extraordinary diligence to ensure it is effectively gauging customer priorities and preferences. As Dave Jeppesen, Vice President of Capital One's direct marketing center, puts it, "We are going after the holy grail of direct marketing–to get the right product on the right terms to the right customer at the right time through the right channel. We believe we are pretty far along."[22]

In his fascinating book, *Maestro*, Bob Woodward explains how Federal Reserve Chairman Alan Greenspan actually increased his power and influence by making the activities of the Federal Reserve (the Fed) considerably less secretive than they had been in the past.[23] In other words, he gave Wall Street and the rest of the financial community visibility into the Fed's machinations and thereby stoked greater interest in its plans, decisions, and forecasts. Similarly, marketing leaders have much to gain from openness.

THE MULTIPLE DIMENSIONS OF HIGH PERFORMANCE MARKETING

High performance marketing depends on excellence in multiple dimensions. This book demonstrates that marketers must manage an ar-

FIGURE 1.1 *Marketing Effectiveness Enablers*

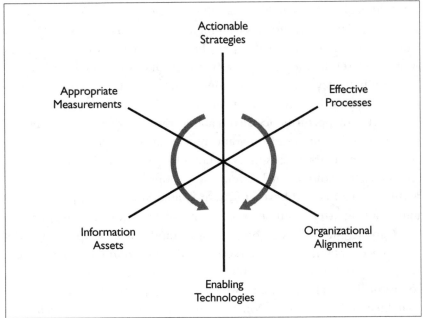

ray of key capabilities, competencies, and enabling forces to realize truly outstanding performance. The following sections introduce and explain in detail six key dimensions that drive marketing performance. These dimensions are shown in Figure 1.1.

Actionable Strategies

Marketers are very fond of strategies. Strategies deal with the big picture, are fun to develop, and play to the strengths common among marketers. Marketing strategies often fail, however, because they were never translated into operational plans that take into account market realities and executional capabilities. We, therefore, stress the need for actionable strategies, with the accent being on the word *actionable*. *Actionable strategies* are those that describe, specifically and in detail, how marketing is going to achieve its objectives.

What does this term mean in reality? Marketing strategies will often aim for what seem like reasonable targets (for example, to increase the penetration of a product by 5 percent within a customer base during the course of a year). Nevertheless, sometimes these strategies do not take into account ground level realities, such as:

- How many customers need to be contacted to achieve that increase?
- How often should customers be contacted, and through what channels and with what messages?
- How much will this communication program cost? Is it in the budget?
- Have past programs been able to achieve this level of increase?
- If these customers own other company products, why haven't they already bought into this one?

One may argue that all this belongs in the realm of marketing planning, which it does. Too often, however, when plans are created and have to deal with the reality of operational and financial constraints, they will take the strategy as a given (which it often is). The plans will focus on target markets and segmentation, advertising expenditures, promotional campaigns, product features and design considerations, distribution targets, and fulfillment plans. These are essential elements of marketing plans, but they beg the question: Does the strategy make sense in the first place?

At one financial services company, which was organized along product lines (as most such companies are), we observed product managers and their marketing counterparts create an elaborate strategy and marketing plan for increasing sales. To achieve marketing's targets and execute their ambitious strategy, every retail branch and call center group had to sell one more product each working day. This sounded very reasonable, until all of the product marketing plans were viewed together. When the company added up the number of outbound calls that were required to achieve the incremental sales, it turned out the branches and call centers would have to almost double their headcount to manage the calls, at a time when they barely had budgets to maintain their current headcount! Marketing strategies all too often do not take into account channel bottlenecks. This is increasingly a problem in these days of multiple, overlapping channels, where a customer can browse on the Web, get advice from a call center, and then actually buy from a store.

Effective Processes

Processes are the vehicle through which an organization can create value and benefits from marketing investments beyond those offered by individual marketing activities. In essence, *effective processes* marshal and manage the resources necessary to meet an organization's marketing objectives. Execution of these processes provides predictability and repeatability of market results. This is the case even as it minimizes the risk that a potential customer segment will not respond as predicted, a product will not be accepted by the marketplace, or a channel will not be as effective as expected. Establishing and following effective processes also make marketing's performance more visible and assessable.

A process also lays a foundation of continuity to ensure a marketing organization can perpetually improve its performance overall. Following established effective processes ensures that marketing's activities are consistent and coordinated, aligned, and executed to create value. Without established processes, marketing departments are perpetually acting in an ad hoc and inconsistent fashion. They diminish productivity and needlessly disperse the company's resources, talents, and energies.

One of the most established processes is that of new product introduction. Most consumer packaged goods companies follow a very methodical testing process, both through market research and in-market testing, to fine-tune a new product's features and marketing program. This process determines, for example, how many coupons of a particular face value should be dropped before a company finally brings a product to market. Using this process has cut the failure rate significantly in one of the highest risk areas of marketing.

Organizational Alignment

Marketing cannot operate on its own. Critical to the success of marketing strategies and plans, then, is the ability to ensure that various operational groups and units within the organization are synchronized. Marketing must span within organizational boundaries and orchestrate the organizational alignment of different functional groups. Whether the focus is a contact center or a sales force, product development or service logistics, marketing must bring the voice of the customer to enterprise operations and ensure the company is always building customer value.

Marketing also must ensure that appropriate talent and capabilities are in place to carry out marketing plans, and that relevant training, development, and reward structures are applied to ensure the success of those plans. Marketing plays a central role in the execution of customer-facing activities and it must have the leadership skills to drive consistent and coordinated execution.

As mentioned in our earlier introduction of the notion of actionable strategies, coordination with multiple, often overlapping channels over which marketing often has no control, is a significant organizational challenge. Aligning internal areas within marketing (for example, analytics and planning, strategy and execution), can also be a challenge. It is essential that marketing meet and overcome this challenge in order for marketing programs to be truly effective.

Appropriate Measures

Marketers are now under severe pressure to measure the impact of their investments. They also need *appropriate measures* to guide their investments and ensure maximal outcomes. Some marketing organizations tend to be quite advanced in the measurement of certain activities and channels. One can find sophisticated market research on advertising, precise direct marketing measurements, or accurate sales close measures. However, marketing organizations generally do not have an integrated approach for measurement, reporting, and investment across operations.

Organizations must devise and implement a comprehensive measurement framework to diligently and rigorously assess various options for these investments, such as alternative channels, media, customer segments, and offers. To the extent possible, these measurements should be linked to key business and financial metrics and connect marketing cause and business effect. Information gleaned from appropriate measurements can help guide judicious investments, enabling marketers to compare and assess outcomes, and then reinvest for maximum returns across these investments. The added visibility gained by these measurements will enable marketers to defend marketing budgets and build corporate confidence. If marketing returns are clear and impressive, they will even invite greater levels of investment.

Information Assets

Marketing success is inextricably linked to the ability to capitalize on the organization's *information assets*. Customer insight is a critical lever that enables companies to engage customers in increasingly powerful, personal, and profitable ways. Knowledge and understanding of customer behavior comes neither easily nor cheaply, however. For years, corporations have been investing heavily in technologies which promised to deliver profound insight into customer behavior and likely responses to marketing solicitations.

Nevertheless, those investments have produced mixed results at best. One reason is that the possession of more information is not necessarily a guarantee of greater insight, particularly insight which is relevant and actionable. The key lies in how information is organized, integrated, analyzed, reported to decision makers, and applied as part of a rigorous process that is aligned with strategic business objectives. This is true not only for information about customers, but also for market information, such as competitive intelligence, changes in consumer lifestyles, or variations in demand patterns across different markets.

Enabling Technologies

The advance of the computing, communication, and database technologies has transformed the nature of company and customer relationships, and this trend will prove even more important in the coming years. Many companies and industries have made impressive strides in using this technology to market differentially across products and customer segments. Most companies, however, have failed to fully leverage the technologies available to them with regard to marketing operations and customer relationship management. The success of marketing depends on ensuring that *enabling technologies* are effectively implemented and integrated, from an organizational and technological perspective. This will require greater leadership from marketing and more effective collaboration with information technology groups.

Developing Dimensions for Maximum Performance

The future of marketing performance, as this book demonstrates, will revolve around the development, linkage, and parallel execution of these various competencies, which together represent the essential dimensions of marketing performance. Some dimensions will prove more critical than others. In fact, some will prove to be key differentiators for marketing organizations and enterprises at large.

Regardless, most organizations must maintain a minimal level of competence and performance in all of these dimensions, just to stay competitive in certain markets. The role of these dimensions in any organization's marketing performance will depend on strategic objectives, industry trends, and other circumstances. While companies need not perform at world-class levels in all marketing dimensions to drive success, they will need to develop their skills and capabilities in each to some degree, excel in a chosen few—and continually improve them all over time.

LEADING THE INITIATIVE FOR CHANGE

As the demand for higher, more visible marketing performance grows, marketing leaders will be required to rethink priorities. This means reinvesting time, money, and resources in initiatives and activities that deliver the highest return. Today's leading marketers are actively reassessing their investments in channels and distribution, media and programs, organization, and operations. Rather than looking for ways to protect budgets, they are seeking opportunities to invest for maximal outcomes. These marketers are taking an active and assertive stance toward performance assessment, not a reactive and defensive one.

However, marketers cannot assume this type of leadership unless they are willing to pursue performance gains with rigor and discipline. Success depends on making the critical linkages between investments and outcomes. It will demand the testing of assumptions and learning from experience. Increasingly, marketing decisions must be grounded in facts and evidence, not intuition and "gut" feel.

This is not to say that there is no room for intuitive and creative thinking in the modern marketing organization. To the contrary, the emergence of greater marketing discipline enables one to realize even greater impact in one's creative endeavors. Just as Procter & Gamble's famous "one page memo" required employees to present their ideas with greater lucidity, the constraints of smart marketing investment promise to liberate new forms of creative clarity.

Rather than dispersing resources blindly, marketing begins to determine which activities are rigorously measurable and which ones must be assessed in terms of nonfinancial goals, and milestones. Brand and image are enhanced, not diminished, by the rigorous management of marketing investments. The power of branding, advertising, and other forms of creative activity, are reinforced and underscored by marketing discipline.

If marketing is to speak with clarity and credibility to senior corporate decision makers, it must speak in a language that is well understood. It must speak of execution, performance, and results, and it must convincingly defend its statements. Marketing must be more than a simple arbiter of campaigns and communication activities; it must clearly show how its investments have built customer and brand value. Ultimately, the marketing challenge lies in demonstrating how customer and brand value contribute to stronger growth, higher profitability, and overall shareholder value. Marketing must make these linkages if it is to realize its full potential, and assume a critical position in the sphere of corporate strategy.

THE PERFORMANCE CULTURE

One way or another, marketing leadership *will* emerge. Such leadership is central to success in an era of customer-focused business. As operational efficiencies and other "supply-side" differentiators are progressively eliminated through competition, companies will increasingly turn to the "demand side" of business as the next frontier of differentiation, growth, and profitability.

One study of 700 CEOs by the Conference Board in 2002 found that "customer loyalty and retention" was their leading management concern.[24] CEOs also are deeply concerned about growth. In a recent survey conducted by Bain & Co., 87 percent of CEOs said they face a more difficult growth environment than they've ever experienced in the past.[25]

As such surveys and studies demonstrate, marketing challenges rank at the top of the CEO agenda. Unfortunately, executive surveys also demonstrate the low credibility and esteem accorded to the marketing function. Marketers tend to be perceived as profligate spenders rather than diligent investors. At a moment when marketing is most valued strategically, it is least valued organizationally.

Senior decision makers "already see their most important challenges as marketing ones—they just don't believe marketers themselves can confront them," writes Nirmalya Kumar in his recent book, *Marketing as Strategy*.[26] "CEOs know that their firms must become more market-oriented, market-driven, or customer-focused. But a true market orientation does not mean becoming marketing driven; it means that the entire company obsesses over creating value for the customer and views itself as a bundle of processes that profitably define, create, communicate, and deliver value to its target customers. Only demonstrated customer value can assure firms of fair, perhaps even premium, prices and customer loyalty."

While the value of "marketing as a mind-set" may be on the rise, it's not apparent that companies can reach their business objectives by simply making marketing "everyone's job." High performance marketing, as our research and analysis in the course of producing this book suggests, demands real leadership as well as clear accountability.

The real question is whether that leadership will come from within marketing or from the *outside*. In some cases, marketing may lack the strategic perspective, organizational credibility, discipline, capacities, and skill sets to rise to the targeted level of performance on its own.

Cathy Bessant, chief marketing officer of Bank of America, is particularly insightful on this question. Bessant ran a large regional operation for the bank prior to assuming the CMO role, but had no formal background in marketing. In a recent interview, she told us her operational expertise is a "huge advantage" in terms of ensuring high marketing performance.[27] "You can almost make the case that marketing is too important to be left to professional marketers," she said. "We have, in fact, completely shifted the leadership within marketing from functional experts to business people. My direct reports do have marketing expertise and knowledge, but they do not have classical marketing backgrounds."

On a similar note, Harrah's CEO Gary Loveman says that his success in the transformation of marketing was linked to his initial entrance into the organization as chief operating officer. He contends this gave him the credibility to persuade property general managers and others with line authority to implement new marketing and service approaches. As he recently explained, "I had the authority to say, 'Here's how we're going to engage customers.'"[28] Most of the conventional work of marketing executives is done internally, as he sees it, "trying to get the P&L people to let them do things. That's a losing battle. And if you're trying to generate change in an operating business, it's almost a doomed exercise."

Indeed, Loveman had the authority to completely overhaul his marketing staff to drive the development of the company's Total Rewards loyalty program. "We took out the entire corporate marketing department," he says. "They were never going to get our program where it needed to go. They were never going to build the decision tools or be able to plot out the mathematics of this program the way we needed. So we brought in the kind of people we have now, who have the horsepower to do this kind of work."

Bessant and Loveman are examples of effective change imposed on marketing from the "outside." While external leadership may, in fact, be necessary to drive such change in many cases, this book also recognizes the power and potential of marketing to drive such advancements and innovations from within.

MOVING INTO THE NEXT ERA OF MARKETING

This book foresees a larger, more prominent role for marketing in the coming years. High performance marketing, in fact, is critical to success in a market-driven company. The mystique of marketing, however, must not lie in its inscrutability; that is, a one-way trip to irrelevance in this era of increasing transparency. Rather, marketing's mystique– the perception of heightened value and importance–must be found in its clear, definable impact on performance and results. The next era of marketing, therefore, requires the marketing organization to rise to a new and higher level in the enterprise. At the same time, it obliges marketing leaders to develop a more collaborative, cross-functional perspective. Here are some of the key facets of marketing in this new era.

- *Marketing as catalyst.* Marketing's future is, in part, a matter of dynamically engaging markets and customers to drive perpetual learning, improvement, and innovation. Corporate leaders are increasingly struggling to determine how best to generate value among their customers. Marketing executives are in a unique position to advise and confer with these senior decision makers in management, finance, and accounting, product development, and operations on the positioning and roll-out of customer-focused initiatives. Marketing, which has an analytical perspective on customer value, is in a position to drive these initiatives and ensure the "voice of the customer" is always clearly heard.

- *Marketing as boundary spanner.* While it's common for marketers to believe "the magic is in the mix" of media and programs, there is also magic in the mix of aligned functions and operations within the organization. Marketing leadership, in this case, is about spanning the boundaries and leveraging the full capacities of the enterprise to build customer value. Whether in the internal mix of enabling forces or the external mix of customer engagement programs, marketing has the opportunity to integrate, cross-pollinate, and orchestrate key resources to ensure high performance is obtained.

- *Marketing as force multiplier.* By leveraging strategic and operational plans, organizational competencies and capabilities, processes and metrics, customer insights and technologies, marketing has the resources necessary to realize high-impact results. Such levers enable marketing to play a key role in customer-focused advancement. But successfully realizing this potential will take clarity and discipline. As an array of stand-out companies are now demonstrating, marketing leaders can realize impressive outcomes by rigorously linking strategy and execution. As we later discuss, marketing can become an increasingly powerful "force multiplier" for the enterprise if senior marketers strive for unmatched performance.

Interest in "performance management" is at an all-time high at present, as companies search for new levels of insight and accountability, as well as new payoffs that such transparency should produce. Companies are investing heavily in Balanced Scorecard, Six Sigma, and other performance-focused initiatives. These efforts will continue to evolve and will eventually converge with marketing performance management practices.

But marketing cannot wait for corporate-wide standards of performance management to emerge. Marketing executives must step up to the current challenge and offer a powerful solution. We must embrace rigorous and resolute decision-making approaches, and must maximize the returns on our marketing investments. Successful marketers are taking steps now to build a performance culture within their organization.

2

THE STRATEGY-EXECUTION CYCLE

From Assessment to Investment

> *"The desire, and the ability, of an organization to continuously learn from any source, anywhere–and to rapidly convert this learning into action–is its ultimate competitive advantage."*
>
> **Jack Welch, former CEO, General Electric**

It has become conventional business wisdom that a debilitating gap separates strategy and execution. In recent years, management theorists have lamented our inability to turn strategy into disciplined action, and their concerns have received much attention. Less understood is the way in which front-line execution influences—or should influence—strategic decision making.

When we look closely, we discover that the business world is full of ivory tower strategists. Too often, strategic mandates are handed down from the most senior levels of the enterprise only to fall apart in the implementation phase. The absence of rigorous planning, robust communication, and diligent follow-up dooms many strategies to failure on the front-lines. Enterprises fall into the "Strategy-Execution Gap" when they fail to build a dynamic and effective link between their business strategies and the execution of those strategies. Whether businesses fail to act on their strategic plan, learn from the results of enacting their plan, or both, the outcome is almost certain to be disappointing—perhaps devastating over time.

But the solution to the problem isn't simply a matter of more effectively translating strategy into execution. It also lies in the ability of organizations to learn from experience. In other words, new strategies must be guided and refined by execution. Through action and experience, we strengthen our strategies. Smart decisions are driven by relevant facts and evidence as well as market experiments and continuous learning.

Success comes when strategy and execution are closely intertwined. Strategy drives execution and execution informs strategy. Whether one is thinking in terms of product innovation, supply chain efficiencies, or customer value growth, the objective is to close the gap, thereby linking strategy and execution in a self-reinforcing loop. We call this the *Strategy-Execution Cycle*. This cycle is illustrated in Figure 2.1.

When the concept of the Strategy-Execution Cycle is applied to the growth of revenue, profit, and customer value, marketing becomes a central factor in performance. The role of marketing, after all, is to acquire, grow, and retain customers. To achieve its mission, the marketing organization must perform with great skill, precision, and effectiveness. Marketing must drive execution and inform strategy. At its best, the marketing organization enables the enterprise to effectively *engage* its markets—customers and prospects alike—and *learn* from them. Indeed, the dynamic interplay of strategy and execution depends on a foundation of strong marketing performance. Marketing performance, however, depends on a core set of capabilities and competencies. As we explain in this chapter, these dimensions of performance lie at the heart of every world-class marketing agenda.

FIGURE 2.1 *The Strategy Execution Cycle*

CLOSING THE STRATEGY-EXECUTION GAP

The challenges associated with addressing the Strategy-Execution Gap are particularly acute in the field of marketing. In many firms, marketing suffers from its own credibility gap. There may be many questions about how marketing invests its resources and what returns it is capable of delivering. In some cases, the marketing organization may have become opaque and bewildering from the perspective of senior leaders and other groups. In other cases, the marketing organization may simply have become synonymous with tactical communications or advertising campaigns or, in sales-driven organizations, a sales support function. Even when marketing plays a strategic role and commands a great deal of respect within the enterprise, there is always an opportunity to attain higher levels of performance. Few companies, if any, excel in all of the capabilities and competencies that high performance marketing demands.

But let's be clear. The objective here is not merely to improve, or even transform, the marketing organization. That is a means, not an end. Rather, the marketing organization's objective ought to be to employ all available resources and capacities to drive profitable growth and shareholder value. It is clear, definable, and measurable performance that will elevate marketing—nothing else.

In the context of customer-focused and demand-side initiatives, marketing is in a powerful position to help close the Strategy-Execution Gap. It is in a position to listen to the voice of the market and learn from customers. It can span conventional boundaries, advising and enabling the rest of the enterprise to act on what it discovers. It can also facilitate and enhance the decisions, interactions, and relationships that will drive growth and profitability.

One of the most significant hurdles that must be overcome involves confronting organizations that have become rigid and complacent. Organizations that are designed to execute one kind of strategy cannot always (in fact, seldom do) turn on a dime to effectively execute a new strategy. Depending on its magnitude, a necessary change can require significant reorganization and retooling to execute with great effectiveness.

Consider an organization that is superb at customer acquisition. It may have to make far-reaching, even wrenching changes in order to become equally skilled in customer retention. Similarly, an organization that is superb at new product development can sometimes be very poor at the other end of the development cycle (for example, at pruning its product line of unprofitable or unsuccessful products). The inherent flexibility or inflexibility of any organization can determine the amount of time, money, and effort the organization will need in order to refocus and reorient its operation to achieve new strategic goals.

Our research suggests that many companies have a problem translating customer-focused strategy into execution. Resources in these companies are often allocated based on past experience (and by the needs of senior managers to protect their budgets and fiefdoms), rather than being driven by the need to meet new strategic goals. Such companies often fail to commit to and measure appropriate goals of specific programs and overall spending. This lack of structure and planning often leads to lackluster performance or arguments about whether a marketing initiative was, in fact, a success or not.

At the same time, companies have difficulty learning from execution and using that knowledge to enhance strategy. They struggle to analyze the impact of their actions and enhance their decision-making approaches. In such companies, execution may be quite strong; it's their strategy and, more specifically, their inability to learn from experience, that is unimpressive. Closing this learning loop is an essential step for any organization that wants to achieve its greatest potential performance.

Marketing has the opportunity to become a catalyst for and an implementer of vital change. Marketing can enable the enterprise to more deeply align itself with its customers and prospects, ensuring the development of compelling experiences and mutually rewarding relationships. Marketing has the potential to become a critical, interconnecting force between organizations, their customers, and market opportunities. It can provide vital insight and assistance to guide the rest of the organization safely across the Strategy-Execution Gap.

The Marketing Performance Framework

We at Quaero believe that marketing results are driven by a set of core performance dimensions. Each marketing dimension represents a distinct competency or capability that marketing must demonstrate in order to generate outstanding performance. Commitment to the development of these core dimensions ensures that outstanding performance is repeatable and predictable and can be improved upon year after year. High performance in these dimensions drives better strategic decisions and more capable and successful execution. By leveraging these capabilities and competencies, marketing can generate visible results.

To help our clients close the Strategy-Execution gap, Quaero has developed and used the Marketing Performance Framework. This framework can be used to break down any marketing problem into its constituent parts and assess the dimensions or proficiencies that contribute to overall marketing performance.

Quaero employs this framework to drive high performance marketing. It has proven to be a powerful tool to assess and improve key dimensional capabilities and competencies that contribute to overall marketing effectiveness. It enables marketing organizations to set a baseline for marketing performance, and to determine where they stand. Once the organization has engaged in a full accounting of strengths and weaknesses, this framework provides a foundation for setting priorities and enhancing proficiency and performance over time. The Marketing Performance Framework is designed to drive rigor and discipline, clarity, and visibility. It encompasses the dimensions of performance that generate superior strategy and execution, binding strategy and execution to create an integrated whole.

We developed the Marketing Performance Framework because we wanted to determine how well enterprises could perform without making major additional investments in key performance-focused dimensions. We also wanted to know what organizations could accomplish if new investments were made in the dimensions that were particular bottlenecks to performance and, hence, where the investments would generate the greatest returns. The framework then has the virtue of helping us understand how to best invest both existing resources and incremental dollars. It can help us identify performance chokepoints that inhibit effectiveness.

The framework is made up of six critical dimensions of marketing performance, which you read about in Chapter 1:

1. Actionable Strategies
2. Effective Processes
3. Organizational Alignment
4. Appropriate Measurements

5. Information Assets
6. Enabling Technologies

These dimensions are the essential capabilities and competencies behind any powerful marketing organization. They are the "accelerators" of organizational learning and the "key drivers" of effective action. Organizations can systematically assess each dimension in the framework to determine the effectiveness of their existing marketing department or program.

Though these dimensions are distinct, they are not rigidly separate in their functions. For instance, customer analytics spans the measurement, information, and technology dimensions in most companies. Likewise, appropriate measurements are an integral part of any effective process. The particular power of these dimensions lies in their interconnection, integration, and parallel application. Performance breakthroughs demand consistent and continuous improvement within each of these dimensions. That does not mean, however, that all of the performance dimensions must be built and managed with equal attention. For any given organization, some may represent greater value—and market differentiation—than others. As we recognize the need to improve capabilities and capacities in individual dimensions, we can make appropriate investments in them.

Some companies tend to shine in particular dimensions. Capital One and Royal Bank of Canada may excel in measurement; Dow Corning and Bank of America may be strongest in effective processes; Tesco and Harrah's, on the other hand, are most successful at leveraging information. What separates high performing marketing organizations from their competitors is an exceptional capacity to leverage all of these dimensions across the board, while playing to particular organizational strengths.

Quaero's Marketing Performance Framework was developed over five years, through more than 150 engagements with Fortune 500 companies across a range of industries. We have found that this framework is very applicable and useful to any company that invests significant resources in marketing. We have deployed this framework through the use of MAST™, Quaero's "Marketing Performance Assessment Survey Tool." Through the use of this tool we are able to help companies define, clarify, and more accurately determine where marketing investments must be made to generate maximum returns and results.

Assessing Dimensional Performance with MAST™

Companies must periodically assess their dimensional proficiency if they are to ensure they have the marketing capabilities and competencies to close the Strategy-Execution Gap. The challenge marketing leaders face lies in understanding and evaluating the state of current proficiencies. Based on these findings, organizations can determine how to enhance effectiveness and make the investments necessary to maximize overall performance.

Initially, Quaero's methodology was to ask our clients (typically, senior marketing or IT executives) to position themselves, based on a self-evaluation, on each dimension. We would also do a subjective evaluation based on our own observations and experience with other clients in the same industry or with similar characteristics.

We quickly realized, however, that this form of evaluation wasn't always effective. Our clients often had no context in which to judge themselves on any of these dimensions; their experience was often limited to a few companies or, in some cases, divisions within the same company. Additionally, while our consultants have exposure to a broader range of companies and industries, they did not always have equal competence across all dimensions. In addition, it was difficult to move beyond the initial assessment to a diagnosis of the underlying factors that were driving the assessment findings. Finally, it was very difficult to measure improvements on an objective basis over time. Recognizing these challenges, we developed MAST as a comprehensive assessment tool and methodology.

Based on our experiences and accumulated knowledge, the MAST survey encompasses more than 200 questions that span all the dimensions of marketing effectiveness. The survey is administered interactively (responses to one question determines whether a follow-up question is necessary) on the Web, and there is an executive version for higher level executives, both inside and outside of marketing, who may not be familiar with the details of marketing operations. We also tailor the survey to segments within marketing when necessary. For example, there is no point in asking creative staff detailed questions about analytical processes. Typical response times can vary from 20 minutes for the executive version to an hour and a half for the entire survey.

As a standardized tool that can be used repeatedly to plot improvement over time, MAST can be used to highlight differences in percep-

FIGURE 2.2 *MAST Gap Identification by Performance Dimension*

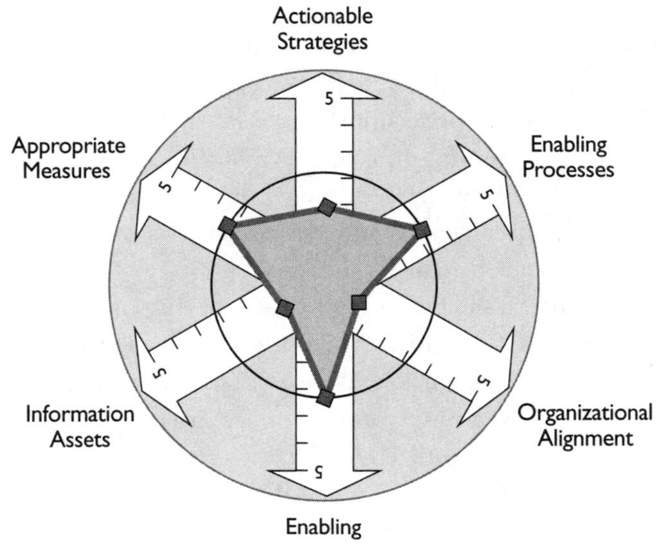

tions across employee groups and different levels. For example, business analysts may view the robustness of a business process differently from product managers, while managers will often perceive performance differently from those who report to them. These differences highlight misalignments, process breakdowns, and opportunities for improvement, as illustrated in Figure 2.2.

MAST is flexible in that not all dimensions have to be measured, especially if the organization doesn't want to open up a particular set of issues or has a high degree of confidence in an area. This flexibility played a key role in the use of this tool by one of our clients. The company had a marketing department that had grown rapidly over a two-year period from a group of 50 to a group of 130 people—growth that mirrored that of the business units. As growth slowed, the company was looking for efficiencies within the organization. There was some conflict about whether marketing was a cost center, and thus a target for cost cuts, or a revenue driver in a maturing environment, and therefore something to be invested in even more heavily. Sound familiar? The company also had some questions about the marketing organization's alignment with the channels and product areas.

FIGURE 2.3 *Perceptions of Marketing Effectiveness*

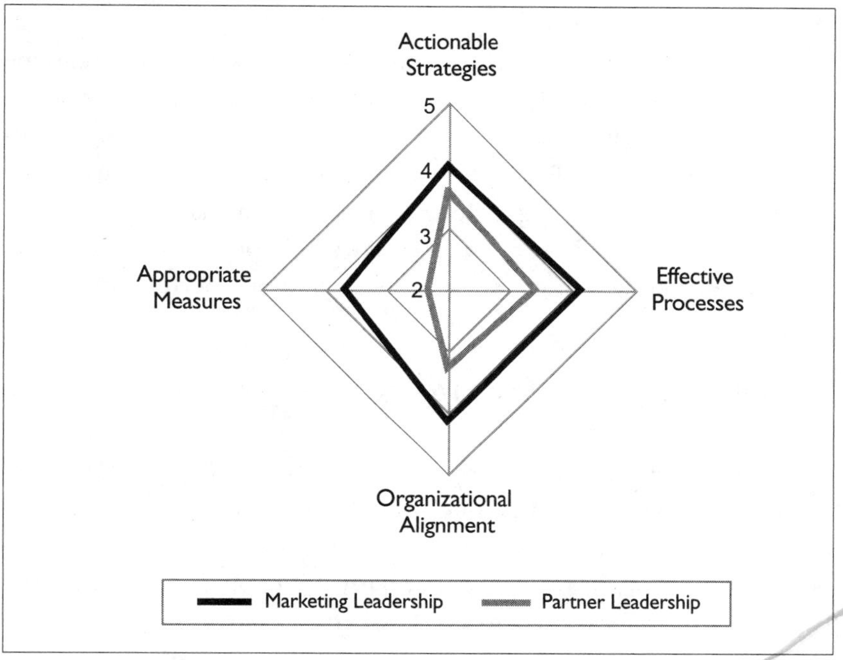

In this situation, technology and information assets were not a major issue, so the organization used MAST to rate only the remaining four marketing performance dimensions. As Figure 2.3 shows, in each of the four dimensions, marketing executives rated themselves higher than did the Partner Leadership (executives who were internal clients for marketing and who funded the marketing budget). The gap was widest in the area of appropriate measurements and the two groups could not agree on whether marketing programs were measured well. This, of course, meant they could not, agree on which programs preformed well either.

It can be very difficult to bridge the perceptual gap in the other dimensions when two groups do not agree on basic measurements. In this particular case, the recommendation was that the marketing group devise a set of measurements that were credible for the business executives. This measurement set could then help frame the discussion for future improvements. Once appropriate measurements were identified as a problem area, the responses to the individual MAST questions were analyzed to understand which areas within measurement were driving the differences in perception. This, in turn, helped to identify specific measurement priorities which, when addressed, would help to bridge the gap between the two groups.

As this example illustrates, it is often necessary to drill down into the individual dimensions of an organization's marketing performance to analyze the underlying factors necessary to effect change. Using a detailed tool such as MAST helps to pinpoint specific areas that are contributing to weakness or strength along a particular dimension. These areas can then be better understood, diagnosed, and improved to move a company to a higher level of marketing effectiveness and performance.

DIMENSIONAL ANALYSIS: A CASE STUDY

Even without the use of a specific tool such as MAST, the Marketing Performance Framework can be used to improve marketing performance. One of our earlier client experiences, which preceded the development of MAST, provides a particularly apt explanation of how the framework describes and drives marketing performance in multiple dimensions.

The client was a prepaid mobile phone company, less than five years old and growing very rapidly. It met its growth goals by adding new distribution channels—new stores and chains that sold its phones and prepaid phone cards. Based on this strategy, the company doubled in size annually for approximately five years.

At the six-year mark, the company hit a wall and growth stopped abruptly. The growth strategy, which revolved around adding new distribution outlets to meet aggressive performance targets, had worked effectively in prior years, but had now reached a logical end point. The major retail chains had all been signed up and sales leveled off. Then, the company discovered its subscriber base was actually in decline. Not only was this no longer a high-growth company, it had become a shrinking one. Now the company was facing financial catastrophe.

Assessing the Problem

What happened? It happened that there was one big problem that no one noticed amid the excitement of rapid growth. While the company was acquiring new customers at a rapid rate, it was also experiencing an enormous amount of customer churn. Ultimately, the customer attrition rate began to eclipse the rate of new subscriber acquisitions, therefore resulting in a declining subscriber base.

Management had acclimated itself to rapid growth and quick decisions. The culture of the company was to introduce new programs first and ask questions later. Without the benefit of any analysis, senior executives assumed that the company must be suffering from a pricing problem. Therefore, they instructed all their customer call center people to give away free minutes any time someone called to disconnect or complain. The potential cost of this giveaway was nearly $1 million per month and there was absolutely no evidence that the program would work. There was no testing of the program, nor was there any historical data suggesting customers were price sensitive. (Prepaid programs tend to be more expensive than traditional annual contract plans with postbilling.)

The company did not have good information systems to help assess its decisions. When Quaero was hired to assess and address the problem, our first task was to build an improvised customer database. This information enabled us to identify patterns and to test hypotheses. We wanted to know which customers were churning and why. Management believed that some of the newer subscribers who bought phones with fewer minutes on their initial card were causing some of the additional churn. Contrary to management's hunches, however, we did not find these subscribers to be churning at a faster pace than other customers.

Instead, there was a correlation between rapid churners and specific distribution channels, particularly the ones that had been added most recently. The cards that were purchased with the phones were only valid for 60 days. After that period, that customer needed to buy a new card to keep the phone active. Unfortunately, no one in the new mass merchandise distribution channels explained this to many of the customers, since these new channels depended on customer self-service. The instructions that came with the phone and card made it very clear that the cards were only valid for 60 days, but, unsurprisingly, few people bothered to read the instructions. Many people bought the phones for emergencies and had no cause to determine whether they were working or not. So, these customers were not really churning by choice. They simply let their cards lapse because they had not been properly informed of the expiration dates at purchase.

Finding a Resolution

Recognizing this dynamic, the company launched a new strategy that would revolve around increasing retention and reducing churn. The prior, ill-conceived approach had been to throw money at the problem by giving customers rebates or benefits. What we found when we looked at the data was that there was a communication problem, not a pricing issue. Customers merely needed to be reminded that they would need a new card after 60 days.

With this insight, the company launched a new communication program. When customers signed up for the product, the call center operators were trained with incentives to obtain customer's e-mail addresses. All customers received a set of e-mail reminders as the expiration date neared and after it passed, if they still had not renewed. The e-mail response rate was greater than 30 percent, which is an extraordinary outcome in direct marketing terms. Meanwhile, the company also launched an outbound phone campaign, both as a control group to benchmark the results of the e-mail campaign and as a way to reach people who did not have e-mail addresses. This outbound phone campaign generated significantly less response, but was still successful enough to pay back its costs. Without money or discounts, the company was able to reduce churn by 70 percent in six months. The value of these strategic campaigns to the company, in terms of saved revenue, was in the hundreds of millions of dollars. The cost was significantly less than the $1 million per month it was preparing to spend on potentially useless promotions.

Happily, the company succeeded in achieving this remarkable turnaround in a short period of time. Central to this success was the CEO's recognition, driven by necessity, that the company required a new strategy and that it must be executed with great effectiveness. He was able to knock heads and ensure that marketing, merchandising, operations, and IT all came together to solve the problem.

This was a major crisis and it could well have sent the company into a downward spiral of lost customers, revenues, and profits as well as layoffs and declining morale. Instead, the company rose to the occasion and demonstrated the leadership to execute a new strategy in a disciplined fashion. Forced to confront a disastrous potential future, this company at last found what it took to close the Strategy-Execution Gap.

Assessing the Marketing Performance Dimensions

As this study illustrates, the strategic direction of a company can change very quickly and very dramatically. Within a period of only a few months, the company went from an aggressive distribution channel strategy to a strategy that was primarily focused on retaining existing customers, while attempting to continue to sell additional subscribers through existing channels.

The execution of the strategy, however, required access to the right information and measurements—access made possible by some short-term technology enablement. The company had to design new processes including revised call center scripts, and realign the organization to meet their objectives. This organizational alignment included bringing on external call center services with expertise in customer retention, as well as training and motivating the company's own service employees in customer retention. The alignment also involved strengthening the internal positioning of the marketing and customer service organizations vis-à-vis the merchandising organization, which had traditionally called the shots. This change resulted in some high level resignations and made for some spirited company leadership meetings.

As you can see, an actionable strategy was critical to the success of this turnaround. Because the company's overall strategy had changed from a focus on customer acquisition to retention, the organization had to rapidly develop a plan that would drive new behaviors. The plan would enable the organization to realign its activities and refocus its resources toward new objectives. In this case, the new plan revolved around customer retention. The company was under severe pressure to act quickly, but it had to act diligently as well. The CEO was able to step back, even in the heat of the crisis, and recognize that shooting from the hip, which is what his management team was inclined to do, would be very risky and might even be counterproductive.

Effective execution of the strategy also required a new set of appropriate measurements. In the past, management had been very pleased with the net subscriber increase levels, without realizing that so much of the overall gain from increased distribution was being lost through the back door in lapsed subscribers. Management also was focused on average revenue per subscriber, which is a very important measure in the mobile phone industry. However, the company was not paying particular attention to the length of time people stayed on as customers. As a result of its new measurement strategy, the organization decided that management would track new subscribers and the number of disconnects and lapsed subscribers separately, rather than just tracking the net change in subscribers from month to month.

While it was important to ensure the management team was identifying the correct metrics, the ability to leverage information assets also was critical. We were able to improvise a database in short order that allowed the company to identify lost customers and understand their behavior in the channels. Ultimately, the database gave the company the right information assets to identify the key variables behind customer churn. We looked at geographic trends. We looked at product features. We also looked at the stores in which customers purchased their plans. This final variable turned out to be the relevant one. The data reflecting where customers made their purchases was critical for assessing what was leading to this company's reversal of fortune.

It has been our experience that information assets in many companies are not always readily accessible to the business leaders charged with making critical decisions, even if it does exist somewhere in the organization. We were fortunate in being able to pull together relevant information in fairly short order. This is not always possible, especially in cases where top management is not willing to force the issue. Our ability to quickly provide these information assets was possible only after we built this improvised database. The database had to be built rapidly, within a period of a few weeks. Building the database in such a rapid time frame was only possible because this was a critical issue for the entire company and the CEO made it a top priority, enabling us to bypass the usual turf battles between marketing and IT.

Of course, the challenge didn't end with obtaining information. Once the company's key strategic challenges had been identified, it became important to put effective processes in place. The company now knew which customers were churning. The question was how to retain them.

First, the company developed a program that motivated call center reps to capture valid e-mail addresses. Then, it designed a new process to communicate with customers. E-mail was found to be both more effective and far less expensive than outbound phone contact. So, the new process revolved heavily around e-mail communication, supplemented by outbound phone calls where necessary. In addition, the Web site had to be redesigned to allow subscribers to buy new cards directly from the company, rather than revisiting the retailer from whom they bought the phone. However, these sales had to be tracked so that originating retailers could be compensated for the sale in order to avoid channel conflict—that possibility had the merchandising managers really worried. It was also necessary to put in place a mechanism to test different types of informational messages to customers in order to arrive at the optimal sequencing and timing of messages to various segments of the market.

Organizational alignment also was important. The performance of call center reps previously had been measured and productivity bonuses were based on how quickly the reps completed calls. This obviously discouraged them from asking for and recording customer e-mail addresses during calls. Under the new plan, they were to be given a bonus for obtaining valid e-mail addresses. We helped them understand that retaining customers is as valuable to the company as signing up new ones. When the project started, the company only had valid e-mail addresses for about 30 percent of its customers, another example of limited information assets. With the proper incentives in place, call center reps more than doubled the percentage of customers with assigned e-mail addresses within three months.

The company's growth historically had been driven by the people that were responsible for convincing retailers to carry the phones. These were merchandisers who had superior sales skills. In fact, they were the corporate heroes. With the strategic focus shifting from opening up additional channels to retaining existing customers, marketing's role became much more critical as did that of customer service. Customer analytics—identifying customers who were particularly valuable as well as identifying customers whose profiles indicated they could become valuable—also became significantly more important.

However, the people in marketing had traditionally been focused on creating free standing newspaper inserts and other kinds of cooperative advertising with retailers, all to drive traffic to the stores that carried the company's phones. These marketers had limited analytical and direct marketing skills for tracking the results of campaigns. They also had no experience working with call centers, developing scripts for outbound calls, and modifying them based on what worked. The company acquired these skills both by training existing staff and by hiring new people.

Finally, it was important to ensure the right enabling technology was in place to execute the plan. In the past, the e-mail field in the database was too small to capture the relevant data, with the result that many addresses were truncated or rejected. The systems had to be modified to capture the complete address and to check that it was valid. Furthermore, the company had no ability to send outbound e-mail in large, targeted quantities, based on timed triggers from the database. We had to temporarily house the company's database and send the e-mails from our servers with a link back to its Web page for card purchases.

STEPPING INTO THE SIX DIMENSIONS

This case study shows how thinking through the six dimensions of marketing performance can enable a company to link strategy and execution for superior results. The Strategy-Execution Gap was closed when this company diligently and dynamically rolled out new plans, put the right metrics in place, developed the right information assets, introduced relevant processes, realigned the organization, and leveraged enabling technology. As we see here, these dimensions are all interconnected.

In the upcoming chapters, we focus on each of these six dimensions of marketing performance in greater detail. All have critical relevance in the establishment of a high performance marketing organization. We can assess and enhance marketing performance by thinking of each one as a window that offers us a particular vantage or perspective. Together, they provide deeper clarity and greater transparency.

These dimensions are concerned with the structure as opposed to the content of marketing. Strategy, for instance, depends heavily on specific circumstances. Customer-focused strategies tend to be quite unique, and are dependent on growth objectives, business context, and market dynamics. This also is true in terms of channels and marketing mix—the tactical approaches that might be undertaken to execute a plan. The marketing mix is highly dependent on particular circumstances. It is difficult, therefore, to provide valuable guidance on strategy or tactical execution without delving deeply into the content of a given company's goals and objectives, opportunities, and constraints.

However, the dimensions of marketing performance discussed in this book are a different matter altogether. Because these dimensions are matters of structure, not content, a tremendous amount of universality is associated with them. The principles discussed in this book, therefore, essentially apply to all organizations, both large and small, direct sellers and indirect sellers, business-to-business and business-to-consumer.

INVESTMENTS IN MARKETING PERFORMANCE

In order to close the Strategy-Execution Gap and deliver high performance outcomes, smart investments must be made in the portfolio of marketing performance dimensions. Organizations should not become overwhelmed by the challenge of building and managing expertise in all of these dimensions at the same time. Instead, it makes sense to concentrate on strengthening capabilities and competencies in certain dimensions at certain times. Some dimensions will demand higher investments than others at given times, and some will prove to be greater differentiators than others.

What's clear is that consistently strong outcomes will not be realized over time without making these investments and building these dimensional capabilities and competencies. As with the challenge of business performance overall, the key to successfully investing in marketing performance lies in discipline and diligence.

With that in mind, it is useful to keep in mind that one must constantly be assessing, developing, and leveraging one's marketing capabilities and competencies. These three phases are part of the Marketing Performance Improvement Cycle, illustrated in Figure 2.4.

When companies are assessing their dimensional proficiencies, they are trying to analyze the strengths and weaknesses of their current organizational capabilities and competencies. They also are determining the future state of marketing performance they wish to achieve. When companies are developing their capabilities and competencies, they are actively engaged and invested in generating the plans required to capitalize on their overall strength. When they are leveraging their competencies, they are actively applying and putting them to work in order to realize the outcomes they seek. Ultimately, these activities are re-

FIGURE 2.4 *Marketing Performance Improvement Cycle*

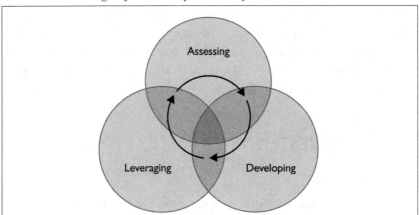

peated in a perpetual cycle as marketing organizations strive for increasingly high levels of proficiency within the various dimensions, thereby raising marketing performance overall.

You may be focused on one dimension of marketing performance or multiple dimensions at once. You may be simultaneously engaged in all three phases of the Marketing Performance Improvement Cycle or merely focused on one. The key is to prioritize your attention, investments, and activities. As you engage in efforts to build strength within the various dimensions of marketing performance, it becomes necessary to map out where you stand in relation to each dimension and what types of activities are being undertaken. Subsequent chapters of this book show you how to do this for each dimension.

The overall marketing performance equation ultimately depends on smart investments in strategy, execution, and the dimensional proficiencies that lie between. As companies become more disciplined and diligent about investing in the levers of marketing performance, they begin to consistently realize the objectives they have set.

3

DECISIVE LEADERSHIP, ACTIONABLE STRATEGIES

"Plans are nothing; planning is everything."

Dwight D. Eisenhower

Marketing effectiveness demands disciplined and decisive leadership. In order to close the gap between strategy and execution, marketing leaders must provide a clear sense of direction to guide action, investment, and improvement. Central to these efforts will be the marketing organization's ability to develop and act on realistic strategies and actionable plans that take into account market realities and the capabilities of the organization.

Through the discipline of actionable strategy development, marketers identify objectives, invest resources, and leverage key capacities. The process involves vigorous communication and dialogue. Marketing leaders must help others in the organization align their perspectives and reconcile differing points of view. The marketing plan itself serves as a binding agreement that sets clear goals and expectations. Strong leadership demands that managers be held accountable for the goals they agree to meet, just as the chief marketing officer will be accountable for results to the CEO and other senior executives. Marketing doesn't operate in a vacuum, of course. The first priority of marketing leaders is to communicate with other senior leaders in the enterprise and act on the strategies and imperatives that are laid out in the executive suite. Marketing must take a company's strategic objectives and turn them into operational plans.

Unfortunately, companies generally don't execute strategy—certainly marketing strategy—as effectively as they might. Asked which areas of marketing merit further attention, senior marketers listed "planning" at the top of their "must fix" lists, according to a survey by the Market Leadership Council.[1] Executive interviews conducted for this book certainly validate this finding.

Through planning, we determine what objectives we must meet and how we will meet them. Just as important, we determine what dimensional capabilities and competencies we must leverage and how we can leverage them. At its best, planning must be seen as a continuous and flexible process—one that encourages a high level of agility, interaction, and accountability. As a key dimension of marketing performance, actionable strategies enable the marketing organization to effectively execute, adapt, learn, communicate, and generate results.

MARKETING'S DRIFT TOWARD INSTABILITY

At present, it seems marketing leaders are under assault from all directions. Fairly or unfairly, marketing has been accused of squandering resources and failing to meet business objectives. Marketing leaders, in many cases, have become the scapegoats for corporate disappointment. Many marketing organizations are in a difficult and unstable position, and a great deal of uncertainty about the value and future of marketing remains to be resolved.

Consider the brief, tumultuous tenure of the chief marketing officer. One study by executive search firm Spencer Stuart found that the average tenure of a CMO at the world's top 100 branded companies is slightly less than 23 months.[2] By contrast, CEOs at these same companies held their positions for an average of nearly 54 months. In fact, only 14 percent of marketing leaders at top-branded companies had been in their roles for more than three years and nearly 50 percent had held their positions for less than 12 months.

The turmoil surrounding CMO placements and dismissals is clearly taking a toll. Spencer Stuart notes that companies face vast productivity losses as paralyzing transitions occur.

"Companies often face financial hardship with incoming CMOs due to changing strategic marketing direction and to being out-of-the-market for an extended period of time," the report states. In addition, morale suffers in the marketing organization as plans and personnel arrangements are thrown into an uncertain state. "By bringing in an outsider to lead the marketing department, it raises questions regarding the career path for the company's star marketers."

What's worse is the "vicious cycle" that ensues in this uncertain environment. When leadership is unstable and executive support is restrained, marketing organizations are less likely to invest for enduring performance gains. The temptation grows to turn to "radical" reorganizations and turbulent change, all to demonstrate short-term, if superficial, returns. This upheaval wreaks havoc on the culture and organization of marketing while failing to set a promising new course. Even when marketing leaders are not bringing in "hired guns" to replace loyal talent, top performers may soon defect for other companies.

One could argue that these are the results of an ill-defined, undisciplined, opaque approach to marketing. When leadership tenure, plans, and investments are ambiguous, the stability of marketing is itself in question. The lack of solid support from the CEO and other senior executives only further imperils the professionals who have invested their careers in marketing roles. While multiple factors play into the present instability of marketing, one key contributing factor is within the control of marketing leaders themselves. This factor is the absence of disciplined planning.

Planning translates strategies into action; it guides the investment of resources and firmly establishes lines of accountability. Without rigorous planning and commitment to established objectives, the marketing organization tends to break down and unravel, or merely becomes static and unimaginative. Marketing executives are often unable to articulate the linkages between the goals they are trying to meet and the actions they are taking. These executives are unable to take the steps necessary to drive necessary changes and improvements. They have limited insights into other customer-facing operations. As a result, they can provide no clear direction to other decision makers in the company, no reliable assessment of the impact of their efforts, and no trustworthy guidance to define future expectations. Without diligent planning, the fragile trust that top executives place in new marketing leaders is likely to erode.

The actionable strategies or planning dimension of marketing effectiveness is complex, because it essentially unites and leverages all the other dimensions. In this context, planning is about developing a systematic approach to guide marketing performance and drive investment decisions. This dimension also is about ensuring that the plan is rigorously enacted and appropriately refined based on learning and experience.

Among the best companies, marketing strategies and plans are prosecuted with great intensity and tenacity. Marketing managers set measurable targets and then take responsibility for meeting them. Their superiors hold them accountable for these commitments and take necessary action to ensure that established agreements are consistently met. Actionable strategies also enable marketing to link up in a meaningful way with other interdependent parts of the organization, such as sales and service. For example, marketing can help define what realistic revenue targets are in specific geographies (down to a retail store level) for specific products, thus helping sales develop appropriate staffing plans and quotas for the salespeople. Similarly, marketing can define the brand experience and set standards for customer service within call centers.

This kind of planning and accountability is relatively rare in marketing organizations today, however, which helps to explain the brief and erratic tenure of the typical marketing leader. Marketing leaders will have to take clear and considered steps to bring discipline to the planning dimension in the coming years. Such steps promise to transform the relationship between CEO and CMO. They also will deeply change and enhance the boundary spanning linkages between marketing and the rest of the enterprise.

PLANNING FOR MARKETING EFFECTIVENESS

When the CEO and the CFO present their expectations to financial analysts, they are putting their companies and their own reputations on the line. They are asked to explain their current results and provide guidance with regard to future earnings. The providers of capital, the shareholders, are a demanding group and they are becoming more so every day. In the wake of recent corporate scandals, shareholders expect increasing transparency and accountability.

Unsurprisingly, the pressure that weighs on the shoulders of top officers is being shifted downward into the areas of the enterprise where performance and productivity are least certain. Top executives know that growth depends on demand-focused improvements in marketing and sales, and they are unwilling to accept mystifying explanations of marketing's impact on overall performance. They want results and they want them to be clearly reported.

Given the growing demand for performance and accountability, it's not surprising that enterprises would seek more disciplined ways of managing their limited resources. This leads us to the centrality of plans and planning. Through diligent planning, marketing can establish the lines of authority and responsibility that are critical to high performance. Planning makes it possible to gain visibility into operational processes and report on the results of actions taken. It is also a key vehicle for communication and collaboration, dialogue, and discussion.

Smart planning encourages marketing organizations to be dynamic and responsive. In a true performance culture, professionals are respected and empowered. They are encouraged to expect the unexpected and to act appropriately. Although implementation is critical, planning provides essential objectives and mileposts, rather than intricate details for execution. The ability to move from strategy to execution is a critical differentiator for many successful companies, including Dell Computers, Southwest Airlines, Wal-Mart, Microsoft, or Procter & Gamble. Too many leaders at too many companies make the mistake of delegating responsibility for execution. They may take a "walk in the woods" at an executive retreat to seek inspiration for high-level, strategic plans and then leave it to their subordinates to "walk in the weeds" of tactical implementation. When senior leaders merely issue strategic decrees and disregard their own responsibilities for execution, they invite failure and disappointment. Instead, executive leaders, marketing leaders, and operational managers must work together to build a sturdy bridge across the Strategy-Execution Gap.

Indeed, disciplined marketing leaders are those that are actively engaged in efforts to link strategy to execution. They are highly interested in and deeply focused on the operational aspects of marketing. They demand clear commitments from their people and hold them to those commitments. They encourage robust dialogue and incisive questioning to surface the key challenges and opportunities that lie ahead.

This high level of engagement enables them to clearly and confidently articulate the role of marketing in the value creation process to other senior leaders. But it also helps ensure collaboration, coordination, and alignment within the marketing organization itself. It draws marketing leaders, managers, and teams into an ongoing conversation about what goals are obtainable and where performance can be improved. Planning is essential for developing and maintaining this level of engagement.

As the lead dimension of marketing effectiveness, planning has a special role. Not only must the skills and capabilities associated with planning itself be developed for superior performance, this dimensional competency must be honed to ensure all other marketing dimensions are effectively leveraged. Through planning, we identify and apply processes, organizational alignments, measurements, information, and technology. Plans articulate and embody our marketing competencies. They explain how these competencies can be deployed to realize the results we seek.

CLOSER LOOK AT THE PLANNING PROCESS

To put planning in its wider context, we must look at the different types of planning and plans that must be managed. Within a disciplined enterprise, planning occurs at three levels: strategic planning, operational planning, and marketing planning. Marketing plays different roles within each process. Through these multilayered planning activities, marketing leaders engage and address their superiors, their organizational peers, and the various members of marketing and customer-focused teams.

Strategic Planning

Whether at the corporate or the business unit level, strategy defines the goals and objectives to be pursued. Senior leaders must come together in a demanding process to determine new growth opportunities and ways to build a sustainable competitive advantage. Strategic planning answers the questions: Where do we want to go? What do we want to achieve?

The strategic plan lays these objectives out at a high level, but it is not divorced from action. Strategic plans are based on clear assumptions of how resources will be brought to bear to hit key financial and strategic targets. Marketing provides perspective on future market and customer trends as well as critical analysis of historical trends. Based on such forecasts, leaders can make better decisions about how to allocate and invest resources, what resources must be cultivated, and what competencies developed.

Of course, strategic plans depend on committed leadership for success. Tesco offers a stellar example of top-down strategic leadership that is committed to results. Terry Leahy, CEO of Tesco, had first championed the Clubcard program in the early 1990s.[3] Haven risen from the retail shop floor to his position as marketing director and board member, he had a strong sense of how the program could deliver value and why it deserved top-level support. Since its initial pilot in 1993 and amidst widespread industry skepticism, Tesco executive leaders built and backed the intelligence-based strategy necessary to vault the company into its current leadership position.

Similarly, compelling strategy leadership has come from A.G. Lafley, Procter & Gamble's CEO. With an operational background, he has strategically focused the company on organic growth and what he calls "the reframing of brands."[4] Deep customer insight and observational research has enabled the company to better serve everyone from devoted pet owners to young mothers concerned about their baby's development. P&G's Chief Marketing Officer Jim Stengel and his marketing organization have embraced this strategy, leveraging rigorous customer research and analysis to enhance product development and brand marketing activities.

Strategic planning has to focus on how best to support the overall company plans. At this level, marketing has to decide on priorities among such options as:

- New customer acquisition
- Cross selling or up selling to existing customers
- Inducing changes in buyer behavior, such as greater loyalty or increased purchase frequency
- Increasing retention of targeted segments of existing customers
- Increasing the profitability of customer relationships within targeted segments
- Increasing, decreasing, or withdrawing marketing support for specific products

- Weighing efficiency versus effectiveness in marketing efforts

Marketing organizations have to make hard choices at this level. Muddled thinking that seeks to spread bets across products, segments and customer life stages will dilute the impact of the entire marketing effort and lead to subpar performance.

Operational Planning

Whereas strategy defines the overall direction of an enterprise, operational planning puts strategy into a framework of executable action. It engages the various functions of an enterprise—finance, manufacturing, distribution, logistics, sales, service, and marketing—in rigorous dialogue to determine what specific actions and programs must be rolled out to meet established objectives. Operational planning answers the question: How will we meet our strategic goals?

Again, marketing plays a critical role here by providing insight into the risks and realities associated with markets. Marketers have a privileged and powerful view of customer dynamics, one that is highly valued by others within the organization. The sharing of these insights is critical to strong planning because it provides real and defensible analysis of the market implications of operational plans. Real-world, customer insight enables the various actors in the planning process to test and validate their planning assumptions.

Perhaps it's no surprise that some of today's most successful marketers come from operational backgrounds. Harrah's CEO Gary Loveman was initially hired into the chief operating officer position, a role he believes was critical in establishing the authority, credibility, and insight he needed in order to test and introduce new operating processes at various Harrah's properties.[5] Loveman has had to win the confidence and commitment of property general managers that might have resisted an executive who had no operational experience or authority.

The top leaders at P&G and UK-based retailer Tesco also have risen to their positions from operational roles within the business. They understand how their companies operate and have deep insight into the operational implications of strategic plans.

Marketing Planning

Marketing plans demonstrate how a company will generate profitable growth by attracting, growing, and retaining customers. The marketing plan is concerned with key issues of customer segmentation, marketing mix, channels, product, pricing, and much besides. It answers the question: How will the marketing organization help the enterprise meet strategic and operational objectives?

Marketing plans feed into operational plans. They provide a critical, demand-side perspective to guide the planning process overall. But they also must be reconciled with the plans laid out by leaders of manufacturing, research, and other units. Together, the groups can build an operational plan that reflects the realities of the market and limitations of available resources.

Marketing plans also must draw on the dimensional capabilities and competencies of marketing performance. These plans should incorporate the best thinking and capabilities with regard to marketing process, measurement, and other areas. Furthermore, marketing planning provides context for investment thinking by helping marketing leaders determine where to invest in order to maximize the return on marketing investment, as well as to effectively achieve marketing performance goals.

Elements of Successful Planning

Of course, planning is itself a key marketing competency. In order to excel in the planning dimension, leaders must be interested and incisive, collaborative and communicative, accountable to others, and willing to hold others to account. Planning is part of a dynamic cycle, not a routine production of static documents that will gather dust on untended shelves.

Rather than engaging in an annual planning cycle characterized by a marketing budget based on a year-over-year percentage increase, leading-edge marketing planning processes are more anticipatory and responsive. Those creating these plans are constantly surveying the market for opportunities that may have gone unforeseen in previous planning meetings and discussions. In some cases, implementation of a continuous budget planning process consists of quarterly marketing budget allocation reviews to ensure continued alignment of financial resources with high-value marketing opportunities.

Marketing leaders, as such an arrangement suggests, must be active and assertive in the planning process. Here are the five key elements of successful planning:

1. Set priorities, objectives, and targets. At the outset of all planning activities, it is vital to be clear about what one intends to accomplish. The parties engaged in the planning process must come together and determine opportunities and risks, and then set appropriate financial targets. Both targets and budgeted resources should be proportional to the size of the opportunity.

2. Determine relevant actions. Based on the objectives and targets that have been set, planners should determine key actions and activities necessary to meet them. Here, marketing leaders will identify relevant measurements, processes, organizational alignments, information assets, and enabling technologies that must be incorporated into the plan.

3. Drive consensus and commitment. Whether the planning occurs outside the marketing organization or within it, key leaders must commit to and hold themselves accountable for certain results. Ownership for outcomes is critical to achieving those outcomes. Trade-offs must be discussed and differing points of view reconciled at this point to ensure consensus.

4. Follow-up and follow through. Planning, as we have stated, should be considered a dynamic process. It doesn't end with a static planning document. Leaders must ensure that commitments are reiterated, widely understood, and kept. Senior leaders will hold operational leaders accountable and operational leaders must hold their own people accountable. Periodic reviews and discussions are critical to ensuring that the plan remains on track.

5. Refine and enhance. Should unexpected circumstances arise, as they usually do, dynamic planning processes must be flexible enough to allow course corrections and plan refinements. Through continuous dialogue, leaders determine where real-world outcomes stand in relation to forecasted ones. With this knowledge, they must take decisive steps to ensure the refined plans, expectations, and market realities remain aligned.

Such discipline is vital to the credibility and success of marketing leaders and the marketing organization overall. In its study of marketing leaders, Spencer Stuart discovered that one of the key reasons that marketing leaders don't last is a mismatch of expectations.[6] Dynamic planning is a key vehicle to enable robust communication and ensure expectations are clear. Another factor in the early demise of marketing leaders is "overpromising and underpromising" by the marketing leader, according to Spencer Stuart. Rigorous planning helps to ensure that promises are aligned with market realities and operational demands. Such an approach also helps to address a final point that undermines a marketing leader's stature: a poor cultural fit between the CMO and the company. Strong planning spans organizational boundaries and unites leaders through mutual commitments. It helps build cultural bonds and deepen relationships that are critical to the marketing leader's ability to drive performance.

Creating a Dynamic, Effective Planning Process

A planning approach that we have seen to be very effective in organizations that have a retail presence across diverse geographies is store or branch-based planning for sales targets by product lines. A large bank, one of our clients, demonstrates the benefits of this approach. Historically, each product line within the company, including deposits, mortgages, home equity, consumer loans, mutual funds, insurance, brokerage, trust, and so on, set their annual revenue and sales volume targets with the general banking organization. The general organization, which controlled the retail outlets as well as the centralized call centers and internet sales, allocated these targets to each region and channel. This process was fairly arbitrary; the outcome usually depended on the negotiating skills of the regional or channel managers, some arm twisting on the part of the general organization, and historical performance. There was minimal input from marketing or consideration of ground-level market realities during these operational negotiations. The process was excruciatingly painful for all involved and the outcome was unsatisfactory as well.

Even though some geographies and channels performed spectacularly well with some individual products, the organization suffered successive years of failure to meet product revenue targets. As a result, the company decided to adopt a more information-driven approach to setting geographic goals and to tie sales incentives more tightly to the achievement of these goals. Marketing was asked to analyze the geographic areas down to the individual branch level to understand the potential in each market for each line of products; marketing based its analysis on demographic characteristics as well as the company's competitive position. Sales volume targets were then tailored for each individual product line within each specific market.

The organization also reengineered the incentive system so that managers and individual salespeople were rewarded for more than just incremental sales. The new plan included incentives for achieving sales quotas for individual products, as well as for retaining existing customers, and growing the book of business. A pilot project testing this approach in one geographic area was highly successful for all of the parties involved, including branch managers and individual sales people as well as the product lines. The organization then rolled out the program to the entire company, encompassing thousands of branches, over a three-year period. The company went from repeatedly missing financial projections to consistently making its numbers.

The effort was not without cost. The number of analysts within marketing who were involved in planning and maintaining the program was fairly large. The investment, both financial and organizational, of going from a top-down decision-making structure to a fact-based, target-setting process was significant. Those who had learned the old system of negotiation and sandbagging found themselves at a disadvantage in the new process. The organization as a whole benefited significantly from the change. Marketing came to be seen as a much more valuable partner in the entire strategic and operational planning process, with a commensurate increase in visibility, budget, and headcount.

CLOSING THE GAP: THE MARKETING INVESTMENT PORTFOLIO

Successful planning requires marketing leaders to diligently prioritize their objectives, initiatives, and competencies. Marketing initiatives may be looked at in different ways by different companies. Some may see them through the perspective of the conventional "Four Ps"—product, promotion, place, and price. Others may look at marketing initiatives in relation to the particular media or channels that compose the "marketing mix." Still others may hone in on customer segments, analyzing how various segments are linked to investments.

Marketing effectiveness revolves around dimensional competencies. As stated previously, these competencies are levers or capabilities that we draw on to realize our marketing objectives. We must have a balanced portfolio of investment in these underlying capabilities in order to achieve true marketing effectiveness. In fact, marketing plans typically encompass and incorporate all of the dimensions of marketing performance. The marketing plan enables us to comprehensively analyze our investment requirements and outcomes in relation to key marketing dimensions.

Investing in Marketing Initiatives

Marketing initiatives can be thought of as a portfolio of investments. We can separate these initiatives along two axes: impact and innovation. In constructing this framework, we assess the business results (impact) associated with various types of initiatives, and the ability of these initiatives to drive new levels of value (innovation) to the enterprise. Marketing initiative investments can be directed to one of four categories based on relative impact and innovation:

1. *Foundational marketing programs* provide a necessary platform for the overall execution of marketing activities. These programs, which may include product brochures or a basic Web site, are almost a cost of doing business and are fundamental to the underlying productivity and effectiveness of marketing. They cannot really be considered true investments since they may not incrementally impact revenues or result in an impact

that is very difficult to measure. They are merely necessary from the perspective of day-to-day marketing action. These programs typically have to be monitored to ensure that they are still contributing some value and are not just cruising along on autopilot. They also need to be fine-tuned from time to time to maintain their accuracy and relevance. Spending on these programs has to be constantly evaluated; but ROI is not an appropriate measure.

2. *Operational marketing initiatives* have an important impact on the delivery of business value. These medium-risk investments are not particularly new or innovative, but they enable high levels of productivity and operational excellence. They may also provide important levels of differentiation in markets where competitors are not particularly proficient in an operational sense. The bulk of marketing spending typically can be classified in this area, regardless of whether it is tied to promotion, sponsorships, advertising, or direct marketing. These are programs that have been shown to work historically but may be reaching the point of diminishing returns. It is exceedingly important that these be executed as efficiently as possible, putting a premium on efficient processes. ROI is an appropriate measure.

3. *Experimental marketing initiatives* are essential to an enterprise's efforts to identify new and incremental sources of value creation. While risk levels depend on the scope of the experiments, most experiments are not high risk. Experimental initiatives may involve new types of marketing campaigns or media. They also may revolve around testing new or adjacent markets for growth opportunities. The bank examples presented earlier in this chapter started out as experimental initiatives with limited funding.

4. *Transformational marketing initiatives* are game changers. While they typically represent higher investment commitments and higher risk, they also are designed to drive highly differentiated, breakthrough growth. These approaches are designed to transform and reframe markets, setting the enterprise apart from its competitors by generating striking new forms of value. Experimental initiatives that are deemed successful at the pilot stage become transformational initiatives when rolled out at a division or enterprise level. The focus of these programs is on effectiveness rather than efficiency.

The Marketing Initiative Portfolio diagram shown in Figure 3.1 illustrates the integral relationships of these initiative categories within the marketing portfolio.

With a balanced and carefully managed investment portfolio, marketing leaders ensure they are meeting operational demands of productivity as well as pushing the envelope of growth. "By employing the portfolio framework, a business executive can make intelligent decisions that provide for a more reasoned, strategic, and efficient allocation of time, energy, and resources," writes strategy consultant Amir Hartman, whose own work on portfolio management inspired the framework presented here.[7]

Hartman points to several key process elements that must be in place if companies are to invest smartly. Among Hartman's recommendations:

- Intelligently compare initiatives across a set of strategic imperatives.
- Prioritize initiatives across the organization on an informed basis.
- Effectively allocate resources to drive successful execution.
- Better understand the ongoing costs and progress of the efforts.
- Gain better visibility into the value (financial and strategic impact) that investments deliver for the company.

Assessing, Developing, and Leveraging Marketing Investments

As previously discussed, marketing effectiveness demands investments in marketing competencies. The three phases that make up the

FIGURE 3.1 *Marketing Initiative Portfolio*

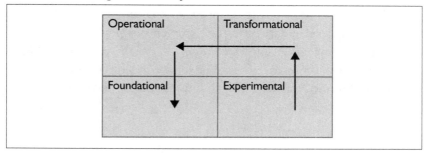

FIGURE 3.2 *Marketing Initiative Portfolio*

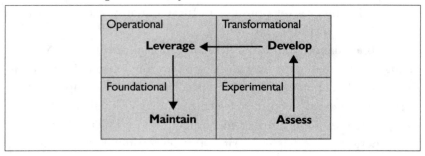

Marketing Effectiveness Cycle are assessing, developing, and leveraging. When a marketing initiative becomes foundational, it must then be maintained in order to remain effective. Using the portfolio framework introduced above, Figure 3.2 illustrates how marketing program categories fit into each of these phases.

As a simple exercise, take a look at your company's marketing budget and classify the different expenditures based on the Marketing Initiative Portfolio matrix. How much are you spending in each box? Is there a balance? Are you spending a small, but significant share on experimental programs that might provide a marketing breakthrough? Answering "yes" to these questions is good. Is the bulk of your marketing budget being spent on foundational programs? A "yes" answer here is probably not so good.

Questions of marketing effectiveness often will become visible through the marketing planning process. Planning is a powerful vehicle for leveraging these dimensional capabilities and competencies and determining relevant actions. Through plans and planning, the various marketing effectiveness dimensions are integrated and incorporated.

While the size of investments that go into these dimensions or competencies will be based on judgments about relative strengths, weaknesses, opportunities, and threats, it is essential that marketing leaders be aware of the level and direction of current investment. They can draw on the result of marketing effectiveness assessment methodologies (such as the MAST approach described in the previous chapter) to track changes and improvements, and guide future investments.

CASE STUDY: THE MARKETING PORTFOLIO APPROACH OF ONE MAJOR FINANCIAL SERVICES COMPANY (MFSC)

A company that I refer to here as MFSC (the real name of this financial services company has been withheld at the company's request) recognizes that prioritization is critical to smart decision making. The company's portfolio approach to marketing investment helps ensure that it realizes maximum returns even as it continues to experiment with promising new approaches.

"Marketing expenditure is absolutely critical to the success of this business," says the Senior Vice President, Relationship Marketing, at MFSC. "Marketing stimulates demand and without that demand we wouldn't meet goals. The big questions are: How much spending is necessary? What works and what does not?"

MFSC looks at marketing "as a portfolio of investments as opposed to an expense or a necessary evil." As the company formulates its portfolio, it identifies multiple types of marketing initiatives. "Reliable initiatives" are those that are clear and measurable and meet a certain threshold for return on investment. Such initiatives are categorized as "operational" in the Marketing Initiative Portfolio context.

In addition, the company considers it important to invest in emerging initiatives—those that have potential to drive new growth. "If we continue to optimize their performance and there is opportunity, they will eventually meet the threshold and become a reliable investment," the MFSC Senior Vice President states. These are the experimental initiatives that have not yet proven to be winners.

Yet another category of marketing initiative is "high potential." These are transformational initiatives, described as bold, big opportunities that require investment in order to learn about and understand them. Finally, there are initiatives that don't presently work, but might deliver strong returns if certain variables are changed. These could be foundational or operational programs that have either outlived their usefulness or have stopped working because the market or competitive environment has changed.

While not all of these investments are rigorously quantifiable, they all lend themselves to rigorous analysis and assessment.

The portfolio perspective enables MFSC to devote the lion's share of its marketing expenditures to investments that are perceived as reliable or operational, while spreading the remainder of its budget around into promising, yet unproven categories (experimental or transformational). "That enables you to avoid overextending yourself on unreliable investments," explains the SVP. "But we need to experiment and try those out."

Perpetual experiments are necessary in order to determine how to optimize marketing across products, channels, and customers. The company recognizes it must continuously test media, offers and messages, and campaigns to determine which approaches yield solid returns. If companies can take the portfolio perspective, small steps can have an enormous impact.

Yet, cultural change remains an ongoing challenge as the company seeks new levels of measurable marketing. "I think the number one issue is culture," says the SVP. "It will take longer to overcome the cultural aspects than it will to put the measures and discipline in place. Visibility [into marketing initiatives] based on understanding ROI needs to be there from the beginning so people understand the potential down the road."

He also acknowledges the danger associated with misapplied measurement and quantification. "..there will always be an art to marketing. We will not be able to measure everything. We must allow for experimentation and creativity and our 'gut'. As an organization, we must be mature enough to ensure a certain amount of spending on things we can't measure. Marketing will be destroyed if the art is taken out of it."

That said, he notes that measurement is essential to the credibility of marketing initiatives, even if it is initially difficult to do. "I don't think the measurement of marketing will ever be complete," he says. "We will constantly be out there trying new things that we don't think we can measure. But in order to keep them going, we must strive to measure them—either through some quantitative or qualitative approach. This discipline of Marketing ROI is not something that a company bakes for a year, takes out of the oven and pronounces 'done.'"

CASE STUDY: SAMSUNG ELECTRONICS, PLANNING FOR VALUE

One of the most impressive examples of how marketing planning can be turned into a dynamic and powerful vehicle for value creation is provided by Seoul-based Samsung Electronics. Where once marketing budgets were controlled by geographically distributed organizations, now investments are directed to areas of fact-driven opportunity.

The challenge of rethinking marketing investment at Samsung began in 1999. That's when the organization gave Eric Kim, former executive Vice President of Global Marketing Operations, the responsibility of turning Samsung into a global powerhouse to rival industry leader Sony.[8] Having long been a behind-the-scenes component supplier, Samsung's brand recognition was fairly low among consumers around the world at that point.

Kim was presented with a marketing budget of $1 billion, to be allocated across 14 product categories in nearly 200 countries. His challenge was to identify opportunities that represented maximum return on investment and redirect marketing resources appropriately. Through the course of an 18-month project, Kim and his team developed a powerful new approach to marketing, developed new decision and investment processes, and built organizational commitment to the endeavor.

Samsung's marketing organization needed to develop a rigorous and systematic way of gathering, standardizing, and analyzing data across countries and product categories so that valid comparisons could be made. This goal largely was facilitated through a Web-based, marketing data repository known as M-Net. While the site enabled the marketing team to capture data on marketing spending trends, media costs and product profitability, other benchmark and trend data was gathered through interviews with brand, category, and country managers.

Relying on analysis technology built into M-Net, Samsung's marketing executives were able to begin assessing the results of past marketing investments on a comprehensive and comparative basis. They also were able to build predictive models that would guide future investments in an intelligent fashion.

Among other findings, Samsung discovered that it was significantly overinvesting in North America and Russia, while underinvesting in Europe and China. The marketing group also discovered that several product categories, including phones, vacuum cleaners, and air conditioning units, were taking up an unjustifiable amount of marketing resources.

Such analysis persuaded Samsung executives that it would be necessary to redirect about $150 million from mature product categories and regions to ones that represented much more significant growth potential. Critically, it was made clear to business leaders around the company that budget reductions, inevitable in some cases, were not a reflection of personal performance. In fact, executives and managers were given opportunities to move to regions and jobs that presented different levels of growth.

The effort has paid off impressively. Between 2001 and 2002, Samsung's brand value rose 30 percent to $8.3 billion, according to Interbrand. Annual sales climbed 25 percent during that period, from $27.7 billion to $34.7 billion. Net income rose from $2.5 billion to $5.9 billion. The company is now committed to dynamically and analytically assessing its marketing investments based on facts, evidence, and comparative data. Samsung has become a global powerhouse in consumer electronics, challenging—and sometimes overtaking—Sony, the hitherto undisputed market leader. Kim and his team have overcome key organizational challenges and changed the culture of the company. They have demonstrated how a disciplined and rigorous approach to marketing investment—one that transcends traditional boundaries of product and geography—can generate extraordinary returns.

CASE STUDY: GILLETTE EMPHASIZES PLANNING, ACCOUNTABILITY, AND AWARENESS

One company that has executed an impressive turnaround in recent years is Gillette. A central element of that turnaround was the company's disciplined approach to planning, which has established powerful new levels of accountability and awareness.

Strong growth in Gillette's market share between the mid-1980s and mid-1990s perpetuated a sense of invulnerability throughout the company. However, a series of disappointing mergers, uneven performance in various product categories, and a perpetual shifting of blame and responsibility eventually began to take a toll on the company's performance.

In the latter half of the 1990s, Gillette started to unravel.[9] Only the manufacturing and product innovations of years past (particularly in shaving systems) enabled the company to continue hiding its fundamental weaknesses. Perhaps the most striking symptom of the company's failing health was its increasing reliance on a practice known as "trade loading."[10] In order to meet unrealistic performance targets, the sales force used discounts and promotional incentives to encourage retailers to purchase more product than necessary. The practice merely drove up inventories, eroded profit margins, and trained buyers to expect discounts at the quarter's end.

In 1998, sales flatlined and profits went south. The company's high profile 1996 acquisition of battery maker Duracell had merely hastened the company's decline. When Jim Kilts was appointed as CEO in 2001, Duracell had suffered nearly two years of declining market share as price wars raged.

Prior to accepting the board's offer to join the company, Kilts, along with longtime associate Peter Klein, conducted research that showed a series of disturbing trends and patterns. In some of his early meetings with Gillette executives, Kilts boldly demonstrated that the company was caught in a "Circle of Doom." It was undermining its market position and destroying its long-term strengths to meet short-term financial targets.

The company, as benchmarking research would later show, was eight-to-ten years behind its competitors in some areas of productivity. "When we arrived, the wheels were falling off," says Klein, now Senior Vice President of planning, business development and global marketing resources at Gillette. Gillette, however, quickly began moving in a new direction. Of his team members, Kilts demanded new measurements and reporting processes, dialogue, and accountability. Klein led the company's development of a new strategic planning process. Performance-based compensation arrangements were introduced, rewarding results instead of effort. Communication and collaboration became essential to groups striving to meet new performance targets. As a result, cross-functional teams and councils were established, and longer-term planning meetings, which were rarely held in the past, became more routine. Weekly operating committee meetings, weekly e-mail updates and quarterly off-site meetings all have become part of the process for setting objectives and reviewing progress.

To managers throughout the company, Klein issued a large book on why to do planning, including templates known as "the bible." (He told readers that they need not read the second book, which explained the reasoning behind strategic planning, if they followed the directions laid out in the first.) Now, managers are responsible for contributing to an annual operating plan and a three-year strategic growth plan that sets performance expectations. Operating committee members discuss the objectives and targets of their own groups, which cascade down to their staffs and are also used in individual performance appraisals. The strategic growth plan looks ahead three years into the future. "Previous Gillette corporate management did not value planning beyond one year," says Klein.

Jim Kilts, who built a name at Nabisco as a branding and marketing leader, has touted the company's new commitment to "Total Brand Value" internally throughout the company, and externally to Wall Street. It was a strategy designed to align Gillette's future with its recognized history as an innovator and value creator. Disciplined marketing, as Kilts has stated, is central to the company's revival.

It is working. Real growth rates have doubled since the entry of the new team. Emboldened by sales of M3Power, the company's new premium shaving system, and several new Oral Care and Personal Care products, Gillette is experiencing record growth levels. "Our powerful marketing programs are fueling new sales and consumer trade-up to premium products, even in the face of competitive offers of steep discounts and product giveaways," states Kilts.[11] Gillette sales were up 13 percent in 2004 after a 9 percent increase in 2003. Not bad for a company selling fairly mature, packaged goods products. Gillette was acquired in 2005 by Procter & Gamble for about $57 billion.

BEYOND ACTIONABLE STRATEGIES

As you've seen in this chapter, actionable strategies enable marketers to translate high-level corporate strategies into specific plans that can help to achieve those strategies. Such strategies are readily translatable into specific actions in the marketplace. In this chapter, we discussed the central role of planning, and how strategic, marketing, and operational planning can be integrated to manage the transition from strategy to execution. You've also seen how the Marketing Investment Portfolio integrates all categories of marketing planning and programs, and you've seen this process illustrated in the case studies of companies that have taken an aggressive approach to evaluating and allocating their marketing expenditures.

Evaluating and allocating marketing spending often requires good measurement, however, which can be a challenge in many marketing environments. This is the topic we address in the next chapter.

4

THE MEASURE OF MARKETING

From Measurement to Improvement

"The most urgent problem facing the newly independent United States was how to pay for the war that won the country its freedom; America's debt was enormous. Its greatest asset was the land west of the Ohio River, but for this huge territory to be sold, it had first to be surveyed–that is, measured out and mapped. And before that could be done, a uniform set of measurements had to be chosen for the new republic out of the morass of roughly 100,000 different units that were in use in daily life."

Andro Linklater, Measuring America

In the early years of America's independence, land itself was an "intangible" that defied clear measurement. It wasn't until the new frontier was accurately surveyed and measured that the country's promise of dynamic prosperity could at last be fulfilled.

We face a similar challenge as we struggle to map out the intangible realm of customer value and measure marketing's impact on growth, profit, and shareholder wealth. Marketing, as we have said, is in a privileged position to identify key market trends and opportunities, to more deeply connect the enterprise to its customers. Marketing, therefore, must act to drive growth.

But marketing also must defend and validate its actions, and the measures of its performance must be clear and definable. Those measures and performance results, rather than allocation-based budgets, will guide the investment of corporate resources in marketing.

The development and application of rigorous new measurement initiatives is a critical step in an organization's move toward high performance marketing. You cannot manage that which is not measured. Disciplined marketing depends on measurement—both as a way of assessing the impact of marketing investments, and as a lever to drive continual performance improvement.

DEMANDS FOR ACCOUNTABILITY

We live in an ongoing era of accountability. Shareholder skepticism and the introduction of the Sarbanes-Oxley Act are rippling through the corporate world, forcing top executives and board members to demonstrate new levels of diligence and transparency in order to rebuild lost confidence.

Marketing, while traditionally one of the least measured functions of the enterprise, is a significant expense in many organizations and the implications of its actions are critical to corporate performance overall. Unsurprisingly, CEOs, CFOs, and board members, who are under more pressure to be accountable themselves, have cast a critical eye on the marketing organization and are demanding more and better reporting.

Marketing is responding to these demands. We see evidence that senior marketers are searching for new ways to measure marketing performance and build credibility within their organizations. One Forrester Consulting study involving 280 marketing executives from an array of industries found that their greatest challenge this year is "measuring marketing effectiveness or ROI."[1] Of the respondents, only 37 percent said their marketing organizations are perceived by those within the organization as being both strategic and capable of delivering measurable value. Another 32 percent said marketing is perceived as strategic, but incapable of measuring its impact, and 30 percent said that marketing is not perceived as strategic at all.

The measurement challenge was underscored by another study from the Chief Marketing Officer (CMO) Council, an association of technology marketers.[2] In a poll of 315 senior marketing executives, the CMO Council found that fewer than 20 percent of respondents have formal marketing performance measurement systems in place. In addition, almost 80 percent are dissatisfied with their ability to demonstrate their marketing programs' business impact and value. These results are especially significant given the fact that technology companies tend to be among the heaviest spenders in marketing. According to a Marketing Leadership Council (MLC) survey, high technology companies spent an average of more than 15 percent of revenues on marketing.[3] This is several times the percentage spent on marketing by companies in many other major industry verticals, including such marketing driven industries as consumer packaged-goods.

The CMO Council study, however, found that nearly 90 percent of respondents believe measuring marketing performance is a key priority for their organizations. "Growing boardroom pressures on marketing departments to justify and account for their spending, as well as more critical and demanding corporate performance environments, heightens this priority," according to the council. As opposed to asserting its own perspective, marketing has reacted to these demands by putting measurement, ROI, and other elements of "accountability" on the front of their agendas.

But measurement isn't just about diligent accounting. In fact, one of the major challenges in marketing measurement is determining what to measure. The range of options is vast, perplexing, and sometimes contradictory. Advertising can be designed to increase awareness, recognition, or recall, to improve consideration, or to drive traffic to a retail center or Web site. So which one matters most? Direct marketing effectiveness can be measured in terms of the response to a mailing or an e-mail campaign, but the quality of the responses may be more critical than the quantity. The actual revenue generated (which can be influenced by price levels as much as by response), can also be a relevant metric. Sometimes the cost of acquisition is the key measure while other times the potential lifetime value of the customers acquired may be more critical. So determining what to measure is a very important, but too often neglected, first step.

The functions of measurement go beyond explaining what has happened in the past; measurement also moves us forward toward appropriate actions and improvements. Useful measurement requires appropriate reporting on the allocation of marketing resources and their investment return, but it also requires that we take action—and intervene—when key objectives are not being met. Measurement should guide us as we invest incrementally in programs that do meet or exceed their targets.

Rather than one more mandate from the executive suite, marketers should see measurement as a critical lever to enhance performance and drive value in a continual way. Indeed, measurement is central to the success of marketers' careers and organizations. Rigorous and appropriate measurement—ultimately linked to financial measures—will earn marketing executives a place at the table with their peers in operations, manufacturing, finance, and sales as well as entry into the boardroom. Just as the Total Quality Management and Six Sigma movements have driven new standards of improvement on the supply side of business, we now have an opportunity to drive performance levels much higher on the demand side of business.

While the economy goes through cycles and the fashion for marketing measurement comes and goes, true leaders will recognize the necessity to build a "measurement competency" as part of a larger performance culture. That is why appropriate measures is one of the key dimensions of marketing performance.

MEASUREMENT MYOPIA

As they seek to improve the return on marketing activities, senior marketing executives ask a number of questions: What is working and what is not? Which marketing programs show promise? Who are our most profitable customers? Who are the least profitable? What is the profitability breakdown of our various channels? How are we aligning our limited resources with our greatest opportunities? Where should we invest? Unfortunately, most organizations do not have any practices, processes, or measurements in place to find and provide the answers to these questions. Without the insight required to intelligently assess investment options, marketing is vulnerable to both underinvestment and overinvestment—the value-eroding misallocation of resources.

Marketers have all sorts of metrics and statistics available to them, of course; but too often, the data is useless or irrelevant and disconnected from the larger objectives of the enterprise. Marketers tend to confuse measured data about specific campaigns, channels, media, events, and activities with a comprehensive analysis of marketing payoffs. Marketing tends to measure isolated silos of activity, but it fails to provide a wider and more rigorous perspective to guide marketing investment decisions. As a result, the most significant indicator of the size of one's annual marketing budget and the particulars of allocation is the previous year's budget. Rarely does a marketing organization rigorously reassess its investments without a precipitating crisis.

Meanwhile, the argument of whether marketing is primarily art or science has continued. When marketers were accused of being "hucksters" and "hidden persuaders" in the 1950s and 1960s, they fought back by emphasizing their grounding in measurement and science.[4] As a result, marketers became particularly proficient in bedazzling their clients with sophisticated measurement techniques and statistical analyses. Today, many of these techniques remain actively in use, especially in the consumer-packaged goods companies.

Complex technique, however, is no replacement for comprehensive perspective and insight. It's clear that, while we do have an array of sophisticated metrics, many companies still have no clear sense of whether their marketing dollars are being invested properly. Most companies do not even differentiate between necessary marketing expenditures that are a cost of doing business versus expenditures that are investments in the future with a longer term payoff.

Marketing expenses are often linked with particular elements of a media mix rather than to the customers we intend to grow. We have budgets for advertising, direct marketing, and supporting the sales force (budgets based on areas of activity as opposed to results and outcomes). Some marketing organizations, in fact, tend to be quite advanced in the measurement of certain activities and channels, such as advertising, direct marketing, or sales. However, marketing organizations generally do not have an integrated approach for measurement, reporting, and investment across operations. As a result, they work with a skewed picture of marketing performance.

Marketers say they are most capable of measuring direct mail and e-mail campaigns, Web site and Internet search engine presence, and telemarketing and contact management programs, according to the CMO Council's research.[5] However, they are least capable of measuring advertising, sales and marketing collateral, and branding. Relying on their "strengths," many marketers optimize the measurement of certain activities, rather than the measurement of enterprise-wide performance. It is not uncommon for companies to focus on the activities they can measure well, emphasizing the ones that can help them meet preset sales quotas, while cutting back on longer term investments in activities that can build brands and enhance shareholder value. This piecemeal accumulation of metrics fails to provide a comprehensive picture that can drive smart management decisions, and is akin to searching for one's keys where the light is best rather than where one might have dropped them. No marketing organization will reach its potential as a force for growth within the company using this approach.

Cathy Bessant, the Chief Marketing Officer of Bank of America, is alert to this danger. "We are very disciplined about our approach to measurement and disciplined processes, but we also want to avoid the tyranny of measurement," she told us.[6] "It is important to measure whatever you can, but it would be naïve and dangerous to focus investment on measurable activities and channels while neglecting those that may, in fact, be more effective but are not necessarily as measurable. Good business judgment, a grasp of the overall marketing portfolio, and an understanding of what you expect from different parts of the portfolio are extremely critical to maximizing overall business impact."

What CEOs Want: Linking Investment to Outcome

Yet another challenge for marketing leaders may be the absence of clear and tested linkage between the marketing performance metrics they employ and the outcomes they seek. This pattern has undermined the value and credibility of many marketing measurement efforts. The sheer act of measuring may not produce value. In fact, poor or careless measurement can prove an enormous misuse of resources.

What the top executives within companies seek is a linkage between investments and outcomes. Financial measures such as revenue, profit, and shareholder value, frame our understanding of overall corporate health, even though they fail to show us the underlying health of a business or support management decision making. Financial metrics offer a retrospective view of results; they do not indicate what actions we must take to drive results. However, these are the results most often reported to the financial marketplace and the investors who have the last word on shareholder value.

Marketing is well positioned to bridge this measurement gap. Measures of customer loyalty, attitude, or behavior can be linked to customer profitability and lifetime value, which, in turn, can be linked to financial measures. Marketing measurement is a constant process that depends on multiple metrics, rather than a single number or snapshot of organizational health. Thoughtful marketing measurement reflects the current state of the organization, even as it influences what the company can do to change its future state.

Bill Moult, founding partner of Sequent Partners and a former president of the Marketing Science Institute, says marketing often produces lists of metrics that are not considered relevant by the CEO and CFO.[7] Such metrics don't work as credible measurements. Marketers, according to Moult, must take the steps necessary to link marketing and financial measurements. "It is critical to demonstrate the underlying structure or relationship between them," Moult adds.

As Figure 4.1 demonstrates, there are multiple ways in which classic marketing metrics can be translated into financial metrics. Through such endeavors, marketing can raise its credibility in the executive suite.

FIGURE 4.1 *Translating Marketing Metrics to Financial Ones*

Context	Key Elements	Barriers	Results

Marketing Metrics ⟶ **Financial Metrics**

Response Rate ⟶	Incremental Revenue
Retention ⟶	Increased Profitability
Cross-Sell Ratio ⟶	Increased Revenue
Cost per Lead ⟶	Reduced Acquisition Expenses
Customer Satisfaction ⟶	Reduces Services Costs

Of course, cultural resistance to measurement and analytic thinking can be problematic, too. Many executives continue to rely on intuition, experience, and conventional wisdom to guide their decisions. One 2002 study by executive search firm Christian & Timbers found that fully 45 percent of corporate executives rely more on instincts than facts and figures in running their enterprises.[8]

While instinct and intuition may be key attributes of leadership, they may not provide the best foundations for the increasingly complex decisions we as marketers are forced to make in an era of global, real-time commerce.

Positioning Measurement at the Core

As today's leading marketers now see it, measurement must be central, not peripheral, to the development and management of a performance-driven marketing organization. Measurement becomes part of one's role and set of responsibilities. It is an essential element of the marketing and management skill set.

This organizational paradigm goes beyond the current array of techniques that are now on offer, although most organizations would do well to adopt some of those techniques as a start toward more effective marketing. In fact, techniques are themselves context-dependent. Some companies will prefer top-down measurements; others bottom-up. Some are concerned about brand equity; others focus on customer equity. Some prefer ROI metrics; others prefer free cash flows. Some theorists believe marketers should take the reins in the measurement arena; still others believe the reins should be turned over to finance and accounting.

These decisions certainly are important, but the current challenge facing marketing is less about technique than mindset, organizational discipline, and culture. In fact, marketing organizations must be prepared to introduce, test, and adapt improvements on a constant basis. Marketers must have the capacity and will to make the necessary linkages between actions and outcomes. Many leading edge companies have created a group within the marketing department that is responsible for performance measurement. This group often functions independently of the managers responsible for developing or executing marketing programs and reports directly to the Chief Marketing Officer or Vice President of Marketing, sometimes with dotted-line accountability to the CFO.

Marketers must lead the way toward an era of rigor and discipline. Facts, as they say, are our friends. Whereas some marketing theorists believe marketing can elevate its place in the organization by embracing transformative initiatives that hold a valued place on the CEO's agenda, the real deliverance for marketing lies in its insight, its command of real-world activities and outcomes, and its special perspective on the customer. Marketing is in a uniquely powerful position to drive innovation and improvement where it is most required, on the demand-side of business. But it can't accomplish this objective without facts, evidence, and actionable insight.

Many companies are already seeing the benefits of positioning measurement at the core of their marketing organization. Through measurement and analysis, a small life insurance company found that that it is more effective to focus on marketing $50,000 policies than $200,000 ones, even though the latter might appear to be more valuable. The company discovered that conversion and retention rates linked to the smaller policy holders are far greater, eclipsing the face value of the policy as a key variable of profitable growth. "We have to consider the revenue stream in relation to the conversion rate," explains the president of the company, noting that the company actively measures cross-sell, up-sell, and other investments to clarify where its marketing investments deliver the best outcome.

The path to world-class marketing excellence lies in a rigorous commitment to measurement, and the performance improvements that measurement makes possible. Indeed, measurement is a critical element in one's efforts to identify the gaps that hinder the execution and enhancement of growth-oriented business strategies, and disciplined marketing is impossible without a clear understanding of the facts on the ground.

LINKING ACTIONS AND OUTCOMES

Although they are critically important to forming a disciplined approach to marketing, "facts" can be difficult to establish and defend. Establishing strong links between actions and outcomes is often quite challenging. Even the linkages that once seemed clear can become less so over time.

Frederick Reichheld, a director emeritus at Bain & Co. and a long-time champion of customer and employee loyalty initiatives, has raised many questions over the years about the validity of customer satisfaction as a meaningful measure of future behavior. Surprisingly, he has even begun to raise questions about customer loyalty as a key measure of progress and success. While he hasn't completely disavowed his past work, Reichheld admits that his theories have never caught on in the real world of business.

As Reichheld now sees it, "retention rates have not progressed over the last decade. Where the rubber meets the road, customers are not demonstrating loyalty.... No one defined what loyalty was. There was no measurement, no link to profitability or growth. There was a lack of definition. What is loyalty? If what you mean is putting up with lousy value or service, do you want stupid customers?"[9]

Now, he is interested in customers who are willing to recommend a company's products to a friend or a colleague. Reichheld believes that, in addition to measuring customer profitability, companies should also be identifying the "promoters" and "detractors" among their customers, with the obvious objective of increasing the number of promoters. "The median 'net promoter score' is just above 10 percent," says Reichheld in *Direct Magazine*.[10] "Most companies have 10 percent more promoters than detractors. But the best companies have 80 percent more. The net of promoters minus detractors doesn't show up in profit and loss statements, but detractors destroy your future and make your employees feel lousy."

A great example of a company that relies on customers for promotion is Amica Insurance. Amica, the oldest mutual automobile insurance company in the United States, actually took this notion to an extreme. It would not accept a new customer unless that customer was "referred" by an existing customer in good standing, although the company has since modified this policy. It still does not advertise or employ agents in an industry where most business is driven by aggressive agents. It relies on word of mouth referrals from customers. At a time when most companies measure customer attrition on an annual basis, more than one-third of Amica's customers have been with the company for more than 20 years. When I have shared the Amica story with audiences, I will often have someone in the audience raise their hand and talk about generational loyalty (saying, for example, "My grandfather and my mother were Amica customers and now I am one, too."). The

CFO of one or our client companies is a passionate advocate for Amica, in addition to being a lifelong customer, due to the outstanding service he received when his home was destroyed by a hurricane.

One enterprise that is rigorously focused on optimizing marketing returns is Cleveland-based KeyBank, which manages assets in excess of $85 billion. It has been investing in "marketing performance optimization," which enable it to match marketing actions and outcomes. Key-Bank has developed sophisticated models for forecasting and scenario planning across media, channels, and geographies. "You can see what happens when you move dollars around," says Trish Mathe, Senior Vice President and Director of Database Marketing.[11] Mathe says that Key-Bank has cultivated a "culture of accountability." In this case, accountability is made visible to all through an array of corporate and departmental scorecards as well as marketing "snapshots" that capture key indicators of performance. "It [accountability] has closed the gaps in our reporting on marketing campaigns and helps us plan the media mix appropriately." Mathe noted. "It forces a kind of scientific rigor and drives more intelligent conversations."

A COMPREHENSIVE, INTEGRATED VIEW

What many marketing executives most need is a comprehensive decision framework to help assess various marketing initiative options in a diligent and rigorous way. This framework can help guide judicious investments, enabling marketers to compare and assess outcomes, and then reinvest for maximum returns. Such visibility will enable marketers to defend marketing budgets and build corporate confidence. If marketing returns are clear and impressive, they will invite even greater levels of investment. Measurement enables us to test our assumptions, discover what is working and what is not, and continually refine our performance.

The following matrix outlines a very simple framework that can serve as a starting point for such an assessment. The first column of this matrix lists marketing elements used by many companies; the rows extending from each of these elements show measurements used to assess the marketing element. As you move across the columns, the measures go from the obvious to the not so obvious, from marketing measures to financial measures, from response to profitability.

Sponsorship	Awareness	Recognition	Influence	Purchase
Direct Mail	Response rate	Buy rate	Revenues, RFM	Profitability, Lifetime Value
Advertising	Awareness	Consideration	Intent	Purchase/ Repeat
E-mail	Open	Click-through	Purchase	Value
Promotion	Response rate	Incremental Volume	Cannibalization	Incremental Profitability

Since companies are interested in ROI and financial measures, why do they not immediately go to the extreme right and focus on those measures? The problem is that as you move from left to right on the chart, the measures are more complex and may require fairly sophisticated analytics. Many organizations do not have these skills and have determined, sometimes quite legitimately, that it is not worth their while to invest in them.

A senior executive at a major direct marketing company told us precisely that. His company considers Recency, Frequency, and Monetary (RFM) metrics, all which have been heavily used in the direct marketing industry, to be effective measures of value, and doesn't see the economic justification for pursuing still more sophisticated and precise measures such as Life Time Value (LTV) of customers.

"RFM measures are our proxy for lifetime value of a customer," he explained. "We realize that there are many nuances that we miss by using RFM, such as the price sensitivity of the customer and the potential future value of different customers. However, the rush to get stuff out the door and the daily operational pressures make it very difficult for us to invest a great deal in testing and R&D into these issues. If we are able to meet our numbers, the pressure to constantly improve how we do things is not felt as heavily."

RFM is a standard measure among most direct marketers and is very good for generating incremental sales through existing customers and others like them. However, it is somewhat akin to driving with a focus on the rear-view mirror. Understanding potential future lifetime value can be valuable in unearthing new and emerging segments and developing new products. It takes effort and investment, but the payoff can be significant.

Let me illustrate this point with another example, this time from one of our previous clients, a publishing company. This company owned a number of major magazine titles and spent a fair amount on direct marketing, mainly on renewal mailings, an initiative with which we are all familiar. The company spent a minor amount of money on cross promotion across magazine titles. It had a small analytical staff, including three statisticians who were very competent statistical modelers, but who did not really understand financial and economic models. Their focus was on the first level measures, response rates. They did test different prices for different mailings, but not to measure price elasticity, per se; instead, they measured response rates. The general manager, on the other hand, was not concerned about response rates to individual campaigns as much as the overall renewal rate and the total paid subscription level, since advertising rates were tied to this metric.

However, an analysis of subscriber LTV led to the conclusion that, for some of the magazines, subscribers who were first solicited with very low introductory rates often did not renew. Therefore, these subscribers did not really add in any significant way to the magazine's ongoing rate base, the paid circulation (what advertisers base their payments on). The incremental advertising revenue gained by having these subscribers in the customer base was not enough to justify the cost of solicitation at the price point at which they were willing to renew.

As these examples illustrate, the very scale and complexity, risk, and uncertainty of contemporary marketing often makes performance measurement much more critical than it might have been in the past. Under the circumstances, marketing investment has risen to an entirely new level of difficulty. As demands for greater performance and accountability increase, marketing leaders are charged with identifying the key drivers of growth and performance improvement. They are expected to be able to drill down into current actions and activities, and vividly demonstrate the impact of their investments.

Laying these options out within a single portfolio provides "the comprehensive perspective necessary to invest with discipline," says the senior vice president at a major financial services company.

Clearly, this level of clarity and discipline raises the credibility of marketing within the enterprise. The CMO council study found that companies that have formal performance measurement systems "consistently achieved a higher level of CEO confidence in the marketing function."[12]

THE PRINCIPLES OF A MEASUREMENT-DRIVEN PERFORMANCE CULTURE

In order to establish a comprehensive and integrated marketing perspective, marketing organizations must have the discipline to measure in a rigorous fashion. These measurements lay the foundations for performance improvement.

The leading marketers recognize that there are a few essential objectives they must set and meet if they are to produce valid measures on an ongoing basis and successfully rely on them to drive action. These three principles must guide a measurement-driven performance culture:

1. Measurement must be relevant
2. Measurement must be visible
3. Measurement must drive improvement

Let's look at each of these principles in more detail.

Measurement Must Be Relevant

The most highly sought-after financial outcomes may include increased shareholder value, revenue, or profit growth. Marketing must target more immediate performance objectives, however, in order to deliver on such financial targets. Therefore, it must make causal linkages between key measures such as customer satisfaction, cross-selling, or campaign response rates and the financial results it seeks to produce.

These links are not as obvious as one might think. In recent years, critics have raised questions about the implications of customer satisfaction, for instance, on overall corporate success. Even marketing campaigns that are apparently successful may not be truly successful if outcomes are misaligned with objectives. (Consider a no-interest financing campaign for a new car that generates tremendous response, but merely eliminates all margin on the purchase. U.S. carmakers are very familiar with that particular impact of their marketing.)

Let us take for example another previous client, a banking institution. This bank had a major deposit generation campaign in which it paid above-market rates for CDs. The bank raised deposits, but ended up cannibalizing money from many of its existing accounts at a much higher cost. As a result, the campaign cost the bank more than $15 million in net income. The bank's increased deposits were directly linked to a decrease in its income. This outcome was not apparent, however, until we were able to analyze the entire customer portfolio of deposits and were able to see the flows from mutual funds and checking accounts to these hot CDs. Prior to this analysis, the executive who was leading the deposit generation campaign looked like a hero for having grown deposits in his geographic region much faster than his counterparts elsewhere. After the analysis, he disclaimed all responsibility for the decision to offer above-market interest rates. [13] To be successful in terms of measurement, marketers must rigorously and diligently test their assumptions. Until a clear linkage between actions and outcomes is established, the relevance of favored performance metrics is merely a hypothesis. Sometimes, marketers merely need to dive deeper to determine the true implications of an action. During the refinance boom of the past few years we have often seen instances of financial institutions advertising mortgage rates and soliciting business aggressively. We found that the ability of their back offices to actually fulfill and close on those loans could not match the demand that was generated, leaving them with irate prospects who failed to become customers.

As linkages are tested and established, it becomes easier to weight the relative importance of one metric versus another, and to decide which marketing activities are worthy of investment within a portfolio of marketing options.

Measurement Must Be Visible

Essential to the continuing success of today's marketing organization is its ability to determine and clearly communicate the impact of its actions. While it is clear that most companies have important benefits to gain from smart marketing measurement, it is hardly certain what the most relevant metrics of marketing performance might be from one company to another.

The level of resources that must be devoted to the measurement task will, of course, vary too. It will depend on industry dynamics, the size of marketing budgets overall, and each organization's existing proficiency in measurement. Marketers must put their best effort into measuring the outcomes of their current activities and investments. This is the critical foundation on which marketing improvement, and, perhaps innovation will emerge. Marketers must measure to determine where they should invest, and where performance improvements are necessary.

Furthermore, marketers must measure and report outcomes to meet the executive suite's growing demands for accountability. Indeed, they must communicate performance outcomes to reestablish credibility with corporate decision makers. Deeper credibility lays the foundation for larger and certainly more effective marketing investments. Performance-driven marketers have nothing to fear from new measurement reporting processes. We have found that these more relevant and effective measures often already exist within marketing organizations, but are not widely shared inside and outside marketing. It is a problem that must be addressed to achieve a successful outcome.

Measurement Must Drive Improvement

As we stated earlier, measurement is not simply about accountability. True, measures should enable us to better determine how investments have played out and assess whether we are addressing our objectives. More importantly, however, marketing measurements should drive new improvements and performance gains. Such measures can help us generate growth in customer value and take the actions necessary to ensure that the marketing organization is performing at peak levels.

Measures represent a powerful lever for organizations that are struggling to drive performance gains. They have the potential to depersonalize and depoliticize change. Objective measurements provide a touchstone to guide actions. Actions can be taken not as a response to the hunches or whims of powerful people, but because the measurement system is indicating that a change must be taken.

On the foundation of measurement, marketing leaders can take action to ensure they are maximizing the return on their marketing investments. They may discover that they need to shift resources from customer acquisition to customer development. They may find they need greater skills and expertise in terms of customer segment analysis and management. They may learn that the marketing organization is not aligned with a key channel such as the contact center.

Such discoveries occur through the application of measurement. Acting upon these discoveries is the next step. When a company acts on the results of its measurements, it demonstrates to the rest of the organization that measures matter. By contrast, marketers that fail to act on the measures that have been implemented tend to create an air of cynicism about measurement, and eventually, the measurement efforts either become meaningless or stop altogether.

The measurement-driven performance culture is reinforced by many other elements. Organizations that want to truly promote this culture must link rewards, compensations, and promotions to measurable results. Communicating the value of measurement and discussing the implications of acting in a measurable, disciplined way also are essential steps in carrying out this cultural shift. Finally, these organizations must provide the training and skill development necessary to measure activity. For many people, measurable marketing will come with an array of unfamiliar requirements and demands. They must not only have the will and motivation to meet these demands—they must also have the necessary skills and expertise.

A financial services company we counseled was very aggressive with its cross-sell program. All of the front-line staff in the retail branches and the call centers were heavily incented to sell additional products to customers. Analysis of customer behavior showed that many customers did not use the additional products and services that were thrust on them by aggressive salespeople. As a result, the company actually lost money on these products, since there were very low balances on these accounts. By adding measures of retention and compensating sales associates for growing the overall balances in the accounts, the company was able to change the behavior of it associates, reduce retention, and increase profitability without proliferating unnecessary growth of products among its customers.

In the 1990s, Procter & Gamble took the bold step of cutting its trade promotion budget drastically (a major part of its overall marketing budget) and moving to everyday low pricing. This move was based on a detailed analysis of scanner data from supermarkets around the country that showed that constant price promotions "trained" customers to buy items on sale and eroded the power of its leading brands to command premium pricing. It was also extremely inefficient because sales volumes shifted dramatically in response to temporary price changes, and led to costly inventory, logistics, and manufacturing variances.

Additionally, the cost of tracking and administering these complex trade promotion programs was considerable for both the manufacturers and the retailers. I know of one midsize supermarket chain in the Northeastern United States that employed more than 150 people just to keep track of rebates and promotions from manufacturers. Subsequent to P&G's move away from promotions, many other companies followed suit, and the result is considerable savings to consumer packaged-goods companies and retailers. This major change would not have been possible without P&G's ability to measure and analyze supermarket scanner data across varying markets over time.

Of course, the development of a measurement competency or dimension is never complete. Markets change. Disruptive innovations are introduced. Customers make new demands. An adaptive, robust marketing organization is one that continually challenges, tests, and refines its metrics. It ensures the linkages between marketing measures and financial measures are clear and defensible. And it acts on what it learns to continually improve marketing operations and outcomes.

CLOSING THE GAP: MARKETING MEASUREMENT SUCCESS FACTORS

The linkage of measurement to action, more than any other factor, drives organizational change and improvement. When the impact of measurement is clear and discernable, the value and importance of measurement can be internalized. To make measurement an essential part of the marketing performance culture, marketers need to have a recognized measurement process to guide activity and continual improvement.

While measurements may be quite sophisticated in various parts of the marketing organization or the front office, the objective in developing this process is to establish a discipline of measurement that can be followed by marketing overall. Achieving this objective requires us to develop a cross-functional, boundary-spanning approach to marketing measurement that can deepen understanding of performance goals and strengthen our ability to meet them

On the following pages, we offer some key process steps that marketing organizations can use to guide their own measurement efforts.

Building a Performance Measurement Model

While this objective is easier set than met, the establishment of a comprehensive measurement framework is central to strong marketing performance. The framework should attempt to encompass all relevant inputs and outputs, actions, and outcomes associated with the marketing organization to be truly comprehensive. It is not enough to simply cobble together a report based on the various silos of measured activity. This undermines the opportunity, and necessity, to measure marketing from an integrated perspective and make relevant comparisons.

While the development of such a framework may seem an intimidating endeavor, it is of course possible, and perhaps preferable, to build it in incremental stages. The model will evolve and become more sophisticated over time, through trial and error, experiment and learning. It need not be world-class in its early iterations. The key to success with the model is to embark on the initiative. Once the framework has been launched, marketing can build momentum and refine the organization's perspectives. In fact, we recognize that marketing will first test and deploy the model internally. While input and comment should be sought throughout the organization, marketing should validate and refine its own reporting framework before inviting others within the organization to use it.

Acquiring Measurement Data

Marketing measurement initiatives cannot and will not survive unless the discipline is in place to gather the relevant data necessary to measure. Many measurement efforts in many organizations over the years have foundered on the sheer difficulty and expense of gathering relevant data. Marketing must ensure that the measurements sought can, in fact, justify the expense of acquiring the data. For example, supermarket scanner data that P&G used to make their everyday low price decision was purchased from a syndicated scanner data company such as IRI or Nielsen, but the analyses and relevant measures that led to the decision had to be developed within the company.

Collecting customer data can be a particularly difficult and expensive challenge for companies that sell through intermediaries, such as retailers or distributors. However, the formation of a customer panel or even a user community can provide a platform for data collection that circumvents the channels. The use of product registration cards by appliance makers and software and hardware marketers is an example of this type of data-gathering, although few of these companies truly leverage this information. Yet another client, an office supply company that sold through intermediaries and retailers, built a large panel of administrative assistants who were able to provide them with market and competitive intelligence that was not otherwise available, giving them a competitive edge. They did so by providing special services to this segment of their end customers who no one else was paying attention to–a very innovative approach to data collection.

Once it is clear that the measurements can add relevant and justifiable value, the marketing organizations must devote necessary resources in the form of time, money, and talent, to acquiring the key data. The organization also must assign roles and responsibilities for carrying out this effort. In many cases, the relevant information may exist in various departments and systems. Finding and aggregating this information is a critical element of this endeavor's success. If it is not consistently gathered, the value of the measures and the initiative overall will erode.

Analyzing Data and Generating Key Indicators

It's critical to recognize that a model is just that: a representation of reality. Its assumptions are merely assumptions until they can be tested and causal links between actions and outcomes can be more firmly established. Even then, measures that proved relevant at one point can prove less so over time. Performance measurement frameworks, however, provide a foundation for testing assumptions. When links have been established, the marketing organization can present its measurements with an appropriate degree of confidence.

Different metrics and indicators will prove to be relevant in different contexts. Andrew Abela, the former managing director of the Marketing Leadership Council, contends that a small number of "leading indicators" might be particularly valuable in terms of smartly investing marketing resources.[14] (For instance, a luxury car company might generate a metric based on a survey question such as "Do you intend to purchase a car in the next 12 months?") Dipak Jain, Dean of the Kellogg

Graduate School of Business at Northwestern University, told us that companies should be actively assessing and measuring how their customers derive value from their products and services. "Once I have those metrics then I also know how to capture the value we have created by pricing the product appropriately," he added.[15]

As linkages between actions and outcomes are established, marketing must generate the key performance indicators that will appear within their marketing scorecard, dashboard, or measurement system. These are the measures that will matter going forward. One can expect significant discussion and debate over the establishment (and weighting) of the actual measures. However, once they are chosen, they can be perpetually updated based on new measurement data. Attention turns to trendlines and performance.

Reporting Performance

The framework promises to provide a strong platform both for performance reporting and management decision making. However, marketers must have a system for communicating the findings from their performance initiative. While all variety of high-tech and low-tech approaches have been adopted for other types of performance reporting, marketing will have to choose the medium and format that is most valuable for this endeavor. Currently, there is a great deal of development going into the actual presentation of performance scorecards and analysis. Tying into existing systems, such as a balanced scorecard, can help make this step easier.

While many reporting options now exist, the critical factor is reporting itself. Once the marketing organization begins to report its performance results, marketing changes the relationship between itself and the rest of the organization. Reporting opens up new conversations and opportunities for collaboration, within marketing and beyond it. Also, while senior management increasingly demands that reporting be done on the basis of accountability, it's clear that such visibility can also strengthen marketing's credibility with senior decision makers.

Leveraging Measurements to Drive Decisions

The value of measurement is inseparable from its impact on management decision making. If measurements are disregarded, then their importance will diminish. The whole objective of measuring marketing performance in the first place is to strengthen management decisions and drive greater investment outcomes. Of course, some measures or drivers will be weighted more highly than others. Predictably, those metrics will have a greater influence on capital and resource allocations.

Performance indicators should prove to be a powerful guide for investment. Consider Frederick Reichheld's notion of "promoters" and "detractors."[16] If a strong linkage has been made between the number of customers willing to recommend one's product and the profitability of the firm, then clearly companies must do more to ensure they have a strong base of promoters. Those are the kinds of actions that must be taken and decisions that must be made if measurement efforts are to have a lasting impact.

Enabling Learning and Performance Improvement

Based on the findings that are generated through performance measurement, marketing is in a powerful position to drive new performance gains. Measurement becomes an indispensable tool for demonstrating in an objective, dispassionate way, the gap between actions taken and outcomes achieved. It provides a rallying point and communications vehicle for driving new levels of performance.

Without measurement, management actions are a matter of political will and executive intuition. In measurement cultures, action and improvement become far more collaborative, and hopefully, clear. Measurement platforms lay the groundwork for perpetual learning and performance improvement.

Just as the surveying of America's uncharted Western territories set the stage for a nation's extraordinary growth, today's efforts in measuring the intangibles of marketing and customer value will lead to tremendous new fortunes. At this transitional moment, marketing leaders have much to gain. If we are willing to rethink the way we measure and invest in marketing, we can differentiate our companies, generate new levels of profitability, and establish enduring relationships with our most valued customers.

Measuring Marketing: One Perspective

At Quaero, we developed an integrated measurement framework–one that allows for retrospective analysis of past efforts and results, and prospective analysis to identify opportunities for future refinements and investments. The framework is the tool we employ to map out marketing investments and returns, plotting them onto a matrix to visualize various causal linkages and relationships.

Charting the Customer Engagement Cycle

This framework maps a set of marketing measurement dimensions to a multistage process we call the Customer Engagement Cycle. This cycle recognizes the development of customers (including prospective customers) within a segment along five stages of engagement: awareness; consideration; inquiry; purchase, and expansion. These are the broad stages through which a typical customer passes as a relationship is cultivated. These stages are described within the Marketing Performance Framework: Customer Engagement Cycle chart shown in Figure 4.2.

FIGURE 4.2 *Marketing Performance Framework: Customer Engagement Cycle*

	Awareness	Consideration	Inquiry	Purchase	Expansion
Business Objective	Breakthrough and recognition	Relevance and inclusion in decision set	Differentiate and inform through two-way sharing	Move to desired action; shared commitment	Ongoing engagement and development
Event Description	Presentation of messages and/or an initiation of contact designed to generate customer awareness of product, brand, or service	Presentation of messages and/or an initiation of contact designed to encourage prospective buyer to demonstrate interest in product, brand, or service	Exchange of information in a two-way dialogue or targeted information request	Actions designed to encourage commitment–purchase, loyalty, etc.,—leading to an exchange of value	Actions designed to encourage additional exchange of value and deepening commitment

By recognizing these stages, we make it clear that marketing actions, or investments, influence customers in different ways at different points of relationship development. Mass media advertising, for instance, might be more successful for reaching out to customers in the awareness stage, while investments in direct selling might be more appropriate as customers enter the purchase or expansion stages. The key here is to ensure that the right actions are taken at the right stages and that limited resources are smartly deployed.

While the Customer Engagement Cycle enables us to see the different stages of customer development, marketing measurement dimensions actually track the actions, outcomes, and implications of our investments relative to the stages of the cycle. Each of these dimensions involves a set of metrics that have specific applications, as illustrated in Figure 4.3.

Here are some of the key marketing measurement dimensions our clients are tracking.

- *Actions and activity.* This set of metrics is designed to identify and quantify the particular actions and activities that have been taken to generate marketing results at a given stage of the Customer Engagement Cycle. As such, this measurement dimension is a

FIGURE 4.3 *Marketing Performance Framework: Measurement Dimensions*

Awareness > Consideration > Inquiry > Purchase > Expansion	
Measurement Dimensions	
Action and Activity	Measures the resources, programs, and activities devoted to achieving marketing objectives. These indicators look primarily at programs, inputs, and investments.
Marketing Impact	Measures the results of marketing activities within each stage of the customer engagement cycle (response rates/conversion rates, closed sales, click-throughs, impressions, etc.).
Financial Impact	Measures the financial aspects of the marketing programs, including cost and return on investment at each stage of the customer engagement cycle. These measures link the results of marketing activities to financial outcomes.
Customer Impact	Measures the impact of marketing activities on customer segments (loyalty, wallet share satisfaction, profitability, etc.) at each stage of the engagement cycle.
Time and Migration	Measures the time required to move customers through the engagement cycle and provides indicators of migration difficulty.

gauge of inputs and investments. Key indicators, for example, may include an inventory of campaigns, media buys, or sales initiatives. Tracking this dimension helps our clients recognize the marketing resources that have been devoted to driving outcomes, which can help them determine whether resource allocation is aligned with stated objectives. Through the exercise of merely mapping out marketing activities, one of our financial services clients quickly realized that its strategy of cross-selling and up-selling existing customers was relatively unsupported. It discovered that the vast majority of its actions and activities were occurring during the awareness stage of the engagement cycle as opposed to the expansion stage. Conversely, we have seen clients realize that they have underfunded customer acquisition initiatives by investing most of their resources in the later stages of the cycle.

- *Marketing impact.* This set of metrics looks at outcomes, or effectiveness, from a marketing perspective. It measures operational results such as response rates, conversion rates, closed sales, even click-throughs and Web site impressions. This information is useful for performing consistent comparisons based on which marketing vehicles or programs are effective in moving customers to the next stage (within a stage of the cycle). The inclusion of market research metrics such as awareness, share of market, satisfaction, etc., can provide an insightful backdrop when viewing programs or campaign-based metrics. Looking at these indicators across stages of the Engagement Cycle can also highlight areas for reallocation of marketing investment. Marketing impact metrics enable us to isolate specific opportunities for improvement and to determine what actions might be taken to realize our goal.

- *Financial impact.* This set of metrics is designed to translate operational marketing metrics into financial outcomes. Costs per activity, such as cost per impression, cost per call, cost per customer, and so on, are building blocks for generating (ROI calculations at each stage of the cycle. Marketers can view sales attributions through this metric, and then map out the impact of their activities on actual profit-by-customer segment. They can use the data gathered through this measurement dimension to assess past results and make future forecasts. Organizations are therefore able to treat marketing decisions as investments and use the Engagement Cycle as a means of pinpointing where and how they will manage their marketing activity portfolio. Of course, financial performance and impact metrics speak the language of the executive suite and provide the types of measures that CEOs and CFOs will expect to receive in future reports on marketing performance.

- *Customer impact.* This set of measures examines the implications of our actions in terms of the customer relationship. In tracking this measurement dimension, we might look at specific metrics such as share of wallet, customer satisfaction, customer loyalty, or customer profitability. The key is to gain a greater understanding of the impact marketing's activities are having on customer value development. For example, a senior marketing executive might consider how certain marketing programs affected share-of-wallet metrics over the time the programs were being implemented. One of our financial services clients looks at patterns of customer development, probable customer migration paths, and paths of greatest value. Marketers can use the metrics within this dimension to hypothesize and investigate causal links between marketing actions and marketing performance, and to make appropriate investments, adjustments, and reallocations.

- *Time and migration.* This set of metrics tracks the amount of time required to move from one stage of the Engagement Cycle to the next. Moreover, it assesses the degree of difficulty associated with enabling that transition. Finally, it measures the cumulative costs of actions, activities, and programs in order to evaluate programs and investments. While there may be programs that have good individual ROI or performance results, the cumulative cost of these activities in moving a customer to a new stage in the engagement cycle may be higher than other programs. The cost of migration is important, but so is the time necessary to accomplish the task. Opportunities must be quickly seized or they will be lost. Considering the rapid rate of change in today's hyper-competitive markets, it is critical to recognize "time" as a component in the overall assessment of marketing performance.

Applying the Marketing Performance Framework

While the framework itself provides context for assessing different decisions, the actual plotting of marketing activities on the map, the measurement of results, and the recognition of timing in the engagement cycle adds texture to our understanding of marketing investment returns.

By separating our actions and outcomes, we gain a comprehensive picture of marketing performance. Customer segment managers can see marketing results portrayed segment by segment and stage by stage. Similarly, program managers can see campaign and program results lined up in relation to segments and customer engagement stages. Such insights can help them refine and improve their spheres of activity.

Chief marketing officers, by contrast, gain the integrated view they need to drive strategy. Not only are they able to disaggregate perspectives by segment and stage, they can gather the results together and see them in aggregated form. They also can assess changes in broad measures such as awareness, customer satisfaction, share of customer, and others that are not comparable within a single period, but can be understood as trends over time.

One of our clients recently transformed its marketing organization through the development and application of this framework. Indeed, this Fortune 100 financial services firm has passionately embraced the opportunity to improve marketing measurement and effectiveness. The marketing organization currently is developing a host of new measures, actively integrating previously unused sources of data, implementing new processes for information capture, and data sharing. At the same time, the company is addressing the organizational and cultural challenges associated with marketing measurement.

Under the leadership of the chief marketing executive, the marketing organization has turned measurement into a critical priority and driving force. The marketing organization recognizes that the implementation of the framework is a continuing journey—one that will change the way it makes decisions and analyzes investments and outcomes. However, the measurement initiative already is having a dramatic effect with regard to how the marketing group thinks, operates, and improves. "Marketing is becoming a measurement-driven culture," said the executive leading the charge. "And we are tying that into an overall learning agenda for the business."

In the past, the marketing organization would have been a customary beneficiary of the corporate budgeting and allocation process. Now, marketing is becoming a key driver of strategic decisions. Through its focus on measurement and accountability, marketing is earning credibility at the most senior levels of the organization. The framework enables the CMO to demonstrate to other corporate decision makers how marketing investments are supporting key business initiatives, which translates to sales, profit, and cash flow indicators. It allows marketing to make the business case for required resources on a clear and stable foundation, but it also enables the organization to measure and validate the impact of previous investments.

Marketing Measurement: Three Schools of Thought

As we see it, marketing measurement has fragmented into three schools of thought: *the ROI school*; *the Brand Equity school*; and *the Customer Equity school*. While these perspectives are not necessarily incompatible or wholly separate, they tend to emphasize different points and pursue different goals:

- *The ROI School:* ROI is widely used, and just as broadly defined. Research suggests that marketers favorably apply the language of ROI to everything from improving incremental sales to enhancing brand perceptions to growth in market share. Guy Powell, author of *Return on Marketing Investment* and one of the leading adherents of this school, defines return on marketing investment (ROMI) as "the revenue (or margin) generated by a marketing program divided by the cost of that program at a given risk level."[17] ROI is the simple approach that reflects the language of project and program justification that is common in organizations. James Lenskold, president of the Lenskold Group and author of *Marketing ROI: The Path to Campaign, Customer, and Corporate Profitability*, concludes ROI is "the ultimate measure for guiding marketing investments, because every marketing decision affects a company's ability to generate profitable sales."[18]

- *The Brand Equity school:* This school focuses on measures of brand equity, or brands, as assets. The Brand Equity perspective seems to be heavily influenced by consumer packaged-goods industry and other sectors, where value must be inferred from the attitudes and actions of vast consumer bases. Connections to the consumer tend to be indirect, mediated by retailers and resellers. Brand measurement champions are continually challenged to show how variables such as consumer attitudes and behaviors, financial investments, and environmental factors contribute to or detract from brand health. Linkages between the various management domains and measurement silos must be established if companies are to understand brand value over time, contend Bill Moult and Jim Spaeth of Sequent Partners.[19] Companies such as Interbrand and Copernicus Marketing have developed approaches to measuring brand equity. Tim Ambler, author of *Marketing and the Bottom Line: The Marketing Metrics to Pump Up Cash Flow*, encourages companies to look at marketing as a generator of brand equity that rises or falls over time. "Marketing is not a once-off capital sum, but a continuous stream of expenditures which the company makes every year," he says.[20]

- *The Customer Equity School:* This school has largely grown up in sectors such as financial services and telecommunications, where databases of specific segments and even individual customers have become a key asset. Robert C. Blattberg, coauthor of *Customer Equity: Building and Managing Relationships as Valuable Assets*, and Roland Rust, coauthor of *Driving Customer Equity: How Customer Lifetime Value Is Reshaping Corporate Strategy*, are among the leading thinkers in this field of inquiry.[21] They believe that customer insight will prove a powerful force in the evolution of business in the coming years. "[C]ompanies that understand the asset value of each customer, and that tailor their marketing efforts (and their costs) to acquire and sustain the highest-value assets, will trump less-focused mass marketers," state Robert C. Blattberg, Gary Getz, and Jacquelyn S. Thomas in their book.[22] That view is championed by Don Peppers and Martha Rogers, the authors of *The One to One Future*.[23] They have recently introduced the term Return on Customer. "ROC equals the sum of a firm's current-period profit from its customers, plus any changes in customer equity (the sum of the lifetime values of all current and future customers served by a firm), divided by the total customer equity at the beginning of the period," they explain.[24] The centrality of customer-focused measures of profitability and lifetime value also is reflected in the work of Larry Seldin and Geoffrey Colvin. In their book *Angel Customers & Demon Customers*, they argue that "virtually every company in every industry will soon have to rethink its way of doing business along these lines, with customers at the center."[25]

CASE STUDY: HARRAH'S BETS ON RIGOROUS MEASUREMENT

One way Harrah's Entertainment has been able to transform itself into a leader in financial performance within the gaming industry is through the rigorous, enterprise-wide performance measurement of its marketing programs. How, wondered its critics, could homely Harrah's compete against the captivating visual experiences promised by its competitors on the Las Vegas strip? The answer, it turns out, was through an intensive, analytical focus on marketing investments and customer relationships.

In years past, Harrah's has launched a set of loyalty programs known as "Total Gold" and "Total Rewards," enabling it to provide deeply personal service to customers and track their behavior in extremely sophisticated ways. In fact, Harrah's can track individual casino and hotel guests across all of its properties (26 casinos in 13 states). This enables the organization to actively monitor individual levels of play and other activities, analyze preferences and interests, assess lifetime customer values, and provide personal offers or services based on those observations.

Through such efforts, Harrah's found that 26 percent of all customers generated 82 percent of overall revenue. However, it also learned that its most profitable customers are not necessarily the high rollers to which all the other casinos attentively cater. They turned out to be "former teachers, doctors, bankers, and machinists—middle-aged and senior adults with discretionary time and income who enjoyed playing slot machines."[26] Instead of rewarding these clients with steak dinners and stage shows, Harrah's found they typically were more inclined to appreciate a $60 stack of chips so they could dive right into the games. Many also valued the luxury of being expedited through lines or receiving differentiated customer service, and took steps to achieve Platinum or Diamond status.

The careful monitoring of gambling and other activities within the casino has been a critical part of the company's efforts to ensure that its resources are being intelligently invested. The reward cards ensure that nearly all activities are tracked. Harrah's can use this insight to present personalized marketing and service offers that reflect preferences and priorities down to the individual level. The organization also closely watches satisfaction scores. It knows through experience that customers that have a good experience increase their spending on gambling by 24 percent a year, while those who are disappointed decrease spending by 10 percent per year.

At a higher level, the company looks closely at same-store revenue growth and "cross-market" revenues that is, revenue growth across properties and geographies. It also looks at growth relative to other competitors within its various markets. "We've not only grown revenues," says John Boushy, Senior Vice President of operations, products, and services at Harrah's,[27] "We've also grown the percentage of cross-market play by managing the customer relationship. We recognized that there was a customer segment that traveled to multiple markets. We believed that if we could extend the relationship with our customers from one property to the entire brand we would be able to capture a greater share of their wallets when they went to other markets, and that is what happened."

CASE STUDY: ROYAL BANK OF CANADA INVESTS IN MEASUREMENT

Central to the overall measurement process of many firms is the necessity of computing customer profitability and customer potential. One company that invested heavily in this effort is Royal Bank of Canada.

Royal Bank is Canada's leading financial services firms with five lines of business: retail banking, insurance, wealth management, corporate and investment banking, and transaction processing. Headquartered in Toronto, the bank has 23 million retail accounts, 700 products,

58,000 employees, and has served 10 million corporate and public sector clients in North America.

The bank has been refining its understanding of customer profitability since the early 1990s when it learned that 20 percent of customers accounted for 100 percent of profit. The company's profitability model employed a three-tier system, recognizing whether customers were highly profitable, moderately profitable, or not profitable at all. It was a relatively unrefined system that helped direct the resources of the sales force and laid the foundation for future evolution toward customer-focused management. However, the system was not sophisticated enough to allow for relationship-based pricing, channel optimization, or to reflect the potential value a customer might contribute.

Richard McLaughlin, who was hired to lead the bank's CRM initiative, sought a "more robust profitability measurement" system and deployed NCR's "Value Analyzer" software in the late 1990s to help the company attain its objectives.[28] This accelerated the calculation of profitability figures which was critical in the bank's high volume, high complexity environment. It also provided much more accurate information on customer "spreads" (the difference between the rate paid to depositors and the rate charged to borrowers), potential risks, and transaction costs, all contributing to a far more accurate understanding of the variances in customer profitability.

Still, the approach was not enough. "We came to understand that customers can be both profitable and have the potential to be profitable, and that the bank needs both kinds of customers," said Gaetane Lefebvre, Vice President of Strategy Marketing Research and Analytics (SMR&A) at Royal Bank.[29] "Our new strategy was to look at our customers' total holdings and figure out how to deepen their relationship with the bank if they had potential. For example, were we losing opportunities to sell products to these customers? Are potentially profitable and profitable customers being lured away?"

With these goals in mind, the bank realized that truly valuable customer profitability models must incorporate activity based costing data (ABC) at the account or customer level. While the bank had been accumulating ABC data since the late 1970s, it was not until 1999 that the bank linked this data to customer profitability models. With that linkage established, the bank could assign costs to each separate product in a customer's portfolio, thus taking into account the transaction usage and channel preference.

With these capabilities in place, the bank began experimenting with measures of customer lifetime value. It approached this challenge in two ways. First, it assumed that the customer's current profitability percentile would remain constant through the lifetime of the relationship and calculated the net present value of profits. Second, it factored in demographic variables such as age, current products, and propensity to purchase new products. This enabled Royal Bank to calculate individual lifetime value scores and aggregate them up to the level of segment.

Based on the bank's ability to calculate current and potential profitability, it has been able to manage its marketing and service investments with far greater rigor than would otherwise be possible. In fact, the customer profitability calculations now guide the development of customized marketing campaigns, pricing arrangements, and the level of service that is offered.

The company's "decision engine" is central to its efforts to provide personalized attention to its customers. The engine contains several components, the most significant of which is based on four key predictive models: profitability, client credit risk, client vulnerability or attrition risk, and lifetime value. As Lefebvre explains, "Depending on how people rate for each model, they are placed in one of 14 categories, for which the bank will have a primary objective: to retain; grow; manage client risk; or optimize costs. We can then use these categories for marketing effectiveness, courtesy overdraft, allocation of rate discretion, and differentiated service."

The Royal Bank of Canada's marketing group has relied on the deep segmentation of customers, based on both profitability and propensity to buy, to generate its campaigns. Similarly, the bank is using its profitability and value measures to determine service treatment. Customer category assignments are used "to determine the length of wait time and the type of customer service representative that the customer talks to at our telephone-banking center," said Lefebvre. "We always want to ensure that our very best clients, in terms of profitability and lifetime value, get the very best service. That's how we retain good customers."

MARKETING MEASUREMENT'S LINK TO PROCESSES

Given the array of approaches and methods on offer, the measurement challenge, quite obviously, will remain a difficult and demanding one for some time to come. The best and most appropriate measures in the world, however, do not add up to much unless they are integral to marketing processes and are used to constantly improve performance. So it makes sense that we now turn our attention to the third of our performance dimensions, Effective Processes.

c h a p t e r

5

OUT OF THE BLACK BOX
From Process to Predictability

"If you can't describe what you are doing as a process, you don't know what you're doing."

W. Edwards Deming

It has been said that marketing is a "black box" to the rest of the organization. But guess what you would see if you were to open up that black box and look inside? That's right: More black boxes. Marketing can be a supreme mystery, even to marketers.

Complexity, fragmentation, and compartmentalization of marketing activity have contributed to this state of affairs and such trends have undermined the overall effectiveness of the marketing organization. At the very least, the opacity of marketing has undermined confidence. There is now a sense in many companies that marketing spending is unrelated to results. The linkages between action and outcome are unclear. Marketers know this. It is not as though marketing has not tried to apply greater discipline to its activities. We have devised sophisticated ways of managing and measuring advertising, direct marketing, public relations, call centers, and retail channels. We have merely failed to achieve this discipline in a wider, integrated sense. We may be rigorously optimizing particular tasks, activities and subprocesses, but we have not provided a comprehensive and connected view of how the work gets done, or what value it is delivering overall. As a result, we are not performing at peak levels.

What's missing, to a great extent, is a focus on *process discipline*. Like other entities within the enterprise, Marketing resides within a network of processes—some that are performed within the marketing organization's immediate domain of management, some that extend beyond it. Effective processes are a critical dimension in the overall marketing performance framework.

Process can be defined as *a structured and integrated set of activities that are performed to achieve a defined business outcome*. Process provides clarity, visibility, and predictability. It drives clear and measurable value for the customer, and thus, produces enduring value for the enterprise. Process is the central means by which we ensure our activities are consistent and coordinated, aligned, and executed to create value. Without process, we are perpetually acting in an ad hoc and inconsistent fashion. We diminish productivity and needlessly disperse our resources, talents, and energies.

Many businesses organize around isolated tasks, which typically leads to efficiency at the expense of effectiveness. Process design must consider issues of both process efficiency *and* effectiveness. As the economy becomes ever more competitive and our customers become increasingly demanding, the predictability of process and process improvement becomes even more critical to our success. Otherwise, we are perpetually running around like headless chickens, and every successful outcome depends on personal heroics. Such behavior is unsustainable. The continual advancement of established organizations depends on the power and predictability of visible process.

As we discussed earlier in this book, marketing often comprises various functions, including market research, product development, advertising, direct marketing, and pricing, just to name a few. Critical marketing activities (such as new product introductions) often straddle many of these functions as well as functions outside of marketing. In this chapter, we argue the need for marketing to focus on developing more rigorous processes by using methodologies that have become well established in manufacturing and other operational areas within world-class companies. We also examine the benefits of leveraging emerging software tools that offer marketing resource management capabilities. We end the chapter with some examples of organizations that have used a specific process approach, Six Sigma, to improve their marketing performance.

CURRENT MARKETING PROCESSES: ISLANDS IN ISOLATION

In the absence of process, we witness the never-ending reign of organizational dysfunction. Disconnected activities lead to ineffective performance or, worse, paralysis. When marketing is unable to predictably deliver successful outcomes, senior executives tend to respond in more predictable ways. They slash budgets and demand headcount reductions. As the abbreviated tenure of the typical CMO suggests, it is often the senior marketer's head that is the first to roll.

Marketing is not a complete stranger to process thinking. In fact, marketing often oversees an array of silos that have their own limited forms of process discipline. We have already alluded in early chapters to the new product introduction process in leading packaged-goods companies, which has been well refined over the years. Even advertising execution is a well-devised process in leading edge companies. In recent decades, there has been an increasing drift toward fragmentation within marketing organizations as new and distinct groups emerge to address advertising, direct marketing, public relations, direct sales, partner channels, online, and other activities. The touch points themselves, from the Web site to the customer service center, can be rigidly separate in many organizations. These groups or units have developed their own languages, own metrics, and perspectives. They have evolved in splendid isolation.

Splendid, that is, unless you are a customer. Indeed, the fragmentation of customer-facing activity has ensured that no integrated view of the customer exists in many companies. As a result, the customer often confronts a virtual "Tower of Babel," across business units, brands, and geographies, as well as across campaigns and communications.

FAILURES IN EFFECTIVE PROCESS INTEGRATION AND MANAGEMENT

Nor has marketing technology enabled us to overcome our process inadequacies. When marketing process improvement initiatives were undertaken in recent years, they typically focused on successfully integrating new technology into the existing way of doing business, often paving the cow path as it were. This does not imply that each process remained entirely intact, however, but rather that the core work activities and the resources allocated to perform each activity did not fundamentally change. Instead, the emphasis was placed on identifying opportunities for streamlining the execution of the existing work activities for the purpose of increasing throughput capacity.

One of the problems with today's marketing campaigns is that they often are not fully integrated with the activities occurring in the channels or at the customer touch points, undermining the effort to drive new business and strengthen relationships. Contact centers may not know how to handle calls that have been generated through a recent campaign; e-mail requests for information may go unanswered. Poor handoffs of this sort impose heavy costs. They undermine marketing performance and, over time, prove toxic to customer relationships.

Marketing does not—and should not—accept the blame for all such problems and inconsistencies. But it does tend to be caught in the middle of the overall customer-interface problem. Marketing itself confines activities within specific functions and units. One often finds weak linkages between advertising and direct marketing, for instance. In many organizations, "creative" and "analytical" marketers seem to inhabit distinct worlds, pursuing separate, often contrary, agendas.

The management of customer information is another activity that has been poorly executed due to weak process, partially because this requires processes that straddle the Marketing/IT divide, which can be a chasm in some companies. While we have seen marketing invest a great deal of effort into acquiring customer information in recent years, their efforts to capitalize on that information have proven less impressive. Some companies have back rooms full of PhDs and MBAs who analyze customer data. However, many of these companies fail to fully leverage this valuable information asset to generate greater customer value. The head of database marketing at one of our clients repeatedly complained to me that her team was compiling some great strategic analyses on the customer base and the broader market, but she was unable to get executive management to pay heed to the results. When I brought this up to the head of the business unit in a later meeting, her comment was, "Yes, we all know the folks in marketing have done some pretty detailed analyses, but executive management is not consulted before these analyses are undertaken and it is not clear what actions should result [from them]. As a result, they are viewed as largely academic exercises [that are] very removed from real work issues facing my managers." She went on to note that this unfortunate waste of capability and intelligence was a failure of process and communication.

Often, marketing doesn't have any disciplined processes in place in order to provide better intelligence to the groups that directly touch the customer. These marketing groups are not enabling front-line service employees to make the discretionary judgments that would strengthen customer bonds and stimulate profitable growth. Some companies have stopped collecting data in the field because of its inadequate use or mis-application, thereby slipping deeper into a well of customer ignorance.

We've seen a notable drift toward integrated marketing communica-tions in recent years. Many companies have made progress in terms of aligning their messages and the mediums in which they are presented. However, even this is inadequate. It suggests to many that marketing is primarily a "marcom" (marketing communications) vehicle, which tends to compartmentalize the organization.

Such thinking ignores the vital role of marketing in product devel-opment, channel management, customer interaction, market and cus-tomer analysis, partner relationship building, and overall corporate strategy. Smart marketers listen closely to the "voice of the customer" and the prospective customer as well. The role of customer advocate is essential throughout the enterprise. However, it has been abandoned by marketing organizations who simply insinuate themselves ever more deeply into the marcom role.

PROCESSES WITHOUT OVERSIGHT OR LEADERSHIP

Without process discipline or leadership, there is no ongoing desire to design, manage, or improve processes. No one oversees the processes to ensure they are performed as an integrated whole. No one has the authority to ensure work is performed in a streamlined fashion from one end of a process to another; some processes, in fact, remain unseen and unrecognized. Work flows are disconnected, and their components are broken up into separate pieces and responsibilities.

In some cases, this abysmal pattern is related to constant leadership changes, organizational restructuring, and the turbulence wrought by corporate consolidation. It may not be the case that no one has ever con-sidered the challenge of developing wider, integrated marketing processes; it's just that such approaches don't stick in an environment of perpetual change and uncertainty. Unfortunately, the lack of process discipline merely perpetuates and amplifies the uncertainty. It's a vicious cycle.

The prejudices that underlie our thinking may be found in our language. The very concept of marketing "department" or "function" is subtly hostile to the overarching concept of process. When companies are designed in such a way that marketing is discouraged from or unwilling to venture onto the "turf" of others, the possibilities of process thinking are severely undermined. When the marketing "process," for instance, ends with the production of the "campaign," the likelihood of success is increasingly remote.

No wonder campaign results everywhere, whether in direct mail or e-mail or via television, seem to be on a steep slope downward. We have designed the customer and the individuals who are closest to the customer out of our marketing processes. We have truncated these processes, keeping ourselves locked in the black box.

These are the result of poor, inadequate, and incomplete processes: falling campaign results, rising customer resistance, and worse still, remarkable ignorance about the erratic swings of value associated with one's customer relationships. At this point, "process-thinking" resembles "measurement-thinking." In other words, we have islands of process discipline just as we have islands of measurement discipline. What we lack are the vital linkages and connections between isolated activities. We lack a truly comprehensive and integrated approach to marketing process.

EFFICIENCY AT THE EXPENSE OF EFFECTIVENESS

Instead of building processes that maximize the efficiency of marketing campaigns, we need processes that ensure the effectiveness of our customer interactions and relationship development efforts. They are not necessarily one and the same. Just as perceived efficiencies in the call center (such as shorter talk times) can undermine relationships when problems go unresolved, so too, can efficiencies in the marketing process.

"Consumer resistance to marketing is a growing phenomenon," according to recent research from Yankelovich Inc.[1] "Response to all forms of marketing is declining at precipitous rates. The market for products to block, skip, or opt-out of marketing and advertising is growing rapidly." It may be efficient to blast out e-mails to a wide sphere of prospects. It may be efficient to conduct a telemarketing campaign at dinner time. One can efficiently reach an extraordinary number of eyeballs on TV during the Super Bowl. The real question is. "What about effectiveness?"

The Yankelovich survey and others like it should lead to extreme discomfort in the executive suites of enterprises today. These findings are telling us that our processes are not aligned with the results that we wish to achieve. They should drive leaders to rethink their current approaches. Their primary challenge isn't about coming up with more creative advertising or more carefully testing direct mail campaigns. Instead, it's about rethinking marketing process as it applies to connections and interactions with customers.

At present, our marketing activities tend to maximize customer interruption and manipulation as opposed to managing processes that promote customer engagement, respect, and loyalty. Our marketing processes must be integrated and extended if we are to build customer value as opposed to destroying it. "I believe today's marketing model is broken," confides Jim Stengel, Chief Marketing Officer of Procter & Gamble.[2] "We are applying antiquated thinking and work systems to a new world of possibilities."

Clearly, there is a mismatch between our efforts to reach customers and their perceptions of the value and desirability of such efforts. While there are certainly exceptions (and exceptional marketers), the overall experience of the customers we are trying to reach seems to be low.

We are not "moving the needle" in any fundamental sense when we maximize process efficiency at the expense of process effectiveness. As many organizations have come to realize, when multiple process improvement initiatives are undertaken over a period of time, the incremental efficiency benefits diminish with each subsequent initiative. The life cycle of efficiency is such that incremental improvements are not sustainable for the long term. Eventually, all processes reach the point beyond which additional "fine-tuning" interjects little or no incremental benefit, particularly with regard to increased output and associated cost-savings. Eventually, failure to look beyond the efficiency factor often leads to the inevitable loss of competitive advantage.

This daunting reality has particularly been highlighted within marketing organizations in recent years. They have come to realize the importance of increasing productivity via the introduction of marketing technologies (e.g., campaign management analytics applications, etc.), rather than in improving the quality of the processes themselves. Add to this other common realities such as diminished returns on existing marketing investments, shrinking budgets, reduced headcounts, increased competition, more demanding and savvy consumers, and the stagnating skills within the marketing organization, and it becomes clear why process efficiency alone is not sufficient. In fact, marketing automation expenditures coupled with judicious investments in upgrading staff and improving processes can result in higher costs but also significantly higher revenues. Too often, however, automation investments and business cases are justified on the basis of cost cuts and improvements in efficiency alone. All too well, we see that "effectiveness" must be modeled into each marketing process in order to truly establish a competitive advantage within the marketing function.

Opaque and impenetrable marketing bureaucracies are becoming increasingly unacceptable, particularly as a new generation of marketers embrace process discipline. This generation is committed to making comprehensive processes visible to superiors in the executive suite, but it also is relying on rigorous processes to present a compelling and consistent experience to customers. As the costs and risks associated with inadequate process ceaselessly rise, those that remain in the conventional black box will simply fail. Expect fortunes to tumble and marketing careers to be ruined as disappointed customers run for the exits.

PATHS TO IMPROVED PROCESS DISCIPLINE: PROCESS UNBOUND

If marketers are to be effective, we must see marketing process as something that transcends the marketing organization. Marketing can best succeed if it embraces a process discipline that integrates both the activities within the organization and those that extend beyond it. It must integrate its own isolated silos of marketing activity and extend the processes of marketing out to the customer. Indeed, the extension of marketing process might wisely cross an array of organizational disciplines to embrace product development, partner development, service logistics, customer care, and other areas where marketing's strategic and analytical perspective on the customer can provide immense insight and value.

As process discipline has proven in areas of the organization such as manufacturing, logistics, and finance, enduring value lies in the consistent, sequenced, and systemic flow of activities across boundaries to deliver a clear business result. Process discipline enables companies to leverage the skills, capabilities, and talents of individuals to consistently deliver a valued outcome, even as it confronts the premises of corporate "star systems." Rather than rely on the extraordinary acts of individuals to get the work done, process discipline embeds excellent execution in the collaborative methodologies of the enterprise and institutionalizes high performance work.

Beyond this clear benefit, mobilizing the organization to work in concert and collaboration enables the achievement of far more with far less. Marketing has the opportunity to elevate its role and impact in the organization through the design, deployment, and enhancement of boundary-spanning processes.

KEY PRINCIPLES OF PROCESS DISCIPLINE AND LEADERSHIP

Of course, some companies will naturally be more attracted to process thinking than others. Established companies, both market leaders and challengers, have the most to gain. Young, fast-growth companies tend to be less concerned about process and systems. They are sustained by their early breakthroughs and growth itself. Established companies, however, essentially must compete on their ability to execute in a predictable fashion.

"I think once you reach a particular scale, such as we have, the key performance drivers are repeatability and predictability," says Cathy Bessant, Chief Marketing Officer for Bank of America.[3] "World-class processes set you free."

Bessant, who was president of the bank's operation in Florida prior to taking the CMO role, sees marketing through the eyes of an experienced business executive. "When I was running a line of business or a territory, I had a great deal of clarity on the levers to pull for success," she adds. "I knew what to expect if I took down CD rates in a market or took them up, what incremental revenues I could generate and what it would cost me. In marketing, business cases are harder to make. Marketing is often the 'last in' when it comes to budgeting and 'first out' when it comes to budget cuts. That's because there is no continuity and predictability in the returns that are generated."

Process discipline, however, delivers continuity and predictability. It is central to the reduction of costs, the enhancement of productivity and the maintenance of steady and profitable growth. Process also lays the ground work for innovation by ensuring that resources are smartly invested in the areas where they can have maximum impact. Most important, process discipline ensures that a company is deeply aligned with its customers.

Marketers now must understand their prospective and existing customers with far more precision, intelligence, and depth. They must build rich profiles that clarify the preferences and priorities of customers, and they must enable customer interactions and conversations that are personally relevant. Customers now expect high levels of professionalism. They demand a consistent experience and consistent improvement. They seek clearly defined value and service levels. What's more, customers will not tolerate unmet expectations or lapses of performance; it is simply too easy to defect–and punish those who have mistreated them.

Forward-looking marketers have committed themselves to extending processes out to the customer in a way that ensures high levels of consistency. These marketers are committed to meeting and exceeding customer expectations. They recognize that process discipline is an essential tool for achieving a high level of precision and predictability in customer experience and communication. Among the key principles of process discipline guiding today's high performance marketers:

- *Effective processes are enabled by an integrated focus on design, execution, and analysis.* Marketing relies on process *design* to establish a clear and visible sequence of activities necessary to achieve the desired result. Process *execution* is the deployment and operation of the marketing process. Process *analysis* is an assessment of performance (relative to targets) and an exploration of potential improvements. While the value of each of these process management activities is inherently unique, it is only through the successful linkage of the three, as shown in Figure 5.1, that any

FIGURE 5.1 *Process Linkage*

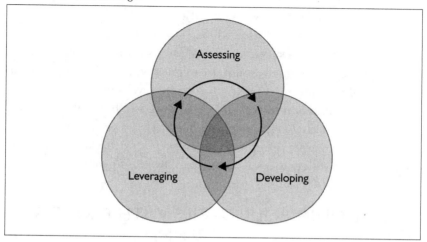

significant degree of marketing effectiveness is achieved. Simply stated, the more successful an organization is in creating dependencies between these three activities, the more likely it is that the effectiveness of its marketing programs and operations will increase over time.

- *Effective processes both create and depend on a visible linkage between actions and outcomes.* When different people do the same things differently, a marketing organization will most likely find that it cannot isolate factors which influence the positive or negative performance of a process. If an organization can't assess the results of specific actions, how can it determine whether or not to repeat the act as it goes forward? Strong process discipline clarifies the connections between activities and results, making them reasonably predictable and manageable. Process discipline helps marketers identify bottlenecks and breakdowns and act quickly to correct them. It is impossible to act with such insight and confidence in an environment that downplays the value of process.

- *Effective processes are defined in relation to their impact on customer value.* High performance marketers prioritize and quantify processes in relation to their impact on customer-facing goals and objectives. These marketers monitor and measure key processes to ensure that defined contributions to customer value are being delivered. They also establish ownership for each process to ensure that the process is continually reviewed and opportunities for enhancements are identified.

As these principles suggest, process leadership is critical to ultimate success. Processes themselves must be aligned with the larger goals and objectives of the enterprise. Moreover, senior-level support is necessary to instill commitment to a process-based approach, but it also helps address the political challenges associated with crossing traditional boundaries. To be fully effective, processes managed by marketing must be interconnected with processes that are run by other groups.

SPANNING BOUNDARIES WITH PROCESS OWNERSHIP

In many cases, marketing must be empowered to design (or redesign) processes that cross conventional boundaries. This can be a challenging task because it may lead to conflicts of status and authority, and it may require new measures and management approaches. New communication, training, and skill development may be necessary for this effort, and may also demand new forms of compensation and reward.

This is the frontier of marketing process design. From a process management perspective, this means that marketers must extend processes beyond campaigns and other areas for which they have immediate *control* out to call centers, sales forces, distribution channels, logistics, product development, and similar areas of the enterprise where their goal should be to obtain greater *influence*. The key to obtaining that influence and using it to elevate marketing lies in leveraging marketing's privileged and strategic perspective of the customer. The marketing organization's insight into customers can open doors and make it a more valued player within the enterprise, and at the same time, a less confined and mysterious contributor. Customers are not concerned about departmental fiefdoms and demarcations. They merely want high-value relationships with their product and service providers. They want value for money and they want their problems solved. It is as simple as that.

Boundary-spanning processes are a vital element of marketing's future. I recently observed the transformational efforts of these process improvements at Juno Lighting, Inc., a leading manufacturer of commercial and residential lighting fixtures based in the Chicago suburb of Des Plaines, Illinois. In a manufacturing oriented company like Juno, it is particularly important for marketing to demonstrate that it can create and lead processes that result in visible improvements in business performance. Alison Zepp, Vice President of Marketing for Juno Lighting, Inc., tackled such a process when she organized the creation of a price list to serve as the reference source for all of the salespeople, distributors, and contractors. In addition to prices, the list includes products from Juno's different divisions, along with product dimensions and specifications. As a result, many people were involved in the creation of the list. The list details had to be accurate because incorrect price or product specifications could result in extremely expensive mistakes.[4]

The original process for this list's creation was not very well planned and had little automation. For example, earlier versions of the list had numerous errors and required over four months to complete. By applying process mapping and control disciplines along with assigning accountability and responsibility, Juno was able to reduce the cycle time for the process to 20 days (less than one month), with far fewer errors (see Figure 5.2). Not only did this benefit the company greatly, it also added to marketing's credibility with senior executives.

FIGURE 5.2 *Juno Lighting: Price List Development Process*

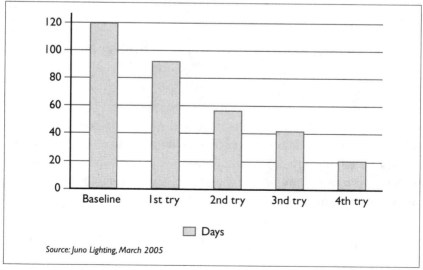

Source: Juno Lighting, March 2005

Zepp's experience and those of other disciplined marketers instruct us that we must commit to clear process ownership, accountability, and support. Process discipline demands marketing *process owners*–individuals who will oversee and assume responsibility for an end-to-end process. While process participants should be incented to ensure successful performance, it is the process owner who monitors performance from a high level and can intervene when necessary to ensure the process works in a consistent, streamlined fashion.

Within marketing, this may mean shifting oversight from geographies, products, brands, channels, or media groups to drive particular customer-oriented objectives. Many companies have begun to raise questions about whether a product-focused structure is the best way of creating a customer-focused organization. Some have shifted process ownership to account or segment managers who can oversee the management of resources on behalf of customers and oversee the performance of customer-facing processes. Team members must collaborate to ensure the smooth and successful operation of the process. Their allegiance, in fact, must increasingly shift toward ensuring the process is effectively performed and separate from their functional groups. They must be encouraged and incentivized to rise above territorial designations and departmental functions to ensure the process is maintained and executed.

IMPLEMENTING PROCESS DESIGN AND DISCIPLINE: SIX SIGMA

Six Sigma is a methodology to improve processes and reduce error rates in manufacturing environments, and was pioneered by Motorola and championed by companies such as General Electric and Honeywell. It has resulted in tremendous improvements in performance for manufacturing organizations. More recently, Six Sigma has found converts in nonmanufacturing companies such as Bank of America, with significant improvements in quality and performance across the board. Six Sigma is one of the approaches businesses are using to implement process design and discipline.

In the past, product or brand managers may have commanded all the resources, maximizing the sale of individual products, irrespective of the value created or diminished at the actual customer level. Product managers might prefer advertising and promotions, even reduced prices, to meet sales targets and grow market share. But a more powerful outcome might actually be achieved through an extension of the marketing process.

ServiceMaster, a $3.6 billion provider of business and residential services based in Downers Grove, Illinois, is a prime example of this principle. It has incorporated the "voice of the customer" into the company's processes in a way that has clearly driven up profitability.[5] When salespeople in the company's American Residential Services division engaged in deep discounting, the company's Marketing and Six Sigma teams decided to test the sales group's underlying assumption that customers were most concerned about price. Customer surveys, in fact, determined that the issues that really mattered were service quality, on-time delivery, and overall professionalism. Ultimately, the company instituted an "on-time service guarantee" and encouraged the sales group to hold the line on prices. By incorporating key insights into the overall customer management process, marketing was able to add $4 million in incremental net profit to the bottom line in 2003–a figure now expected to double.

In this case, Six Sigma provided the framework to drive corporate performance improvement and Marketing embraced the approach. "This was all about culture change," said John Biedry, Senior Vice President at ServiceMaster. "If it weren't for the Six Sigma process working with Marketing, we would never have seen the opportunity to drive both satisfaction and profits so dramatically."

Process design ensures that activities will be performed the same way every time. It provides a critical level of repeatability and predictability vital to successful management in an era of complexity and turbulence that would otherwise prove overwhelming. Predictability is particularly essential in relation to customer-facing performance. Customers, after all, are becoming the least predictable factor in the whole network of value creation. Many companies see their customers defecting in large numbers. In many cases, customers are *changing channels* on a regular basis, deriving information in one channel (such as the Internet) that is then used to strike a better bargain in another one (such as a car dealership).

Predictability becomes increasingly critical in an era of rapid and continuous change. Companies depend on it to ensure they are successful. While breakthrough innovations and transformative changes are a constant, it is predictability and execution that enables established organizations to perpetually thrive.

Marketing organizations are embracing this opportunity to deliver predictability. They are providing process leadership in both design and discipline. Smart marketers realize that they possess valuable insight in terms of customer intuition and they are rigorously incorporating this insight into processes that span the enterprise, whether sales or customer service or product development. These leaders are not merely introducing new processes. They are infusing them throughout their own organizations and beyond them, ensuring that marketing processes are extended to "touch" the customer directly and influence the wider customer experience.

A growing number of marketers are taking the lead in ensuring consistency and continuity as it relates to customer-facing processes. They are engaged in efforts to provide robust performance reporting and commitment to continual improvement. Some marketers, for example, at companies such as General Electric, Dow Corning, and Johnson & Johnson, have embraced Six Sigma as a methodology to infuse their own organizations with process discipline. While they are not necessarily attempting to achieve the 99.9997 percent effectiveness or "practical zero" defect rates that are expected in manufacturing, they are embracing Six Sigma's hardy process discipline and commitment to perpetual improvement.

Two areas where marketers have had distinct success with the Six Sigma methodology are in "process mapping" and in leveraging the "voice of the customer." Marketers report productivity gains of 25 percent or more as a result of such endeavors. "Mapping the work process helps people understand that there are, in fact, patterns buried in the seemingly random nature of the things they undertake each week," writes Pat LaPointe, Editor-in-Chief of *MarketingNPV*.[6] "In the end, process mapping shines a bright light on the value-detracting steps which slow you down, add cost, or prevent you from seeing the real opportunities."

Meanwhile, the emphasis on incorporating the customer's voice into various business processes, a Six Sigma mainstay, tends to empower and elevate marketers (who are in a position to listen to it very carefully). "By leading the dialogue on how the voice of the customer is heard and measured throughout the organization, Marketing can ensure that customer-centric business decisions become the norm and inspire the organization to higher levels of challenge in producing better products and services," writes LaPointe. "This in turn creates more opportunities for differentiation in brand marketing and better coordination through all owned and third-party channels."

Marketing Resource Management Software: An Evolving Resource for Improving Processes

In the coming years, enterprise software will increasingly enhance and automate marketing processes. Today's application frameworks tend to isolate and freeze process within the inflexible operations of the application itself. While this may be a huge advance over the ad hoc and home-grown efforts at automation of the past, the future revolves around dynamic, manipulable, "composite" solutions that give business people greater control over the design and operation of process flows.

Today's marketing software providers have made powerful improvements in techniques for applying customer information in multichannel marketing campaigns and communications. It is becoming easier to design and redesign processes, for example, by implementing new alerts, triggers, and business rules to facilitate real-time marketing response. This is where we are headed. Beyond the slow, lumbering marketing practices of the past to an era of real-time customer engagement. Indeed, significant efforts are now created to leverage customer insight through software, enhancing the decisions and dialogues that take place on the front-lines of customer engagement and operation.

Marketing Resource Management (MRM) software may prove particularly important in terms of the advancement of process discipline and thinking in the marketing organization. MRM software is now enabling marketers to visualize and better manage processes, work flows, and investments.

Traditionally, Aprimo has been considered the leading player in MRM software and was a pioneer in this business. Recently, Unica Corporation, the leader in campaign management software with their Affinium Campaign product, has focused on developing its MRM offering called Affinium Plan, and is starting to emerge as a leader in this space as well. The larger suite vendors such as Oracle, Siebel, and, especially SAP, also have some of these capabilities built into their offerings.

VALUING PROCESS AS AN ASSET

Process is an asset, albeit a relatively intangible one. It is a form of intellectual property that captures, sustains, and embeds our thinking and action as well as competitive advantage. It persists, even as time passes, talent moves, and markets are transformed. As an asset, process must be defined, documented, and managed. Nevertheless, the intangible value of process can be as great as the value of more tangible assets. The value of process is certainly reflected in General Electric, which has long prided itself for its systematic development process associated with management talent. It is also reflected in the leadership of Dell, Inc. Dell's ability to let customers design their own computers on the Web and then to deliver these within a very short time frame has become an enormous competitive advantage. This process aided Dell in becoming a leader in the PC market, surpassing giants such as IBM and Hewlett Packard. Companies such as General Electric and Dell consider exceptionally executed processes to be the beating heart of corporate value.

Though the assets of process may not be reflected in the balance sheet, they are a powerful force in the value creation process. Organizational processes provide a very defensible and long lasting competitive advantage, because the process is less visible and harder to copy than design and communication elements. Some observers have noted that, over time, companies may increasingly seek to establish "process repositories" that hold or contain the intellectual property associated with organizational processes. These repositories can make processes increasingly accessible and visible, and give them a form that is more open to management and leverage.

All processes, whether embedded in software or culture, provide vital predictability to marketing. Just as CEOs and CFOs must offer Wall Street analysts "guidance" into earnings expectations, so too, CMOs must offer "guidance" to senior executives and the remainder of the marketing organization in regard to what to expect from marketing processes and programs. Marketing leaders must make future behavior and performance increasingly predictable, and process is a central tool in this overarching effort. Superior execution depends on it.

CLOSING THE GAP: THE PROCESS PERSPECTIVE

In order to develop firm commitment to process discipline within Marketing, companies must be prepared to take several key steps. Among them:

- *Aligning process resources and required work effort with customer strategy and corporate objectives.* All processes are not equal. Some will be more valuable than others for helping the organization define and implement effective strategies, meet stated revenue and profitability goals, etc. As marketing organizations map out and design processes, they must be clear about how those processes align with higher strategic and business goals.
- *Documenting marketing processes to ensure they are fully understood by everyone involved.* Maintaining accurate documentation is central to the goal of creating greater visibility into the workflows that produce value. Such efforts can help to create a shared understanding within and beyond marketing about what and how it is to be achieved.
- *Leading and supporting necessary transitions and change efforts.* The way that process change is introduced is critical to the successful adoption of the new process. Smart and comprehensive change management is paramount to the successful introduction of a new process. Successful change management requires a critical focus on communication, collaboration, training, development, and support. It may also require a rethinking of reward, compensation, and incentive structures.
- *Developing process measurement and improvement systems.* The ultimate success of a marketing process depends on the ongoing measurement of process owners to ensure that they are meeting performance goals. Marketing must therefore adopt and monitor appropriate measurements. Based on outcomes, the marketing organization can determine where opportunities for improvement lie, whether through fixing an existing process or setting the bar even higher.
- *Establishing executive management and customer buy-in.* If the individuals who are the intended beneficiaries of the process being

performed do not consider the end result valuable, then it is not. High performance marketing organizations understand this and make sure that the processes are appropriately aligned with the stated objectives of senior management, and the needs, priorities, and expectations of customers.

Organizations with well established, effective processes engage in these behaviors, all of which can serve as benchmarks against which other organizations can measure their own progress.

ANATOMY OF AN EFFECTIVE MARKETING PLANNING PROCESS

While there are many processes within Marketing's control or, at least, within its sphere of influence, we focus here on a single process, marketing planning, to illustrate the importance of process discipline.

An effective marketing planning process can be characterized as a *systematic approach to assessing and prioritizing potential marketing opportunities relative to corporate and customer objectives*. Ultimately, the objective of planning is to develop an actionable blueprint that will guide how the organization defines and executes marketing programs.

The value of an effective marketing planning process lies in:

- Helping marketing organizations make decisions that are aligned with corporate objectives and overall customer strategies.
- Providing the basis for ensuring appropriate allocation of limited resources based on estimated value of the marketing opportunity.
- Communicating the objectives and expectations of the marketing organization to the remainder of the business.
- Identifying the specific tasks that must be performed, and the level of detail that allows activity ownership, schedules, and timelines to be assigned.
- Quantifying the estimated ROI of marketing campaigns and programs so that sound budgeting decisions can be made.

The introduction of a defined and rigorous planning process can enable marketing to adopt dynamic, responsive budgeting processes. Traditionally, budgets have been assigned as a straight percentage of corporate revenue or as the result of adding or subtracting a set increment based on the previous year's budget. The rigidity of the budgeting process makes companies loath to revisit plans throughout the year, even when market circumstances change or new opportunities are identified.

However, a growing number of companies are beginning to explore new ways to allocate resources. Many of them, in fact, have adopted "zero-based" budgeting structures, which enable them to reassess and reprioritize their marketing investments in relation to changing markets. Some organizations use "rolling forecasts" that allow them to make a rapid evaluation of changing needs throughout the year, and invest appropriately. Still other companies rely on perpetually monitored consumer or customer metrics to shape their investments.

Clearly, companies are seeking new ways to dynamically match marketing investment to opportunity. At the heart of such dynamism is a commitment to agile processes. However, process discipline is the foundation of all such efforts. Without rigorous processes that enable marketers to continually prioritize, reassess, and measure their potential investments, the budgeting and planning process remains relatively static.

MARKETING PLANNING FRAMEWORK AND PRACTICES

As we mentioned earlier, developing a marketing plan typically involves three phases of process activities: *analysis, design,* and *execution.* Although many variations exist, an effective market planning process framework typically consists of the components shown in Figure 5.3.

Having had the opportunity to witness and study world-class marketing planning processes, we at Quaero have seen a number of key practices emerge. Among them:

- *Identifying win-win opportunities.* Smart plans should create value for both the customer and the enterprise (incorporating processes aligned with corporate strategy/objectives).
- *Approaching the process as a continuous event, rather than an annual event.* Although the onset of the planning process is typically ini-

FIGURE 5.3 *The Marketing Planning Framework*

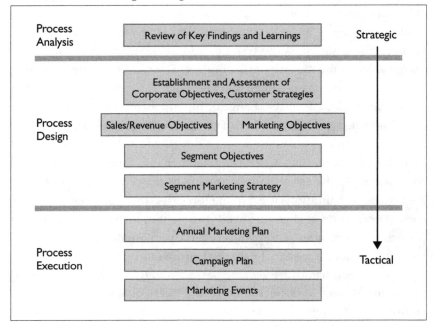

tiated with an annual planning session, in order to be truly effective, it should consist of regularly scheduled events (quarterly at a minimum) that include reviews, updates, and revisions of marketing plans.

- *Validating in the reviews whether future campaigns should remain part of the marketing campaign calendar.* These decisions should be driven by the ongoing analysis of the value of a marketing opportunity (such as campaign performance to-date against the previously established objectives, estimated ROI, and so on). Newly available research revealing a change in the competitive landscape or relevant shifts in customer preferences, needs, or attitudes are among the factors that might justify changes in the plan.

- *Making decisions based on facts.* The objective is to move beyond intuitive planning and decision making and toward approaches based on solid evidence and insight. This decision-making process begins with a review and thorough understanding of key influences from prior marketing campaign programs, as well as insights gained from other means such as research and customer dialogs.

- *Engaging key representatives throughout the enterprise.* Representatives from key departments such as Finance, Sales, and Service should also participate in the planning process. These critical organizations often lend valuable insight from both the company and customer perspectives. In addition, a collaborative approach fosters a sense of shared ownership which is critical to securing buy-in and cooperation in the plan's execution. This approach also helps ensure consistency in customer-impacting strategies and processes.
- *Presenting customer and financial metrics along with the requested marketing budget in order to quantify the value of each proposed marketing opportunity.* Marketing planners should present the opportunity's metrics so that they are relevant and appropriate for the given audience. For example, it is common for Marketing, Sales, and Finance departments to value opportunities using different ROI models. As a result, each department often views the financials developed by the other departments as flawed and, therefore, less credible. As such, it is critical to the budget approval subprocess that planners establish credibility.
- *Embracing an "opportunity-based" budgeting approach to ensure that the budget allocated is in proportion to the estimated value of the opportunity itself.* Investments should be actively linked to perceived outcomes, whether those outcomes are financial or nonfinancial. This approach helps organizations ensure that they get the "most bang for their buck."
- *Establishing and enforcing a "learning agenda" to generate critical insight.* By carefully assessing past performance (much as the army conducts an "after-action review"), the organization learns how to invest more intelligently in the actions that will deliver success in the future. Of course, the future is a moving target. For that reason, the learning agenda must be attuned to current trends and patterns that might influence decisions. The individuals responsible for planning should be actively involved in reviewing and, perhaps, managing performance reports, market research, and other ongoing analyses.

These are some of the winning practices that are guiding marketing planning processes today. By attending to these various elements of the overall process, smart organizations are ensuring they invest limited resources for the greatest effect, continually adapting in hypercompetitive and constantly changing markets.

BARRIERS TO EFFECTIVE MARKETING PLANNING

The introduction of an effective planning process framework, however, does not guarantee that the planning process itself will be improved. This is a reality that many organizations fail to sufficiently acknowledge and anticipate. All too often, marketing organizations assume that once the process itself is defined, the organization will become inherently more effective at performing the activities involved in the process. Reality, however, indicates that the overall quality of the process can be adversely impacted by organizational issues such as the following:

- Lack of support from senior management or other key constituents across the organization;
- Inadequate understanding of the purpose of process activities or how to complete them;
- Underdefined subprocesses upon which the primary planning process is dependent (such as the application of key process measures);
- Ineffective assumptions/inputs to the planning process, such as limited analysis of key learnings upon which sound decisions can be made;
- Insufficient communication infrastructure within the marketing organization itself and with the other parts of the organization;
- Lack of incentives appropriately aligned to the objectives.

As mentioned, it is critical not only to introduce a new process, but to infuse that new process into the culture of the organization. This task requires leadership and commitment.

THE INCREMENTAL REVOLUTION

By and large, process management is an evolutionary–not a radical–approach. Rather than trying to reinvent all processes in their entirety, marketing organizations should first identify the importance of each process relative to the organization's goals and objectives. Furthermore, organizations must establish the potential value and contribution of every work activity within each valuable process. They should examine activities that hold high potential, determining the most appropriate means for completing the activity, and to appropriately allocate valuable resources to high value activities. Organizations also should review activities that are deemed low-value, to ensure that they do not consume a disproportionate amount of resources. Fundamental process changes may be necessary, but they need not be overwhelming and agonizing. Process provides a disciplined, driven revolution in increments. It is not shock therapy, but rather a blueprint for rigorous execution and continual improvement.

Among many of today's world-class companies, process leaders and owners within marketing are encouraged and given incentives to drive continual performance improvements. Current measures and outcomes may set the bar, but they must constantly raise it in order to keep adding value to the enterprise. They also are encouraged to perpetually rethink the elements of true effectiveness.

Customer expectations will rise. Competition will intensify. Products that once were innovative and differentiated will become commodities. Given these dynamics, progress is inextricably linked to process. Process discipline is critical if marketing is to be a powerful force for growth.

CASE STUDY: SIX SIGMA DRIVES MARKETING PERFORMANCE AT BANK OF AMERICA

Bank of America has embraced process discipline and the results have been powerful. Relying on Six Sigma methodology, the bank's relationship marketing group has established visible and measurable processes that build credibility within the organization overall.

"Although Six Sigma emerged primarily from manufacturing, we have applied that discipline to financial services specifically in the marketing function," notes Rose Corvo, Senior Vice President of the bank's relationship marketing unit.[7] "It ensures people are focused on solving business issues, and disciplined in their approach to execution, and provides the ability to produce measurable results at the end of the process."

The unit's objective is to provide the bank's various Lines of Business (LOBs) with clear, defined, and measurable options for marketing investment and revenue growth. The marketing unit's success is dependent on having disciplined processes in place for modeling and measuring outcomes. The unit can then advise the LOBs on expected returns on their marketing investments. The LOBs then have information necessary to consider the trade-offs and opportunities associated with direct-marketing approaches.

Corvo's group relies on a marketing "dashboard" to determine whether it is meeting its performance targets. Key performance indicators are presented on the dashboard as red, yellow, and green "lights." If the dashboard turns red, the group will open an "MBF," Six Sigma lingo for "management by fact." The MBF is a document that "provides a methodology for solving the apparent problem and closing the gap," she explains. "It provides a specific problem statement, and it defines the root causes, which leads to a very rigorous, methodical way of managing to expectations."

Six Sigma approaches to marketing also engender challenges. "The difficulty lies in education and the use of the appropriate tools," remarks Corvo. "It does take time. You are required to work on a project. The good news is this process and mindset provides us with a very disciplined approach to transparency and accountability."

The ability to measure and report performance in a transparent fashion is a powerful aspect of the relationship marketing unit's value to the bank. The unit's approach provides predictable returns and outcomes.

The group also expects to be applying its disciplined marketing capabilities toward the choreographing of customer interactions and communications. As new legislation limits marketing options and customers become more resistant to conventional marketing, communication processes that recognize and encourage individual preferences and are "triggered" by particular events become increasingly critical to success," concludes Corvo.

CASE STUDY: DOW CORNING'S EXPERIENCE WITH PROCESS ENHANCEMENT

Dow Corning, the $2.5 billion provider of silicone products and other performance solutions, has embraced Six Sigma as a methodology to enhance its marketing processes. The company, which is a joint venture between Dow Chemical and Corning, Inc., initially relied on the Six Sigma approach for manufacturing and engineering. However, it has discovered that the same discipline that drives quality processes in those areas can also have a powerful impact on customer-facing parts of the enterprise.

"Six Sigma works for marketing in a lot of different ways," says Scott Fuson, Corporate Executive Director of Marketing, Sales and Customer Service.[8] "First of all, it brings the voice of the customer to the company. It's a terrific starting point because it brings marketing to all corners of the company without actually saying the word 'marketing.'"

In addition, Fuson points out that adopting the Six Sigma methodology has provided "discipline in setting strategic improvement goals for all levels of the company." Finally, he mentions Six Sigma's impact on the improvement of marketing processes. Fuson notes that the methodology embeds new capabilities in processes and work flows, which don't change if someone changes roles. As he puts it, "We use the tools for every facet of performing our daily jobs."

In the past, the company concentrated on maximizing the value of capital resources. However, Six Sigma has transformed the company, encouraging it to adopt a "marketing model." The company is now listening closely to its clients to meet its key priorities and enhance growth, productivity, and customer service. Even "back office" groups such as Finance and Manufacturing have extended their processes beyond "internal clients" to consider linkages to the ultimate customer. Fuson says this has had a powerful impact on the culture of the company. "Now, we let the facts and data and the voice of the customer do the talking," he adds. "It's the trump card of everything. It's undeniable."

DISCIPLINED PROCESSES AND THE WELL-TUNED ORGANIZATION

In this chapter, we have argued that improved processes are a critical step toward improving marketing performance. Marketing has much to learn from other corporate disciplines. Many companies have applied these proven disciplines to marketing and achieved tremendous improvements in cycle times and accuracy, contributing greatly to the overall performance of their companies. Of course, to develop and manage great processes, you need skilled people working within an organization that is tuned for success. That is the topic of our next chapter.

6

ORCHESTRATING THE ORGANIZATION
From Alignment to Engagement

"I find the great thing in this world is not so much where we stand, as in what direction we are moving: To reach the port of heaven, we must sail sometimes with the wind and sometimes against it, but we must sail, and not drift, nor lie at anchor."
Oliver Wendell Holmes

Bewildered executives often ask themselves why it is so difficult to get everyone in the organization moving together in one direction. As enterprises grow, it is not unusual for them to become slow and sclerotic. When market circumstances change, these organizations often are incapable of responding in a rapid and agile fashion, and when new strategies are formulated and unveiled, they execute them poorly.

While these problems may afflict many parts of an enterprise, the challenge facing marketing leaders revolves around aligning sometimes disparate functions to maximize customer value. Too often, marketing focuses merely on building an image through advertising campaigns or manipulating customer behavior through price-oriented promotions. Demanding activities such as these may pull marketing organizations away from the wider challenge of analyzing and driving customer value.

Marketing, therefore, faces a significant test. If it surrenders authority and influence over the customer's experience to other functional units, it risks further erosion of its credibility within the enterprise. The value of the marketing organization depends on a disciplined and integrated management of customer value, something that marketing, more than any other functional unit, is positioned to influence. Revenue reversals and customer defections always will hit marketing hardest. In a de facto (if unrecognized) sense, marketing is accountable for such downturns.

It is critical that marketing take the steps necessary to make certain that the customer experience is seamless and engaging, while also ensuring that it is profitable for the company. But marketing cannot act alone. Meeting this set of objectives hinges on organizational alignment and unified action. In order to lead, marketing must reach out to the rest of the organization by assuming the roles of both *orchestrator* and *boundary spanner*. Marketers also must help create more powerful and engaging connections to customers, therefore deeply aligning the enterprise with its markets.

In previous chapters, we have focused on issues such as strategy, measurement, and process. Encouraging people throughout the organization to work effectively toward shared objectives is what this chapter entails. After assessing the current state within many organizations, we will examine a number of specific ideas for improving organizational alignment. Case studies later in this chapter illustrate specific examples of organizations in which marketing has aligned itself effectively with finance and operations. The chapter ends with a personal anecdote drawn from my own experience with some intangible aspects of organizational alignment.

MARKETING TODAY: SEEKING AUTHORITY AND INFLUENCE

Organizational Alignment is a critical dimension of overall performance. It is the means by which organizational units, resources, and assets are marshaled to generate unique and compelling value. Unfortunately, companies too often lack the wherewithal to pull together in a united fashion for the purpose of meeting certain objectives. They often flounder in the face of core initiatives. One of those key initiatives is the acquisition and growth of customers.

Many companies are extremely conflicted over the question of how best to organize in relation to this challenge. Some company leaders publicly tout the vital importance of their customers, while their companies are a chaotic and overlapping mix of product-driven units that provide an inconsistent and fragmented customer experience. It is not unusual to see companies that proclaim their commitment to customer relationships devote their organizational energies to acquiring new customers rather than tending to existing customers. It is also not uncommon for a customer who is immensely valuable from the perspective of one product-focused unit to be treated with little regard by other units within the same company. Consider the example of a wireless phone customer that has proved immensely profitable for a phone company, experiencing multiple hand-offs and drop-offs from the customer service department of the same company's landline phone service division.

Other companies destroy value by wasting the customer's time. As an example, consider the common situation that occurs when a pharmaceutical company employs a different representative for each drug, and all of them converge on the office of single physician. Still, other companies waste resources and undermine relationships by bombarding their existing customers with undesired marketing messages that are meant for prospects, largely because the prospecting side of the marketing department does not talk to or have access to the company's customer-side information. We have discussed the backlash that is occurring as companies increasingly experience "marketing resistance." The onslaught of poorly targeted ads, direct-mail pieces, and e-mail messages can undermine customer perceptions, just as surely as smart marketing can enhance them.

While the marketing organization can legitimately claim that many of these problems are beyond its immediate authority, it has the most to lose as a result of them. In most organizations, marketing is the de facto owner of the customer relationship and experience. Companies look to marketing to drive profitable growth and enduring customer relationships. While interactions that occur in retail stores, call centers, or with salespeople certainly strengthen or weaken these relationships, marketing, more than any other group, is accountable for the outcome. Fair or not, that's the reality. The question is whether marketing will accept these inevitable circumstances and rise to a role of greater authority and influence. Many organizations suffer a leadership vacuum with respect to customer-focused initiatives. Marketing has an opportunity, therefore, to assume a leadership role—even if the role is an unofficial one.

Otherwise, the organization remains adrift, constantly destroying the customer value it has worked so tirelessly to build. Customers are acquired at great cost only to be lost in the next round of defections as competitors offer a new round of discounts. The lack of visibility and coordination across the entire customer relationship and life cycle can cause serious damage to efforts to increase customer satisfaction and retention. Indeed, one study by CMAT, a global organization drawing on the resources of the Ogilvy Network and WPP Group, found that only 14 percent of organizations share customer objectives across departments.[1] Marketing has an opportunity to reposition itself in the enterprise by addressing this challenge head on. By stepping up to take a leadership position and uniting disparate units, it can help strengthen customer value, enhancing overall growth and profitability.

Customer service, field sales, and partners tend to have a limited perspective on the customer. While these groups' customer interaction may be direct, it tends to be from an operational point of view. These groups find it difficult to consolidate data points, analyze key trends, and view customers from the strategic vantage of profitability or potential. Marketing, more than any other group, has a strategic, bird's-eye view of the market and customer. It is in a strong position to analyze customer profitability levels, interactions, and experiences. Customer value, after all, cuts both ways. The enterprise must receive profits as a result of its customer relations and the customer must receive value to justify an investment or purchase. Marketing is in a position to analyze the key elements that contribute to a profitable and mutually satisfying value exchange.

Through such analytical activities, marketing can identify which market segments and which customers represent high profitability or potential, and which do not. Such analyses enable the organization to redirect its customer-facing resources to the areas where they can deliver the greatest payoff. But marketing also can analyze operational activities to assess their impact on customer relations. It can identify where weaknesses lie, where processes fail, and where the customer experience is inadequate. Marketing also can assess interactions across channels and suggest ways to enhance customer-facing processes. By analyzing customer behavior, attitudes, needs, propensities and profitability levels, marketing can help the rest of the enterprise understand customer value. Because it can look at the enterprise through the eyes of the customer and communicate what it learns, marketing can play a powerful role in alignment of units and resources that will strengthen customer value.

"Marketers often complain about the lack of authority and lack of influence over their colleagues in engineering, operations, or finance," writes Mohanbir S. Sawhney, an influential Marketing Professor with the Kellogg School of Management.[2] "The simple fact is—nobody will give you a seat at the table; you have to *earn* it. And the best way to gain power is through knowing your customers better than anyone else in the organization."

Unfortunately, many organizations tend to handle these types of efforts in a very fragmented and ad hoc fashion—or they simply don't undertake them at all. Too often, marketing is being driven to simply generate awareness, drive acquisition, or manipulate buying behavior through promotions and discounts. Marketing is not being encouraged or incented to represent the voice of the customer within the overall enterprise. No one, in many cases, has stepped up to enable organizational alignment, and customer value perpetually suffers.

IMPROVING ORGANIZATIONAL ALIGNMENT: BRINGING THE MARKET INSIDE

With respect to building customer value, world-class enterprises increasingly cast marketing in the role of organizational orchestrator. In these organizations, marketing can develop sophisticated customer insight and help facilitate intelligent action that reflects what it learns. Marketing spans organizational silos and functional boundaries to ensure the enterprise is engaging the customer in a consistent and compelling way.

"Marketing is the function in an organization that is usually best suited to 'bring the market inside the company,'" explains Jerry Noonan, a partner with Spencer Stuart and former Chief Marketing Officer at 1800Flowers.com.[3] "This role requires unique cross-functional leadership abilities to ensure that the 'head, heart, and gut' of every employee understands the market instinctively and translates it to the countless decisions they make everyday that cumulatively result in the product or service. Marketing's ability to do this well is based on the premise that their fundamental view is from the end customer's perspective back through the whole business system."

While some will argue that marketing has always managed market research, what Noonan is describing here is an expansive new role for marketers. This role requires far more interdepartmental outreach and engagement than marketing is typically expected to undertake. Marketing, in effect, acquires an ambassadorial role within its own enterprise. Once it has generated customer knowledge through rigorous market assessment, it must share its findings and insight with other parts of the company, relying on facts, evidence, and analysis to make the case for particular actions. As marketing generates deep understanding of the customer, it gains the credibility necessary to advocate the establishment of new processes and actions that will generate new value.

Of course, politics and culture may stand in the way of all such efforts. Indeed, it would be naïve to believe that marketing has the power to drive other functional units to take actions that they are inclined to resist. Senior leadership must clasp the reins in far-reaching organizational and cultural change initiatives. Nevertheless, marketing can influence change in important and consequential ways.

Marketers can use their special insights regarding customer-facing activities to influence the strategic perspectives of CEOs, line-of-business executives, and other senior leaders who have authority over the functional units, processes, and budgets that contribute to customer value. But marketing can only have that kind of influence if it begins investing its resources in activities that enable it to better understand the customer experience. Furthermore, marketing must span boundaries within the organization to ensure its findings are widely understood.

Gaining Authority and Accountability

In the quest to establish a greater, more effective organizational alignment with respect to customer value, marketing must pay particular attention to the dynamics of *authority* and *accountability*. Those who have oversight responsibility for customer-facing processes must be deeply engaged in efforts to enhance those processes. This may involve bringing different groups together, such as sales and customer service, to address a vexing challenge. It may possibly require process redesign efforts that establish new lines of authority and accountability, even creating process owners whose management influence stretches beyond conventional silos.

If marketing is to successfully enable such efforts, it must have the dimensional proficiency to drive organizational alignment. This capability and competency demands skill in several key areas. Among them:

- *Analysis and insight.* This is the capacity to rigorously assess and make sense of customer and market data of all kinds. Whether the data is quantitative or qualitative, the capacity to dynamically learn and discern enables marketing to provide perspective on market trends and potential developments that would otherwise be ignored or misunderstood.
- *Communication and guidance.* Based on the knowledge it generates, marketing must then enable the balance of the organization to understand key market trends, opportunities, and challenges. Marketing must speak the language of the audience or organizational unit it intends to reach. Marketing's ability to present its insights in an accessible and actionable form is critical to success, but so is its ability to listen, learn, and refine its perspective based on the views of the stakeholders it engages.
- *Engagement and orchestration.* Spanning boundaries is an essential aspect of alignment. To build a coalition for customer-focused action, marketing must cross functional barriers to engage other organizational units. This type of engagement and orchestration is a form of leadership based not on coercion, but on persuasion and credibility. In order to influence and guide future action, marketing must prove itself a valuable advisor and collaborator throughout the enterprise.

Marketing has a unique and powerful vantage point on customer value. It can use this position to provide valuable assessment and advisory capabilities to leaders and managers throughout the organization. It can assess customer-facing processes from the perspective of the customer, and then advise executives within the enterprise on how to realign and address identified problems. While there is no guarantee that such insights will in fact drive change, they at least lay the foundations for fact-based action and enable marketing to build bridges and credibility within the enterprise.

One company that has performed exceptionally in terms of organizational alignment is Wells Fargo. The company's marketers are considered highly accountable because their activities are deeply integrated within the business. A decentralized company, Wells Fargo delegates responsibility to the regional and local level for most of its growth and performance. Marketing, too, is largely decentralized. The incentives of marketers are directly linked to the performance of the business.

"Marketing here is considered a support and a line function," explains Meheriar Hasan, Executive Vice President in Wells Fargo's Consumer Credit Group.[4] "It is much more integrated and operationalized than marketing as a stand-alone function. Whether it involves customer insight, brand awareness, or value propositions, marketing is integrated with all levels of the business."

This level of integration generates all sorts of payoffs that would not be realized if marketing was treated as an independent function, as Hasan sees it. "The moment you integrate marketing, it becomes more apparent and quantifiable," he adds. Noting the close linkages that are developed between marketing and other groups, "Marketing plans are not created in a vacuum."

The next challenge for Wells Fargo, acknowledges Hasan, is to determine how best to share marketing insights, experience, and best practices across regions and business lines. "As each region is optimizing, there is a risk of suboptimization at the global level," he explains. That has encouraged the company to invest more deeply in brand awareness and corporate marketing. One key initiative revolves around creating greater synergy throughout the company. "We have successfully integrated marketing *within* the line of business," says Hasan. "Now, we have to integrate *across* the enterprise."

ALIGNING MULTIPLE PERSPECTIVES

To be effective in its efforts to align and orchestrate the organization, marketing must consider, understand, and speak to various perspectives. Through its understanding of these many perspectives, marketing positions itself to help align not only the organization itself, but the organization and the customer.

The Customer Perspective

This is where marketing begins to build a platform for credibility within the enterprise. Marketing's expertise in customer and market knowledge sets it apart within the organization. Its insight is a currency that should create interest throughout an enterprise and open doors for the marketing group.

To build this expertise, the group must assess the market to identify current trends and forecast new possibilities. Analytical rigor is critical. Marketing must analyze and engage existing (and prospective) customers in a disciplined fashion and diligently develop quantitative, qualitative, and anecdotal insight. Marketing also must define and assess customer segments. Only through such focused efforts can marketing gain a credible understanding of the customer's perspective and experience.

The customer perspective must be married with the enterprise's objectives for profitability and growth in the ensuing analysis. After all, it is of no use to provide a compelling, loyalty building experience for customers that are unprofitable and unpromising. Customers that do represent significant current and potential value, however, must be carefully assessed and monitored. It is the role of marketing to bring the "voice of the customer" to the balance of the enterprise.

The CEO Perspective

Marketing must be guided by the objectives of the enterprise's top executive. The CEO establishes the strategic goals that marketing will be measured against. With this in mind, it's critical that the CMO and other senior marketing leaders be deeply aligned with the CEO and help to carry that officer's perspective forward in their initiatives and activities. This can sometimes be a challenge, however. In one large organization I was involved with, the CEO repeatedly referred to marketers as "balloon blowers," thus denigrating the entire function in the eyes of the executive team. Needless to say, it proved difficult to align marketing with his vision. The company's $100 million-plus marketing budget bought a little more than a few balloons, to say the least!

Notwithstanding these anomalous situations, the CEO's imperatives can prove a powerful lever in marketing's efforts to influence wider organizational alignment. Marketing faces the challenge of linking the

CEO's high-level strategic objectives and the more tactical and operational actions that must be taken to meet them.

Marketing's role, however, is not merely to follow the CEO's strategic orders and relay them to the rest of the organization. It must provide a feedback loop from the front lines back to the CEO's office by reporting on trends, challenges, and opportunities. Senior leaders also need to know where organizational hurdles have been raised or problems persist. While excessive detail would not be welcomed, it is clear that senior level support will be necessary as marketing asserts itself within the array of groups that must collaborate to provide a successful outcome in the market.

The CEO can be a powerful advocate for the group, but marketing must first address the goals and objectives of the CEO. As William Thompson of the Thompson Group points out, "[T]he chief 'customer' of the marketing department is the company's Chief Executive Officer.[5] His or her responsibilities—driving critical CEO needs—must be fully understood, even anticipated, by the CMO and the entire marketing department."

The CFO Perspective

Perhaps no relationship is more important to, or less understood by, the marketing organization than the relationship with the chief financial officer. Andrew Abela, former Managing Director of the Marketing Leadership Council, contends that most high performing marketing organizations have a strong relationship with finance groups.[6] The MLC's research, he explained, found that there was a "powerful correlation" between perceptions of marketing success and the strength of the relationship between marketing and finance.

Finance executives look to marketing to help them meet their goals for shareholder and revenue growth and predictable cash flow. To the extent that marketing can help create outcomes more visible and predictable, it can win the trust of finance. In turn, finance becomes a healthy supporter of marketing investment priorities and marketing budgets.

However, marketing must take the initiative to understand the CFO's perspective and translate marketing activities in terms that finance can understand. It also can educate finance on the financial implications of conventional marketing metrics such as customer acquisition, customer retention and loyalty, and segment penetration. Together, these two groups can develop credible models of marketing performance and measurement.

To achieve this alignment, marketing must commit resources to the rigorous and quantitative analysis of marketing activities. These analyses must extend beyond easily measurable areas such as direct marketing and promotions, to incorporate sponsorships, advertising, public relations, and other activities that may be difficult to measure. Through such efforts, marketing and finance can develop common frameworks, language, and measurement systems that help drive clear and recognized performance gains within marketing and beyond.

The COO Perspective

While not every organization has a chief operating officer, marketing success depends on addressing the objectives and challenges of operational leaders. It cannot maximize customer value without the assistance of operational groups such as sales, service, logistics, product development, and IT. Front-line groups, in particular, have a direct connection with customers and they contribute heavily to the customer's overall experience. Unfortunately, marketing endeavors often are undermined by misalignment at the operational level. Marketers may try to build the long-term value of certain customer segments only to have their objectives undermined by salespeople judged on short-term quotas or customer service representatives that are incentivized to keep calls brief.

With this in mind, some management theorists have long contended that marketing and sales should be under the leadership of a single individual, thereby consolidating responsibility and authority over the revenue management process. However, placing these two groups under the leadership of a single individual can also result in problems. Too often, tactical sales considerations can outweigh long-term marketing objectives and reduce marketing to a sales support role in this situation. Marketing often needs a distinct champion. Forrester Research, completing its own research, extended this point by arguing that "marketing should own the contact center."[7] As Forrester illustrates, "Contact centers should relinquish control over the customer interaction—via phone, e-mail, chat, direct mail, or self-service—to a marketing executive who owns and manages the overall customer experience." This solution offers its own difficulties, however, because many marketing organizations do not have the competence to manage call centers. Both of these approaches are organizational fixes for what are essentially process problems. We recommend process fixes, ensuring communication and coordination between these functions, rather than centralized control.

While marketing will always have various levels of authority in different organizations and circumstances, the success of marketing revolves around operational execution. Therefore, it must engage operational leaders from all areas to ensure customer-facing processes are designed and managed with great proficiency.

The Marketing Perspective

The final alignment challenge facing marketing leaders lies in keeping their own house in order. The organization, itself, has become terribly fragmented and misaligned within many companies. As markets evolve and become more complex, marketing often has become more opaque and unmanageable. Its activity, too often, becomes an end by itself, several steps removed from the objective of building customer value.

Advertising groups follow complex branding formulas to justify ad buys. Marketing price and promotion teams follow "models" representing analyses that have drifted beyond the comprehension of other marketing teams. Direct marketers may also follow their own imperatives, generating campaigns that do not reflect larger branding initiatives. Indeed, the left-brained direct marketers may have no idea what right-brained creative marketers are doing on the advertising front.

When marketing is misaligned, it sends mixed messages to the market and confuses and frustrates potential customers. Undeniably, it destroys customer value—the one aspect that marketing is most responsible for building.

Marketing's Role as a Catalyst for Organizational Alignment

To successfully orchestrate organizational alignment, marketing leaders must build a shared perspective and forcefully drive consistent behavior. These leaders must marshal marketing resources with consistency and precision if they are to invest in them for maximal returns. In many organizations, marketing is able to help drive alignment through the establishment of a centralized marketing council to provide a forum for sharing strategies and insights across customer-facing departments and business units.

Organizational alignment is a primary factor in the credibility of marketing. Marketers, however, must span boundaries to build this credibility. The tendency has been to expect many marketers to constantly roll out their own marketing strategies, as if the growth strategies of the business were somehow a separate issue. Clearly, the careless usage of the term "marketing strategy" tends to isolate, not elevate, marketing. Similarly, many marketing organizations have developed increasingly complex approaches and models for addressing the "marketing mix." While these models, properly deployed, do enhance effectiveness, they also increase the risk of making the group seem increasingly obscure and opaque to the rest of the organization at a time when marketing most needs to develop even greater transparency.

Nor can trust and credibility be earned by merely following the current fashion for ROI. It is not difficult to employ analysts or consultants to develop quantitative models, metrics, and reports that generate an aura of authority. Such actions can create an appearance of diligent activity while obscuring the underlying truth. Marketing, in many cases, is merely trying to discern what actions it must take or what metrics it must produce to appease its critics, in a passive and reactive approach to a critical and continuing problem.

Marketing needs to abandon this policy of appeasement in favor of a policy of *engagement*. Marketing can strengthen its position and enhance its performance within the enterprise by engaging the various constituencies that contribute to customer value, whether these constituents are inside the organization or the customers and prospects outside. Its leaders must invest their time and resources in analysis, learning, and dialogue. New marketing plans, measurement models, and process designs should arise through these efforts, not precede them.

As world-class organizations are demonstrating, marketing must span boundaries, engage various stakeholders, and drive consensus on the management of customer value. These are the core activities of performance-focused alignment.

CLOSING THE GAP: THE ALIGNMENT INITIATIVE

If marketing is to play an influential role in the orchestration of today's customer-focused initiatives, it must take several decisive steps that establish its credibility within the enterprise. More specifically, it must actively align groups inside the organization with customer segments outside. Marketing, as we have discussed, is in a strong position to assume this boundary-spanning and value-creating role.

While marketing may decide to address these challenges in a formal or informal way, it has much to gain by launching an "alignment initiative." In other words, it should plan out and execute a clear plan to influence the alignment of the organization while maximizing customer value. Here are some key steps that marketing leaders can follow as they embark on this effort.

- *Build a foundational plan.* Marketing can begin this initiative by setting alignment priorities, focusing on the objectives and efforts that are most readily important, and then building a sense of urgency around them. The foundational plan might identify a key customer segment that is in danger of turnover or a set of customer-facing processes that appear broken.
- *Obtain senior-level support.* Once the plan has been established, marketing must turn to senior level management for support. If the marketing unit is to be an integral authority in the alignment process, it will need the backing of top leaders. The plan presented to senior leaders should be linked to key corporate objectives and initiatives. Ideally, this would include financial backing of the initiative, although marketing has a stake in the outcome of such an initiative with or without senior-level monetary support.
- *Engage internal organizations.* With senior-level backing for its alignment initiative, marketing can proceed to engage opera-

tional and other functional groups. Through interviews and conversations, the group can gain a better understanding of each organization's perspective on various customer-focused processes and activities. It can identify potential concerns, challenges, and objectives.

- *Engage customers and prospects.* Even as it is building greater understanding of other organizational units and their processes, marketing should begin analyzing and surveying customers to gain a better understanding of their experiences, attitudes, and behaviors. Through disciplined research and analysis, marketing can increasingly see its own enterprise through the customer's eyes.

- *Report findings and provide recommendations.* Based on its research findings, marketing should report their findings to internal units, including its analysis of customer (and prospective customer) experiences, attitudes, and trends. It might even provide some preliminary recommendations for operational units to consider. The key, however, is to assess customer perceptions and behavior in a rigorous way thereby setting the stage for internal action and improvement.

- *Invest resources in alignment efforts.* Marketing gains credibility within the enterprise by committing some of its own resources to the enhancement of customer-focused processes. By building internal relationship teams dedicated to managing relationships with other groups and staffing them appropriately, marketing sends a very strong message to the remainder of the organization. As opposed to merely recommending how others should solve problems, it takes joint ownership in them.

- *Monitor progress.* Marketing can and should play an important role in the ongoing monitoring of customer interactions, experiences, and behaviors. Through such efforts, it can assess how well the organization responds to identified challenges.

- *Report on outcomes.* Having an influential role in the enhancement of processes that build customer value, marketing must perpetually report back on its findings both to the operational units collaborating in the endeavor and to the senior leaders supporting it. This can easily be done through widely available "performance dashboards," as described in Chapter 4.

- *Identify new alignment opportunities and challenges.* Based on the outcome of initial alignment projects, marketing may decide to go further. For example, new projects can be identified and embarked upon, whether they revolve around other, unaddressed customer segments, processes, or business objectives.

Of course, many enterprises already conduct a great deal of market research and customer satisfaction studies. The opportunity here revolves around leveraging this research further to enhance the alignment of the organization, rather than having the research "sit on the shelf" as it too often does. While there may be tremendous variance among organizations in terms of process and proficiency, the activities outlined above are the essential steps that marketing units must undertake if they are to help orchestrate the creation of enduring customer value.

Nine Symptoms of a Misaligned Organization

How good are you at spotting misalignment in your own organization and what can you do about it? We have identified a few telltale "symptoms" of a misaligned organization.

- *Internal competition.* You hear an excessive amount of *"we versus them"* tales of organizational conflict (as if *"them"* were competitors and saboteurs rather than others in the organization sharing the same goals).
- *"What" does not lead to "How."* When you ask personnel two or three tiers down in an organization if they understand "what" the strategic vision of the company is, they answer your question well. But, when you ask them "how" it is being accomplished, their responses fall apart.
- *Lack of organizational planning.* The closest your company has ever come to planning for change is to restructure and communicate a new organizational chart.
- *Rigid silos.* Departments work in isolation when defining their roles, goals, and success metrics.
- *Dysfunctional incentives.* Departmental rewards and performance measures are at odds with each other. Take a peek under the covers of your incentive and performance plan. You might find, for example,

that your company's IT department is judged by whether or not it makes deadlines, which causes it to pad time estimates. At the same time, your marketing department may be judged by how quickly it delivers value to customers, which causes marketing to move up deadlines.

- *Weak linkages between intent and actions.* The road to poor performance is paved with great visions. You've been asked to contribute to the wording of a value statement, but cannot recall being asked to create mechanisms to ensure that the values are being lived up to. Similarly, many companies say that innovation is important, but how many companies give their employees an innovation line item in their budget?

- *Absence of workflows.* You have great processes defined within departments, but there are no clearly defined interdepartmental workflows. Your good employees spend more time "not stepping on toes" rather than getting the work done.

- *Workarounds are the only things that work.* There is a tendency to create "extra-organizational" units to complete work because the existing structure or processes are not working. In fact, if leveraged correctly, the existing organizational units could and should be accomplishing their own tasks and responsibilities.

- *Lack of trust and integrity.* Employees believe that senior leadership has gone "back on its word." Nothing creates greater misalignment in an organization than a breach of trust. If you make a promise, fulfill it, and celebrate it. Integrity in leadership inspires that special kind of loyalty that moves mountains and market share.

CASE STUDY: KEYBANK'S CMO/CFO ALIGNMENT

In an era of diminished credibility, no relationship may be as important for marketing as its relationship with finance. In Ohio, Cleveland-based KeyBank manages in excess of $85 billion in assets, and has demonstrated that a strong relationship between the CMO and CFO can prove a powerful means of building and sustaining momentum for critical marketing initiatives.

Karen R. Haefling, who joined the bank in 1995 as Marketing Director of the Great Lakes region, now holds the position of Chief Marketing Officer.[8] Having rolled out far-reaching marketing measurement and organizational change initiatives in recent years, she is deeply aware of how important it is to have trusted allies. Indeed, Haefling credits much of her success in building credibility to a solid foundation of support from the CFO.

Openness, directness, and clarity were critical to the development of this relationship, she explains. "I had to come out and say, 'I want what you want. Let's just get that straight. We need to be partners in figuring this out together.' I broke that down as, 'Here are my beginning assumptions. I need your help.'"

Haefling recognizes that many marketing leaders will chafe under the extra scrutiny and oversight that comes with an open relationship with the CFO's office. But she considers this oversight something to embrace rather than resist. Her advice to her mentors and to even those who are leaving for other companies has always been the same, "'The first thing you should do is go make friends with your CFO.' They are going to help you—and they can hurt you. They can be annoying. They can get on your case—and that's their job. That's fine. Because we do need their input. We can't do it by ourselves."

KeyBank uses a method of corporate measurement known as Economic Profit Added or EPA. While this approach was introduced by the CFO's office, the marketing group has been quick to adopt it and align its own measures with the approach. "We just took up the charge when everyone started doing EPA," says Haefling. "It wasn't as though they came and said, 'You must do this.' They were trying to get that discipline going throughout the company and so we embraced it and started doing it."

As a result of such active moves, the measures and outcomes that marketing presents to the balance of the company have gained a high level of credibility. "That was the idea behind the partnership," explains Trish Mathe, Senior Vice President and Director of Database Marketing at KeyBank. "The way to get people to believe the numbers is to say, 'We partnered with finance and we continue to partner with finance.' As a result, they believe the numbers."

The alignment of the marketing and finance organizations clearly has paid off. Despite a relatively wide geographical and market spread, the marketing group has been able to diligently prioritize, track, and measure the impact of its investments. Her organization now has visibility into the results of marketing projects and programs throughout the enterprise, overcoming the unmanageable, decentralist tendencies of the past. "We are excited about progress we have made," remarks Haefling. "Now I can say that 77 percent of spending has some kind of measure and 44 percent of spending has an economic profit added (EPA) measure. So that's a brand new thing. I can say that to my CFO. That is monumental. Not too many people can do that."

CASE STUDY: SUNTRUST BANKS' ALIGNMENTS AND INNOVATIONS

One of the great alignment challenges that marketers face concerns the inherent tensions that arise when simultaneously pursuing both product-focused and customer-focused business objectives. The challenge lies in ensuring valuable customers are retained and grown even as product sales quotas and targets are met.

Atlanta-based SunTrust Banks, Inc., one of America's largest commercial banking organizations with total assets of in excess of $128 billion, has had some significant success reconciling these often conflicting challenges. When compensation and organizational structure place emphasis on maximizing individual product sales, SunTrust's marketing organization is taking steps to keep attention focused on activities that build long-term customer, or household, value.

Consider a standard checking account. Sales representatives, whether in the branch or the call center, may be primarily compensated to sign up customers for new accounts. However, the bank's research demonstrates that checking account customers remain prone to defection unless they become what SunTrust calls "transactors." These are customers who use the bank for direct deposit, online bill paying, debit card transactions, and other activities. So, while the individual sales representative may not have a strong incentive to make the extra call encouraging an existing customer to use direct deposit or online bill paying, the bank has an interest in the customer's continuing loyalty, and, over time, expanded profitability.

The bank's marketing organization has positioned itself as a solution provider in instances such as this, producing customer segment and household profitability analysis that justifies new customer retention and activation programs. Such programs bring new sensibilities, metrics, and incentives to the organization. But the programs depend on alignment between the financial goals of the enterprise and the needs of the customer. "One of my objectives is to gain a broader sense of the customer in our service and sales efforts," explains Greg Holzwarth, Senior Vice President for Database Marketing at SunTrust.[9] "There is still a lot of missionary work to be done to develop a customer-focused approach and see that it is embedded in our strategies and scorecards."

Holzwarth acknowledges that branch and call center sales reps are not necessarily compensated on customer profitability and household value. Therefore, he concentrates on taking "customer centric initiatives and recasting them to align with their [the sales reps'] goals." Cultural change, of course, takes time. Holzwarth points out that the organization has now begun to internalize the importance of customer retention metrics, although he believes it will still take some time get it properly weighted within the overall compensation schemes that drive behavior. Part of the challenge lies in building business cases for new programs that reward customer reps for taking the steps necessary to encourage higher customer retention, even if those steps come at the expense of new product sales or higher sales efficiency scores. Operational sales managers "need help because even though they know in their gut that this is the right thing to do, it still has to be quantifiable and tracked."

Moreover, SunTrust has increasingly factored in the analysis of the database marketing group with regard to meeting customer needs. Specifically, the group has developed a customer segmentation model that recognizes the number of customer needs met by the bank, whether those needs relate to day-to-day transactional activity, savings, loans, or investments. Through this "needs matrix," Holzwarth's team has demonstrated that customer retention and profitability rise as new needs are addressed.

Essential to the marketing team's success at SunTrust has been its ability to span boundaries and speak the language of the groups it addresses. Reframing customer segment-focused concerns in terms that match the "vernacular" of the line of business is especially important. But Holzwarth's database marketing group also is actively involved in the training and support necessary to ensure that call center reps and branch sales reps are well prepared to execute the customer retention initiative. Coaching them to engage customers in conversations that will elicit key insights into needs, problems, and life changes is an effort particularly linked to customer retention.

Traditionally, budgeting within SunTrust has been heavily weighted toward product sales. However, budgeting approaches may be starting to change. Holzwarth points to what he calls a "shadow budgeting process," whereby his group will create a pro forma budget focused on particular customer segment objectives. That said, segment objectives must be mapped back to product goals. "This remains very much a missionary process," says Holzwarth.

BRINGING TECHNOLOGY, ANALYTICS, AND MARKETING TOGETHER: A PERSONAL STORY

One of the major issues we often see within companies is the difficulty in communications between IT departments and business areas. This is particularly so between Marketing and IT as they seem to speak different languages, have different objectives, look at the same problem with very different eyes, and generally seem to have a difficult time collaborating. While there are exceptions to this rule, I would say that the majority of companies suffer from this problem.

The IT/Marketing misalignment is not a new phenomenon. Back in the early 1990s, as a McKinsey consultant, I worked with various companies to help them evolve from traditional, list-based direct marketers into database and analytics-driven marketers. This was a time when data warehouses, data marts, and CRM were just emerging. Marketers and IT had no idea how to work together and I envisioned several disasters in the making. Numerous projects were way off track, over budget, and nowhere close to any semblance of completion. This often happened because the marketing executives were ignorant about IT, did not want to bother to learn the issues that were so critical to their success, and had no control over their IT support groups.

When I was recruited to build a Knowledge Based Marketing Group at First Union (now Wachovia), I realized this issue of control over IT development was going to be a major factor in my success. As a condition of employment, the CIO of the company agreed that I would have control over my IT budget and would be allowed to hire my own IT people, if I chose to do so.

This control did, indeed, play a critical role in my success at First Union, in two ways. Because my IT support team knew that I controlled the budget and hiring, they cooperated with me in hiring a director of data warehousing. I was on the list of interviewers and had veto power in the decision. The person who was hired ended up becoming a very close and trusted colleague, even though he did not report directly to me. He fought to protect the business's interests, even when his colleagues in IT were pushing him to do things that were counter to our needs. In addition, I also built a dedicated team of IT staff within my own group, who acted as a liaison between my business area and the IT data warehousing and operational groups. These special IT team members also provided supplemental development of their own and managed some internal departmental systems.

My entire group had approximately 100 people, one-third of whom were technologists. The remainder consisted of analysts, modelers, direct marketers, account managers (to deal with lines of business and different geographic territories), and those in charge of dealing with our direct-marketing agency. Initially, each of these groups sat clustered around their managers. Although all of these managers reported directly to me, they were located on different floors and various office buildings. As part of a reorganization, we consolidated all of our people on one floor, and physically interspersed the different functions with each other. It happened that it was very possible for a business analyst to be sitting next to a database administrator or a direct marketer to be sitting next to programmer or a statistical modeler.

The physical proximity did wonders for the improvement of communications. These people with different skills (and disparate personalities) now found themselves interacting with each other, not only in the office but also in social settings. The newfound familiarity and friendliness between these people had an enormous impact on their willingness, ability, and propensity to work together to solve common business problems. Rather than dealing with each other through e-mail and formal meetings with dozens of individuals, employees now reached out across their offices and discussed issues in the coffee room and corridors, over lunches, drinks, and late night pizzas.

A true sense of camaraderie and ownership of the project emerged and the interdisciplinary team embraced the challenge of getting the job done. Their relationships continued long after the data warehouse and marketing data marts were built, and made for a much more productive and enjoyable work environment.

The lesson I learned through this experience was that sometimes softer alignment issues, such as physical proximity and shared interests and friendships, can matter a great deal more than formal structures or the boxes you draw on organizational charts.

MOVING FROM ENGAGEMENT TO SHARED INFORMATION

Communication is often the biggest challenge in many organizations, and getting people to talk to each other in informal settings can only help toward achieving the shared objectives. Such alliances also contribute dramatically to an organization's ability to capitalize on the knowledge it contains within its individuals and departments. The value of this ability is the topic of the next chapter.

7

CAPITALIZING ON KNOWLEDGE

From Information to Impact

"For knowledge, too, is itself power."
Sir Francis Bacon

Information is an intangible asset, and is potentially quite valuable. But one cannot realize information's value by hoarding it or keeping it locked in a vault. To capitalize on the asset value of information, it must be built, maintained, and leveraged. Leave customer information alone and its value will diminish. Employ it actively, with great skill and precision, and it can generate tremendous wealth.

Many companies face significant problems with regard to managing information effectively. What's more troubling is their myopic perspective, the inability to see how important information is to their survival and success. Even most marketers who tend to be more attuned to the value of customer information than others in the enterprise, don't fully recognize the enormous potential wealth that is just within their grasp.

Many companies, for instance, are run by leaders who choose not to base management decisions on facts and evidence, and prefer instead to act on their "gut" and intuition. Others might be focused on building great products or cultivating their brand image as opposed to deeply understanding their buyers. Still, other companies find themselves mired in a complex array of technical and organizational problems as they attempt to build the infrastructure of customer insight.

Failing to manage and leverage information represents a costly missed opportunity. Customer information, in particular, can be a powerful differentiator in the marketplace. The more a company knows about the particular needs and interests of individual customers, the more effectively it can differentiate its products, services, and solutions from those of its competitors. Personalized attention also can strengthen the loyalty of a company's most valuable customers, thereby making it exceedingly difficult for competitors to draw them away.

As a number of outstanding companies can attest, the ability to effectively manage information assets is a dimensional competency that contributes heavily to outstanding marketing performance. As you learn in the case studies at the end of this chapter, some of these world-class companies have tremendous insight into the preferences, priorities, and potential profitability of their customers. But just as important, they have the skills and capacities to act on this vital information.

True marketing effectiveness depends on establishing a disciplined approach toward the management of information assets. This discipline separates companies that annoy and interrupt their customers from those that engage them in mutually rewarding relationships. It rewards companies that focus on their most valuable customer opportunities, rather than those that waste their resources. High performance marketing depends on the ability to dynamically learn and adapt, anticipate, and act. Customer intelligence lies at the core of market leadership.

THE CHALLENGES FACING
INFORMATION MANAGEMENT

Some companies already are realizing tremendous marketing success in terms of leveraging information assets. In some cases, customer information has provided a clear and measurable contribution to the bottom line. A growing number of companies have actively leveraged key information to offer a more compelling solution and experience to their valued customers. But even among the leading lights, significant work often remains to develop a disciplined and comprehensive approach to information management.

In recognizing the strategic importance of information, for example, one of our clients recently created an information plan mapping out the key data necessary to build and strengthen customer relationships. However, this company needed to replace or significantly enhance key components of its technology infrastructure in order to leverage these new data sources.

The reality is that very few companies have come close to fully tapping into the potential locked in their data in a robust and sustainable way. Doing so requires organizations to confront and overcome a number of challenges in a variety of areas, including their corporate culture, strategies, infrastructure, and operation. The challenge requires coordination and agreement among many units within the organization. Marketing and IT must certainly work together, but the initiative also involves Sales, Customer Service, Product Development, and Finance. Any undertaking that requires such a high level of coordination and co-operation offers a significant number of challenges.

The Cultural Challenge: No Common Foundation

In many companies, decisions are driven by instinct and inherited wisdom. These cultural foundations can prove to be a distinct barrier to marketers that are intent on developing fact-based approaches to decision making that rely on the rigorous analysis of information. Indeed, the unwillingness of many executives outside of marketing to value, assess, and actively manage information may undermine efforts to build and leverage information assets from within.

Of course, not all companies can find great value in detailed customer information. Their marketing investments may tend toward activities such as mass advertising, whose impact may be difficult to measure or analyze. Their business models and value propositions may revolve around sophisticated product designs or efficiently run operations, rather than leveraging market or customer information. Still, other businesses may sell through retailers or resellers and consider information about the final customer to be too hard or expensive to acquire, or may be of limited use.

Marketers that do expect to generate value from customer information, however, may have to confront cultures within their organization that do not perceive this value. These marketers must expect resistance on many fronts because they will be challenging the way business always has been done.

The Strategic Challenge: Battling Droughts and Floods

Even companies that recognize the vast potential value of their customer data do not necessarily have a strategic method of approaching the information management challenge. Some do not embody the ability to match marketing objectives with information acquisition and management activities. Rather than determining their objectives and collecting the information necessary to achieve them, they begin by collecting data and then try to decide what value they can draw from it.

Unfortunately, such behavior can waste resources and undermine the entire effort in the process. Like the "Sorcerer's Apprentice," marketing executives watch helplessly as more and more data is collected—overflowing its buckets and spilling uselessly onto the floor. CFOs eventually look around and ask why so many resources were committed to collecting data that was never used.

And while companies often suffer from a flood of data, they may, paradoxically, also suffer from a drought in terms of actionable information. We are familiar with a leading financial services company that has implemented a state-of-the-art, lead management capability. However, this capability is still not fully integrated in such a way that hot prospects can be quickly and seamlessly handed off to the right sales and fulfillment channel. Customers must repeat information about themselves to multiple representatives, all the while diminishing the quality of their experience.

Such oversights occur in the absence of a clear and workable strategy for information management. Such a strategy demands that the organization determine the objectives and anticipated value that they intend to achieve through the management of customer and marketing information. Based on this strategy, the marketing team can build operational plans that define how relevant information will be gathered, integrated, reported, analyzed, and acted upon.

Too often, customer data analysis teams end up mired in reactive, low-value projects that are initiated by various lines of business. No strategic prioritization is placed on information management activities. As a result, too few resources are invested in projects that promise strategic, high-value benefits. Driven to provide "rear-view" analysis and reports, data analysis groups are not given time and proper resources to identify trends and patterns across business units, or to generate predictive models and valuable insights that will drive future outcomes.

Without a strategic perspective on information, it becomes exceedingly difficult to value or invest in information in any meaningful way. No one builds necessary information assets in this case, or else, the value of those assets evaporates as they go unused.

The Ownership Challenge: Misaligned Objectives

Customer information, like other forms of data, is a resource that often has no clear owner. Unfortunately, the absence of leadership and stewardship ensures that the information's value will go unrealized. "With our new CRM systems we now have huge amounts of data that could help us drive better marketing decisions," said one senior vice president of marketing at an insurance company.[1] "But how can I get my teams to start using that data? Right now, nobody's responsible and everybody has a day job."

In many companies, the customer data management role falls primarily on the IT group. Unfortunately, this group may have little understanding of how to put the data to use. Meanwhile, marketing may try to divorce itself from the underlying data, requesting reports and analysis without taking any deep interest in how the information was collected, aggregated, and transformed.

When no clear lines of accountability are drawn, corporate politics also can intrude. In the real world, any objective requiring the participation of multiple organization units must face and address this risk. The problem stems from the fact that all of the units that need to be involved in capturing, sharing, and using the data have their own areas of responsibility and, typically, their own targets and objectives. Where politics manifests itself as a barrier to progress, the cause often lies in a misalignment between those targets and objectives, and the manner in which behaviors in pursuit of those objectives are rewarded.

In some companies, product development units are reluctant to share information with marketing that might reflect poorly on product or service quality. Unfortunately, such barriers prevent marketing from crafting customer-focused approaches that might lead to more positive outcomes. Similarly, marketing often is accused of evading responsibility by resisting efforts to assess and measure its performance. Without this information, the enterprise and the marketing organization itself are prevented from making the changes necessary to realize more favorable results. Beyond these problems, the dearth of leadership tends to ensure that resources are poorly invested, skills are underdeveloped, and no meaningful effort goes into assessing and measuring the progress of the endeavor.

The Infrastructure Challenge: Misused Resources

Once there is commitment to the value of information and the necessity of managing it as an asset, the question then emerges of how to acquire, integrate, distribute, and apply it to enhance decisions. This challenge has vexed companies in recent years. Many organizations have thrown money at the technologies designed to harness customer information only to experience grave disappointments. Upon closer inspection, it becomes clear that CRM technology has not failed to perform in any key technical sense, but has merely been misused, mismanaged, and misapplied.

Many of these failures can be attributed to companies ignoring or downplaying the other challenges mentioned here. These organizations, for example, may have failed to determine who will integrate the data, who will produce the reports and analytical models, and who will train front-line talent to act on key information and insights.

That said, technology remains vital to the management of information assets. If marketers are to enhance their understanding of customers, they need systems that will acquire customer data, integrate and aggregate it, distribute it, and present it (we will address this particular issue in the next chapter). Moreover, marketing today depends on skilled individuals who can integrate data and those that can transform it into relevant insights.

Marketing Drives Growth at Mutual of Omaha

Mutual of Omaha, the well recognized insurance provider, has demonstrated growing success in its knowledge-driven, direct-marketing business. Indeed, the direct marketing group is on a steep climb and expects to triple its direct premiums, from $400 million to $1 billion, within the next few years. While there is growing demand from the agency and brokerage sides of the business for direct marketing and lead generation support, the group is challenged to develop the analytical, creative, and operational skills necessary to meet that demand.

Tom Graham, the company's general manager for direct distribution, explains that the "issue is scale...It takes time to turn the ship. We have to build the necessary skill sets, deliver training, and educate the organization."[2] Mutual of Omaha's direct marketing group is currently engaged in efforts both to recruit top flight people and to develop its current staff. The organization also is relying on external service providers to provide certain analytical and data management skills. "As a mutual insurance company, we have enormous surplus capital," Graham said. "We are constrained in terms of human capital. We can't simply substitute will for skill."

The Operational Challenge: Putting Your Assets to Work

It's not enough to possess strong customer intelligence; one must also *operationalize* it to realize its value. Despite their large departments of analysts, statisticians, and data modelers (decorated with MBAs and PhDs from prestigious schools), many companies are failing to perform in today's hypercompetitive markets. "If you can develop valuable insights about your customers, and then act on them, you are going to beat a rival that ...can do the analysis but can't turn it into actionable advice," states Scott Nelson, Vice President and Research Director with Stamford, Connecticut-based Gartner.[3] Winning strategies, he believes, are "not only about how much you know about your customer, but how well you can act on what you know." While intelligence certainly matters, the real challenge lies in putting it to work.

Surprisingly, sophisticated analytics and models are not the key to leveraging information assets. A truly disciplined company designs and drives its marketing programs based on facts and learning that emerge from past experience. It disseminates customer insights across the organization, so decision makers can apply them to new campaigns and front-line service people can use those insights to make discretionary judgments about how they ought to treat individual customers.

One company that has concentrated on addressing this challenge is CIBC, the Toronto-based financial services provider. Daymond Ling, Director of Modeling and Analytics at CIBC, recognizes that customer intelligence is useless if it is not operationalized.[4] Ling has encouraged the bank's customer marketing group to actively collaborate with sales and service operations, while establishing strong relationships with channel partners. "Our challenge lies in our ability to bring focused insight and stories about customer behavior to the table to enable customer-centric decision making to happen," said Ling. "It's not about customer analysis, per se. It's about getting people used to [applying the analysis] and having them talking about customer considerations as a culture."

The Public Relations Challenge: Confronting the Backlash

Against the backdrop of organizations struggling to manage their information assets, one discovers a sense of growing customer and consumer dissatisfaction with marketing. While some dissatisfaction at being interrupted for commercials and having one's mailbox filled with unwanted direct mail packages has long existed, there is evidence that "resistance" to marketing messages is growing.

Yankelovich Partners recently released a report demonstrating just how tired consumers have become with regard to the assault of marketing messages and interruptions.[5] In the survey, 60 percent of respondents said that their opinion of marketing and advertising has become more negative in recent years and 61 percent think advertising has "gotten out of control." In fact, 70 percent confessed that they "tune out advertising more than they did just a few years ago."

Recent legislation covering consumer privacy and placing heavy restrictions on telemarketing has been enormously popular. "Do not call" lists attracted tens of millions of people as soon as they became available. Similar legislation is now being considered with respect to unwanted e-mail messages. Such legislation raises the cost of customer acquisition and makes it increasingly difficult to build new customer information assets. Because of identity theft threat (criminals posing as small businesses to obtain individual consumer data from information brokers such as ChoicePoint), it is more likely that legislation protecting this information will pass in the State and Federal legislatures. This development makes it all the more imperative for companies to manage, safeguard, and marshal the information they have about their current customers, since this type of information is less likely to be impacted by legislation.

Clearly, next generation approaches to managing customer time and attention must perform better than present ones. The next era will revolve around engagement as opposed to interruptions. We must leverage information to address existing and prospective customers in a far more relevant, precise, and personalized way. If we manage customer information as a valuable asset, it will enable us to engage in the high-value and high-impact conversations that deliver the performance we seek.

THE INTELLIGENT ENTERPRISE

Enterprises that successfully capitalize on information develop a strategic mindset. They recognize that marketing is not merely a "resource" to support key decisions and actions, and they consistently view and manage information as an asset. These assets are within the purview of the marketing organization. As the perception of value associated with information climbs, so does the prestige, credibility, and power of marketing.

World-class marketers understand that information assets must be managed and leveraged if their value is to grow. They have invested smartly and dedicated resources to information management. Then as successes are realized and value becomes increasingly clear, these marketers are actively communicating the importance of information assets to the rest of the company, and beyond.

At diverse companies such as Harrah's Entertainment, Gillette, Capital One, and Tesco, the strategic management of information is paying off handsomely in marketing terms. These and other organizations have transformed their respective sectors through the disciplined, rigorous, and relentless leverage of information: customer information, in particular. Organizations that successfully manage information are not merely parading high-minded strategies; they have made the crucial connections between strategy and execution. Information is the asset that differentiates them in profoundly challenging markets.

Leveraging Information Assets

Many companies make the mistake of approaching information from a technological perspective. They build elaborate strategies based on acquiring, aggregating, and disseminating information. They then proceed to make large investments in customer relationship management systems that "capture" information out in the field. Finally, they invest in data warehouses that pull the information together for analysis and application.

In almost all cases, this approach leads to disappointment. What companies often find when they get around to auditing results, is that their resources have been misdirected and misspent. Lost in the elaborate piping and plumbing is any sense of why the information-gathering initiative was undertaken in the first place. Unsurprisingly, deep cost cuts ensue, experienced people are let go, and the infrastructure begins to weaken.

If companies are to make the most of their information, they must be intimately aware of the goals and objectives they are trying to reach. Based on these objectives, they can work backward to develop the proper sources of information and conduct necessary analysis and reporting. Whether the objective is to acquire new customers, enhance cross-selling, or retain valuable customers, smart companies ensure that their imperatives drive information, not the other way around.

Today's leaders in intelligence-driven strategy recognize that the asset value of their information will not be realized unless they concentrate, first and foremost, on three key factors: *Decisions*, *Actions*, and *Outcomes*. After establishing objectives and devising strategies to reach them, these three factors are the most critical to leveraging information assets. All other information management activities must be seen in relation to and in support of these central factors.

- *Decisions.* To provide value, information must drive decisions, intelligent decisions. Information provides value by enabling smart decisions in all areas of the enterprise, including marketing decisions about targeting, segmenting, and engaging customers; customer assessment and valuing; and campaign offerings and interactions.
- *Actions.* Smart organizations carefully identify and map out the linkages between information and action at an operational level. They clearly identify how information will be applied and by whom. These companies consider information not merely as something to be tended and analyzed in the backroom, but as a

vital force in the retail channel, in the contact center, on the Web site, and among the members of the sales force. Without a strong and deep understanding of the linkages to operational activities, the value of information erodes.

- *Outcomes.* In order to complete the loop and ensure information is meeting objectives, savvy information managers monitor and measure the impact of information in the field. Carefully tracking the impact of information as a force to support operational activity clearly reveals whether the information is enabling the enterprise to meet its performance targets or not. If performance outcomes are not being met, it is time to step back and reassess the investments that are currently made in information, and determine how they can be enhanced to meet the plan.

Successful Information Management at Work

Clearly, companies must address all the challenges that we have previously outlined if they are to fully leverage information. Even when the culture is receptive to change, they must concern themselves with leadership and stewardship, processes and roles, skills and infrastructure. If these organizations do not focus clearly on decisions, actions, and outcomes in relation to information, they will fatally undermine their overall efforts. Fortunately, a number of high performing companies are now giving us a glimpse of the future of successful information management.

Harrah's move toward fact-based decision making. One company that demonstrates the power of information assets is Harrah's Entertainment. While other gaming companies have attempted to grow through acquisition and large investments in physical amusements, Harrah's has bet its opportunities for growth on a multiproperty loyalty program. Dubbed "Total Rewards," this program allows Harrah's to track an individual's play and activities across all of its gaming properties, and use that data to create and market custom trip packages and deliver personalized treatment.

Over the past five years, Harrah's CEO, Gary Loveman, has radically transformed the casino business's culture, processes, and structure. In addition to a strongly controlled marketing function, Loveman cites a shift towards an analysis-based and fact-driven culture as a key catalyst for fundamental change at Harrah's. As he explains, the company has employed "database marketing and science-based analytical tools to widen the gap between us and casino operators who base their customer incentives more on intuition than evidence."[6]

Information is now a prized asset within the company. "We collect a tremendous amount of information on what players do with us," said Loveman. "We know when you arrive at a casino, what you do there, and when you leave ... We measure everything." Indeed, the culture of Harrah's has closely linked intelligence and analysis to operational action. "When our employees use the words 'I think,' the hair stands up on the back of my neck," added Loveman.[7] "We have the capacity to know rather than guess at something because we collect so much information about our customers. And if we say 'I know,' let's really make sure we know."

Gillette and Tesco leverage the power of information. As mentioned earlier in the book, Gillette's marketing organization has contributed heavily to the company's stunning turnaround since 2001. The group is relying on Innovative Marketing Intelligence (IMI), which is defined as "a disciplined, fact-based approach [used] to enhance consumer brand preference and build sales profitably."[8]

Central to the effort to grow categories and brands is the company's analysis to determine relevant value propositions as well as its market modeling efforts to optimize advertising, promotion, and pricing. The objective of IMI at Gillette is to apply standardized analytical approaches and metrics across brands and thereby realize scale advantages in areas such as sourcing, SKU rationalization, and capital requirements. The company also actively learns and generates valuable insights through its management of marketing intelligence.

"We will know more about and have a deeper understanding of the buying habits, desires, and motivations of our consumers," said CEO Jim Kilts with regard to expected results from the IMI initiative. "We will know what works where, why it works, and how we can make it work every time."

Still another impressive story in terms of the power of information is the UK-based retailer, Tesco. The company's Clubcard loyalty program generates more than one hundred million pounds of incremental sales each year, and has more than 10 million members. In fact, Tesco has passed Sainsbury to become the country's number one grocer.

"[Tesco] started with a belief that understanding customers was fundamental to running a successful retail business," explains Clive Humby, coauthor of the new book *Scoring Points* and a consultant to the retailer.[9] "Because they understand their customers, they hope they can serve them better... [Tesco has] looked at the program as a way of learning about how consumers shop, and what they want from their retailer."

As the Tesco experience demonstrates, successful execution depends on a commitment to key objectives and outcomes. "One of the accepted principles of the program is that there is no such thing as a complete success or a complete failure," according to *Scoring Points*.[10] "Everything that happens to Clubcard is seen as an opportunity to learn, to refine, to improve, and move on. There is constant monitoring and measurement of how well the card has been working and how it hasn't. Clubcard is a reflection of the attributes of the business and its management: a strong team ethic, a commitment to serving customers, and most of all, top-to-bottom retailers' pragmatism. Tesco made customer loyalty marketing work, when every other major British supermarket loyalty program in the late 1990s failed, faltered, or never got started."

Tesco also offers a stellar example of top-down strategic leadership that is committed to results. Terry Leahy, CEO of Tesco, had first championed the Clubcard program in the early 1990s. Having risen from the retail shop floor to his position as Marketing Director and board member, Leahy had a strong sense of how the program could deliver value and why it deserved top-level support. Since its initial pilot in 1993 and amidst widespread industry skepticism, Tesco executive leaders built and backed the intelligence-based strategy necessary to vault the company into its current leadership position.

Capital One's approach to information application. Another recognized leader in the application of information is Capital One. Indeed, it conducted 80,000 market tests in 2003—on everything from marketing copy to price points to credit lines—to ensure it was investing its resources wisely. The company, which posted revenue of more than $9.8 billion and net income of more than $1.1 billion in 2003, relies on this extraordinary diligence to ensure it is effectively gauging customer priorities and preferences.

"As a statistician, I love this because it gives us the rigor of testing appropriately and doing predictive modeling [to ensure success] going forward," stated Dave Jeppesen, Vice President of Capital One's Direct Marketing Center, in a keynote speech at the National Center for Direct Marketing Winter Conference in Orlando.[11]

One sophisticated, data-driven campaign enabled the company to determine it was sensible to increase customer credit lines and offer an extremely low fixed rate (4.99 percent) on a new card. "We saw $3 billion come onto our books because of one offer in one quarter," says Jeppesen.[12] "It was because of the insight we found through use of our technology."

Two academics, Eric Clemons from the Wharton School and Matt Thatcher of the University of Arizona, contend that the turning point for Capital One came when it adopted an experimentally oriented or "test and learn" approach.[13] This enabled the company to build models to determine which combination of product, price, and credit limit could be profitably offered to customers who could be segmented by a wide range of publicly available credit and demographic information. Through the test-and-learn tools, Capital One produced innovative pricing and balance transfer approaches customized to the needs of specific segments they identified.

"It turns out that this transfer of balances by customers from higher APR credit cards to a lower one provides the card issuer with an important signal," Clemons and Thatcher write. "Customers who do not carry balances find no value in a lower APR and will not take the time and effort to switch cards. More importantly, the customers that the balance transfer product will attract are those customers who have a balance they cannot presently pay off but which they will eventually pay off slowly. Therefore, they care about the lower APR."

This innovative approach, combining testing and learning with segmentation, has enabled Capital One to acquire significant market share in the credit card business. Interestingly, the company, which had promoted its products almost exclusively through the use of direct marketing and very intelligent call centers, has become a heavy television advertiser over the past few years. Capital One brings the same analytical discipline to advertising as it does to direct marketing and call center routing. It did not take the company long to figure out that having a strong brand (created through television advertising) helps to raise response rates to direct marketing efforts.

Such efforts demonstrate the clear payoffs to be derived by linking strategy to outcomes in a disciplined fashion. Information management among the successful companies mentioned here is not a distinct activity. Rather, it is infused throughout the enterprise to realize a powerful and measurable impact. The outcome is not merely an output that lies at the end of a long line of technical activities. Decisions, actions, and outcomes all are crucial markers of the relevance and value of information. At a high level, marketers must place their attention here to ensure they are capitalizing on it.

The 10 Best Things You Can Do with Your Data

1. *Keep it clean.* Accurate data is critical to quality analytics.
2. *Keep it current.* Timely data is becoming more important as tools become available to analyze data "real time" and to act on triggers that can react instantaneously to customer behavior or changes in behavior patterns.
3. *Combine it.* Make sure that data from all lines of business and from all channels of contact with customers are brought together, providing a complete view of the relationship. Be careful not to supply too much data or data elements which you do not have a clear idea of how to use.
4. *Enhance it.* Add external data that can be useful, geodemographics, usage of partners' products and services, anything that can help add insight and knowledge about customers.
5. *Transform it.* Convert simple measures of responses, transactions, and revenue to measures that are meaningful to business, including margins, profitability, share, and customer retention.
6. *Analyze it.* Analysis of data should be pragmatic, with a clear vision of business goals and focused on helping to achieve these goals. Too often, analysis becomes a theoretical exercise that does not go anywhere.
7. *Use it.* It is important to deploy models and use insights gained from analysis in marketing to see if they have an impact on critical metrics, such as response rates, risk reduction, or increase in profitability.

8. *Learn from it.* Structure changes in marketing campaigns in such a way that it will be possible to learn what worked and what did not. These types of analysis can be done by the clever use of holdout samples, control markets, in-market testing, and so on, and reveals information that is critical to successful information management.

9. *Communicate it.* The insight gained from analyses and from in-market testing should be communicated widely to all stakeholders throughout a company. That will increase the perceived value of both the data itself and the actions that stem from leveraging that data. It will also lead to an increase in fact-based decision making in the organization.

10. *Keep it simple.* The processes of gathering and analyzing data and deploying the learned results in campaigns are not rocket science. Too often, however, organizations undertake unnecessarily convoluted processes that are controlled by a "quasi-priesthood." Keeping the processes simple and goal-oriented makes for a much more effective and defensible marketing program.

CLOSING THE GAP: SURVEYING INTELLIGENCE ASSETS

Having established the high-level priorities of intelligence-driven enterprises, it is now appropriate to turn our attention to some of the key resources, capabilities, and infrastructural elements necessary to manage information as an asset. In this section of the chapter, we observe the key assets that must be surveyed, assessed, and built if marketing is to put information to work. First, we catalog the various types of information that drive decisions, actions, and outcomes. Next, we outline the workflows necessary to harness data and manage information. Finally, we discuss the alignment of marketing and IT groups that must occur if the endeavor is to be successful.

Categorizing Information Assets

We can think of the information assets themselves as a portfolio of sources, data types, tools, rules, and models. Different types of information assets exhibit different characteristics and often have distinct purposes. As marketers attempt to assess or audit their current assets, these are the key types they must survey, and ultimately, build.

Content Assets

To a great extent, content assets represent the underlying data and records that will be used to frame decisions and drive actions. *Operational and Enterprise Resource Data,* for example, is the transactional data that records activities that have occurred in relation to customers, products, suppliers, and other sources. It can be pulled from operational systems that manage sales, service, and marketing activities. Operational and enterprise resource data can also be drawn from "enterprise resource planning" systems, such as SAP or PeopleSoft (now Oracle), that typically capture financial, manufacturing, and human resource data. Depending on the company, a host of operational systems may cover everything from logistics and supply chain management to project and professional services activities. To make this data more accessible, many companies have built "data warehouses" and even focused "data marts."

We also recognize *Customer Records and Profiles* as a distinct content asset. The "master" record is the place into which key information about the individual customer will be housed. It might include not only contact and demographic information, but information about past transactions, interaction, profitability, even propensity to purchase certain products or services. Critical customer information and metrics can be used as effective barometers for measuring progress toward customer-centric strategies and marketing tactics. The typical contents of a best-in-class customer information portfolio are shown in Figure 7.1.

The accessibility and richness of this information can be critical in determining whether an interaction is successful. To the extent that companies build their own customer profiles, these assets become valuable and differentiated intellectual property that only they possess. Of course, some companies also choose to purchase data that can be ap-

FIGURE 7.1 *Customer Information Portfolio*

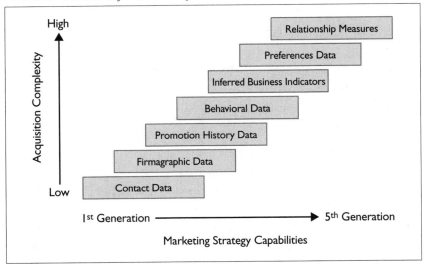

pended to their records and provide a fuller, more up-to-date perspective on the customers they intend to reach.

Yet another key content asset is *Marketing Media and Research*. While this information may be managed separately from more operational and customer-focused information, it is vital to the management and execution of marketing activities. This type of information may include key messages and creative work associated with various campaigns, scripts, training materials, and other resources that are helpful in supporting the front line. Marketing Media and Research data also includes market research such as awareness and usage studies, attitudinal surveys, and competitive intelligence.

Reporting Assets

While not always recognized as such, the presentation vehicles on which marketing depends should also be considered key information assets. Reports are one of the most notable of the many forms the presentation of information can take. Whether information is presented as a document (printed or electronic), a spreadsheet, a marketing "dashboard," or in some other format, the quality of reporting is important to overall decision making within an enterprise. Typically, reports produce static views of specific aspects of the business, such as sales by region, campaign response by segment, and so on. These reports provide a structured view of the business area, without necessarily highlighting key issues or pointing toward their root causes.

To a great extent, the reports themselves are difficult to separate from the medium in which they are accessed. For this reason, Web-based portals, intranets, performance dashboards, reporting software, and customer-focused applications all are part of the presentation layer. These tools have asset value in relation to their ability to present information in an accessible and actionable way.

Analytical Assets

To add value to data and information, you must be able to analyze it to determine trends, opportunities, and challenges. Analytical insights are typically expressed in the form of models. Marketers and other decision makers rely on *Retrospective Models* to assess historical trends and *Prospective Models* to make assessments and predictions with regard to the future.

Retrospective Models assume several forms, all geared to developing a greater understanding of previous activity. Online Analytical Processing (OLAP) allows high-level information exploration, and provides limited support for diagnostic analysis of the issues highlighted in more static views of data. Whereas a report may suggest a sales problem in a particular region, an OLAP tool will allow some contextual analysis which might point, for example, to a specific underperforming sales outlet or team. *Ad-hoc Analysis,* often described as a "slice and dice" approach, provides structured paths of analysis which a user can follow to explore a given business issue. However, deviation from those predefined paths is not well supported, hence the need to explore "raw" data using query languages and other analytical tools.

Prospective Models are typically based on advanced statistical techniques, often applying previous past learning and experience to shape future marketing actions. Two of the best known prospective modeling techniques in marketing circles are *customer segmentation* and *predictive modeling*. What these techniques have in common is that they apply advanced algorithms to the identification of patterns and the relationship between data which have business impact and value. For example, the application of predictive modeling to past campaign response patterns may enable marketers to prioritize recipients of a future offer based on their ability to accept.

Performance Management Assets

As the demand for accountability and performance reporting becomes more important to the marketing operation, we are beginning to see the introduction and improvement of new systems to meet these objectives. While Six Sigma, Balanced Scorecard, and other initiatives are framing how performance should be reported to recognize key intangibles and drive improvement, new technologies are emerging to present this information in a dynamic and accessible fashion. These technologies and their presentations form the organization's performance management assets.

What executive decision makers increasingly are seeking can be described as *Dashboards, Scorecards,* or *Key Performance Indicators.* They want a visual window on performance trends and expectations. Moreover, they seek the ability to "drill down" into the information and look for relationships between actions and outcomes. Such systems hold much promise in terms of driving greater alignment, better decisions, and more agile behavior—both within marketing and beyond it. As such, performance management systems represent a key asset in their own right.

Activity Monitoring Assets

As companies increasingly seek "real-time" agility and action, they need decision-enablement and decision-automation capabilities that drive intelligent interaction on the front line. Whether a customer is engaged on the Web, through a call center, or through a sales force, the success of marketing increasingly depends on the development of approaches that anticipate unarticulated customer needs and enable rapid response to articulated ones. Immediacy in responding to these needs is vital; the opportunity may be fleeting. Monitoring activity facilitates decisions and actions, enabling a company to address the customer's needs in a rapid, personal, and powerful fashion.

Through a host of alerts, rules, and triggers, companies are able to perform exceptionally at "the moment of truth," the point of engagement when customers have a request, a concern, or potential need. For example, a customer makes $5,000 payroll deposits each month and suddenly makes a deposit of $50,000 into their checking account. This activity may warrant an investigative call to the customer to see if they need help handling the money or if it was placed in the account for easy access (i.e., planning to make a major purchase). If the purchase is a house, then it might offer opportunities to sell insurance or a home equity line even if they have already selected their mortgage company. Trigger-based marketing tools, such as MarketSoft's "DemandMore Triggers" helps companies accomplish this goal.

Similarly, if a frequent visitor to a Web site is indulging in a browsing pattern different from their usual surfing activities, they might need an additional level of care and help that closes an "up sell" deal immediately. There are real-time analytical products in the market from companies such as Unica, Chordiant, Epiphany, and SPSS, aiding marketers to identify trends and turn on a dime. Marketers are learning how to provide the right offer at the right time in the right channel. Such capabilities are especially vital when an "inbound" opportunity, those initiated by the customer, presents itself.

Managing Information Assets through Smart Workflows

Having gained a better understanding of the information assets themselves, it is important to now take a closer look at the context in which they are built, managed, and leveraged. We recommend a seven-step process that can drive disciplined information asset management:

1. *Acquire.* Companies must have processes and systems in place to capture the data that will be used to develop greater understanding of markets and customers. This stage of the process roughly corresponds with the operational systems, whether they are "customer relationship management" or "enterprise resource planning," into which the underlying data will be entered. With this in mind, it is necessary to ensure that this information is gathered at the appropriate touch point or within the right channel. While most of the valuable and proprietary

data will be acquired within the organization, such data may be purchased in some cases from third parties.

2. *Integrate.* In its most raw form, customer and market data are rarely very useful. It may lie in various data "silos" and operational systems. Therefore, companies must integrate the data to make it accessible and applicable, gaining a more complete picture and understanding of the trend, segment, or customer that must be analyzed. This stage of the process roughly corresponds with the "data warehouses" and "data marts" that aggregate data in a production format.

3. *Analyze.* Once information has been aggregated and made accessible, it then becomes possible to analyze it. Whether the objective is to generate reports, a retrospective analysis, or prospective analysis, this is the stage at which value is added to the information by putting it in a relevant context. Analysis may come in high-level summaries produced by managers or sophisticated models created by "data jocks." The key to this step in the workflow is to close the "analysis gap" that lies between the rapidly accumulating base of data and a company's ability to interpret that data in relevant ways.

4. *Decide.* Based on the analysis that emerges, marketers and other professionals can make decisions on what markets to target, what customers to assign highest priority, what campaigns to conduct, what offers to generate, and what promising activities in which to invest. Assuming research groups have been given an opportunity to perform strategic analyses, companies can set the stage for more anticipatory and forward-looking decisions. Models and analysis will not make decisions for us, but they can enable us to make more intelligent, disciplined, and fact-based decisions.

5. *Act.* Companies too often manage information in a vacuum far removed from the context in which it should be applied. As a result of this fragmented approach, the value of the information asset is never truly realized. The value of information and intelligence ultimately lies in one's ability to act. Marketers who have a strategic view of market activity and the customer relationship must take a leading role in ensuring that analytically driven decisions are translated to action at the front-line, operational level. Key aspects of support, such as incentives, training, and

resources may be necessary to ensure valued information is leveraged in the field and on the front lines.

6. *Learn*. Analysis must precede and follow action. It is vital to conduct a type of "after action review" to determine how information has influenced real-world performance. Strengths and weaknesses can be identified making it possible to fill necessary gaps. The "learning agenda" revolves around having the commitment and discipline not only to take action, but to determine the impact of the act and learn how to improve performance.

7. *Adjust*. Based on findings in relation to outcomes, the organization must improve and adapt. Marketers can be a powerful catalyst by guiding and leading this process to ensure new actions are strengthened by past experience. The process also comes full circle as it becomes clear what new types of information must be acquired in order to engage the market in increasingly successful ways.

Each of these steps and their interaction in a collaborative information management workflow are shown in Figure 7.2.

ALIGNING MARKETING AND IT

Many of the information challenges faced by marketing are rooted in the organization's relationship with IT. If the marketing/IT relationship is dysfunctional, many of the challenges described earlier become apparent, draining resources and capital as opportunities slip away.

FIGURE 7.2 *Collaborative Information Management Workflow*

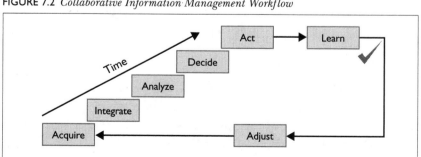

Donovan Neale-May, Executive Director of the Chief Marketing Officer Council, says marketing and IT must collaborate if they are to effectively leverage information to drive growth and strengthen customer relationships. "Marketing has this rich media content, but the challenge is to become tech savvy," he says.[14] "The challenge is to gather data from within their organizations ... and for that, they have to partner with IT." Neale-May contends that cultural and organizational hurdles have hindered collaboration between the groups and their ability to successfully work on projects. "There is not a lot of close cohabitation and integration, but I think that's changing," he said. "The nature of the business pressures and demand on marketing will require them to have deeper access to organizational data. All these demands will push marketing closer to the IT organization."

CMO Magazine reports that only 25 percent of businesses have synchronized relationships between CMOs and CIOs.[15] However, 40 percent are currently engaged in efforts to strengthen these connections. One 2003 survey by Aelera Corp. on the degree of shared understanding and objectives between CMOs and CIOs tends to re-enforce a picture of misalignment.[16] From the perspective of IT presented in this survey, upcoming marketing initiatives tend not to be presented in time to successfully implement solutions. Marketing respondents stated, in most cases, that their organizations did a "good job of explaining the business requirements behind its requests for IT support."[17] However, merely one-quarter of IT respondents agreed with that statement. Based on Quaero's extensive experience in this intersection of marketing and IT in both large and small organizations, this picture of discrepancy between marketing and IT rings very true.

The marketing/IT relationship is critical to ensuring the right infrastructure is in place to support production and maintenance of the right information assets. So how can the gap in understanding be so large? Experience suggests that the following factors lie at the heart of this issue and need to be addressed.

- *Mutual understanding of roles and goals.* The responsibility for capitalizing on marketing and customer information must lie primarily on the shoulders of marketing. However, marketing executives rarely communicate effectively with IT executives. In a world where there is so much technology innovation, the partnership must be enhanced. Only then can the two groups identify opportunities to leverage the latest tools to generate business value. That requires a conversation about mutual roles and expectations which should be an ongoing dialogue between the two functions, at all levels.

- *Prioritization of projects.* One key source of frustration cited by many business units, including marketing, is waiting in the IT queue. The fact is that IT services multiple functions and often does not have the proper measurements to distinguish and prioritize the most critical projects. Ideally, IT will prioritize business functions which are willing to devote the time required to prepare robust business cases. All the while, it must be responsive and flexible, recognizing that priorities can change, often at short notice. One potential solution to dealing with an overloaded IT function is to outsource the management of information assets or parts of the process. In one illustration, many companies outsource their prospecting database, market research, and analytic functions, but will keep customer information, profitability, and value information in-house. Some organizations also outsource their customer database as well as many of the routine marketing operations. Not having to deal with the creation and management of the asset can help to focus an organization's resources on exploiting the insights and business value derived from the information.

- *Measurements, rewards, and motivations.* Too often, business planning is done without any regard for the changes in technology infrastructure that will be necessary to support those initiatives, which is one reason the initiatives often fail. In many financial services companies, for example, product development is essentially a question of changing features and prices on an operational system, since there is no physical product. The key to ensuring success in the management of information assets lies in deep collaboration between marketing and IT. A commitment to the partnership ensures continuous and open communication around shared priorities and objectives. It enables the groups to determine the key measures of success, and establish the rewards and compensation that will drive sustained performance.

Marketers that intend to capitalize on information must assess and audit their existing assets to determine how they can leverage them further and what new assets they will need to meet their objectives. They must evaluate their processes of information management to determine where weaknesses lie and how workflows might be enhanced. But marketers also must look closely at the relationship between marketing and IT. This relationship, more than any other within the business, will determine whether the supporting foundations are in place to take information to a higher level of value.

CASE STUDY: KEYBANK TURNS ANALYLSIS INTO ACTION

Strong marketing performance depends on intelligent analysis. One company that is demonstrating this is Cleveland-based KeyBank, one of America's largest financial institutions with $85 billion in assets under its management. Trish Mathe, Senior Vice President and Director of Database Marketing, says that such efforts have cultivated a "culture of accountability" within the marketing organization.[18] As you learned in Chapter 4, "The Measure of Marketing," marketing at KeyBank is held accountable through an array of corporate and departmental scorecards that present key indicators of performance.

KeyBank invests roughly half of its marketing budget in database and direct-marketing initiatives. Indeed, the database marketing group recently has added new analysis and reporting specialists. "The discipline of database marketing is highly valued at KeyBank," says Mathe. As she explains, the group is actively producing scorecards and dashboards as well as conversion analysis on the movement of leads to transactions. The reporting group also regularly produces a series of reports on "economic profit added" associated with various marketing initiatives throughout the company. "The idea of marketing ROI is one we are focusing on," she adds. "We want to know what is working and what is not."

Mathe's group calls one of its more leading edge analyses "marketing performance optimization" or MPO. The group developed this sophisticated analysis, planning, and forecasting tool that draws on an array of data including market share, account openings, and program results. Based on its analysis, the marketing team can more effectively forecast the likely impact of campaigns, programs, and promotions in various channels and media.

"So we have models we can use for forecasting and we built a scenario-planning tool on top of it," explains Mathe. "We can analyze a segment or geography to help plan the media mix appropriately. We can assess the tradeoffs of outdoor advertising in Buffalo versus radio in Akron. We can see what happens when dollars are moved around."

The MPO tool enables the group to test its hypotheses, learn from market experience and collaborate on the development of data-driven campaigns. "It forces a kind of scientific rigor," she adds. "People are excited about it. It drives more intelligent conversations."

In the past, marketing teams at KeyBank—acting in a more decentralized fashion—failed to report or follow up on the effectiveness of marketing campaigns and initiatives. That has changed. After three years of diligent data collection, the group now is able to drill-down on details, make valid comparisons, and generate rigorous forecasting models.

Such skills also are vital in terms of making a transition from a product-focused to a customer-focused organizational structure. "The company is trying to get to a segment management architecture," says Mathe. "Our teams are aligned with those future segments and we are helping to map out where we are going on segmentation work."

CASE STUDY: THE AT&T WIRELESS STRUGGLE WITH FRAGMENTED INFORMATION MANAGEMENT

As the deadline for federally mandated "number portability" loomed in November 2003, AT&T Wireless discovered just how devastating the costs of poorly managed information could be.

At the time, the company was engaged in a difficult upgrade of its customer relationship management software, one that would require a complex array of links to legacy systems. Unfortunately, the company had no fall-back plan as the software continued to crash, and project teams found their work poorly integrated. Meanwhile, service representatives were unable to sign up new customers without problematic and costly delays. It took approximately 20 minutes of setup time to handle five or six screens while accessing information from as many as 15 legacy systems. As a result, AT&T had the second highest cost-per-sub-scriber among the top national carriers, according to analyst reports.

The Siebel software upgrade was designed to cut through these problems and accelerate customer care efforts. "As we needed to handle more transactions, more customers, we needed a more robust system," explained an AT&T spokesman.[19] "So we upgraded. [The upgrade] was going to make it easier for our representatives to get access to information and give them a fuller array of information on the customer."

The company's IT unit, however, failed to account for the vast complexities associated with implementing the project. Fragmented project teams contributed to the complexity by engaging in continual code updates without stopping to test the system's stability. As rumors of layoffs and offshore outsourcing swirled around the organization, the CRM system repeatedly failed to perform. And, on top of these problems, the company struggled to resolve technical hurdles that prevented it from porting numbers to and from other wireless phone companies—yet another setback that would undermine its ability to acquire new customers.

Ultimately, word got out about the company's difficulties and customers started defecting en masse. "It took most of December to expand the systems capacity so that the customer care reps could have as much access as they needed in order to manage customer calls at the same time the salespeople were processing new orders," AT&T Wireless President and CEO John Zeglis said in a conference call with analysts on Jan. 22, 2004.[20] "Frankly, our customer service went pretty far south."

Despite heavy discounts and incentives, independent cell phone retailers, who represent 60 percent of industry revenue, also abandoned the company. Having placed fifth among top providers in the third quarter (adding 229,000 customers), the company added a mere 128,000 in the fourth quarter. placing it dead last.

The breakdown had cost the company thousands of new customers and an estimated $100 million in lost revenue. Worse, its inability to manage information crippled customer confidence and, eventually, market confidence. In February 2004, AT&T Wireless was acquired by Cingular for $41 billion, less than half the company's market value when it went public four years earlier.

CASE STUDY: SUPERREGIONAL DIVERSIFIED BANK (SD BANK)

The experiences at SD Bank (the real name of the bank has been withheld at the request of this client) clearly demonstrates the power and value of customer information. The bank offers a full range of financial services products and sought out our expertise in driving growth through cross-selling.

When the initiative was launched, frontline salespeople were heavily incentivized to sell additional products and services to existing and new customers. Given these heavy incentives, sales staff took to loading up customers with unwanted products (for example, dispensing qualified customers a credit card whenever they opened a checking account or offering a free checking account to customers who opened a home equity line of credit), without regard to whether the customer needed or wanted the product.

Once the company had implemented a sophisticated system for assigning revenues and activity based costs to individual customers and households, it had control on individual customer profitability. Through this analysis, it became clear that almost 40 percent of the bank's customers were unprofitable, as shown in Figure 7.3.

The analysis also revealed other surprises. The bank assumed that these losses stemmed from customers who only owned one product or service. When this profitability information was broken down by the number of products and services customers owned, however, SD Bank discovered that most profitable customers, ones who contributed a disproportionately large share of profits, owned only one or two products. In fact, more than half the bank's best customers only bought or used one or two of its products (see Figure 7.4). Moreover 35 percent of the bank's most unprofitable customers, those who were a fairly large drain on profits, actually owned three or more products.

This revelation led to a number of changes within the company. One impact was that management started tracking customer profitability and retention of portfolio assets (a key driver of profitability) in addition to cross-sell ratios, which had historically been the focus. Top management also moved very quickly to realign sales incentives so that they were designed to increase profitability, rather than focused on selling additional products and services. Commission plans were changed to reflect the

FIGURE 7.3 *SD Bank Household Profitability*

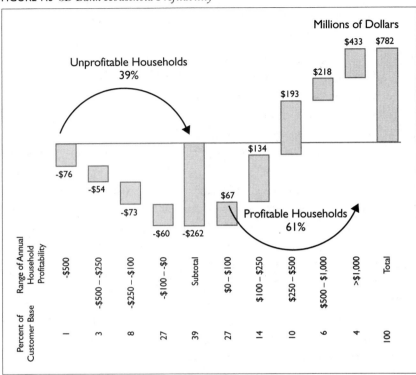

ability of different units to retain profitable customers and maintain and grow an existing book of business, in addition to rewarding new sales, which remained a vital and most important feature of the business.

These changes led to a significant decrease in the bank's unproductive and value-destroying sales and marketing activity, as well as significantly reducing costs. The approach has simultaneously increased revenues, which was greatly appreciated by the entire management team.

TECHNOLOGY'S LINK TO MARKETING AND INFORMATION MANAGEMENT

This chapter has demonstrated the benefits of effectively managing customer and market information, the lifeblood of a High Performance Marketing culture. As you've seen, marketers have to understand how best to leverage information to enhance business value. They must be

FIGURE 7.4 *SD Bank Most Profitable Customers*

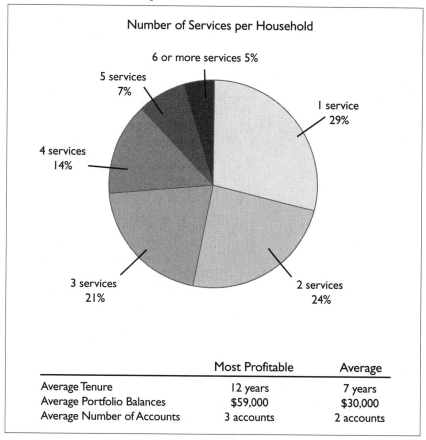

	Most Profitable	Average
Average Tenure	12 years	7 years
Average Portfolio Balances	$59,000	$30,000
Average Number of Accounts	3 accounts	2 accounts

comfortable communicating their needs in very clear, precise ways to their IT counterparts so that they are able to obtain the information they desire. It is also important to not "boil the ocean" in the search for information, because it is easy to get lost in the deluge of data. It is important to be able to see clearly through the data and to be able to take the appropriate actions necessary to enhance business performance. For marketers to be comfortable in their conversations with their IT counterparts, it is helpful if they have familiarity with the underlying technology. This is the last of our effectiveness dimensions and the subject of our next chapter.

8

THE ARCHITECTURE OF ACTION

From Technology to Enablement

"Infrastructures should be invisible..."

Donald Norman, *The Invisible Computer*

Technology is a powerful force. In the realm of marketing, it has enabled companies to greatly enhance the precision of analysis, the productivity of campaigns, and the personalization of customer interactions.

But technology also can be a very disappointing force. In recent years, marketing and customer-oriented technology such as CRM (customer relationship management) software, often failed to meet expectations. In the process of choosing and implementing marketing technologies, many companies failed to focus on the enhancement of business processes and the delivery of clear business value. While these businesses committed big money to software and hardware implementation and integration, the demanding, tactical activities associated with deploying the technology often distracted from the larger, strategic mission. In most of these cases, relatively fewer dollars were directed to communication, training, and the management of change. As a result, the performers themselves become estranged from the tools designed to help them perform and executives reported poor returns and paybacks on many implementations. In some circles, the term "CRM" is now hopelessly tainted.

Marketing automation was often a low priority for many CRM initiatives; the number of "seats" or users in marketing tends to be much lower than in a call center or in the sales force, making it a much less lucrative arena for CRM software vendors and large systems integrators. As a result, marketing departments have had to either live with the existing technology or buy technology that is tailored to their specific needs—an outcome that has worked toward marketing's advantage. As CRM environments mature and second generation efforts become more successful than initial attempts, it is important that marketers prepare to employ that technology with three objectives in mind:

1. They must have the right technologies in place to maximize marketing's effectiveness across all performance dimensions.
2. They need to integrate their technology more effectively with larger CRM efforts within the organization.
3. They must acknowledge that many of marketing's needs are unique and that they will diverge, legitimately, from larger corporate technology choices. They also must understand that compromise is important in the interest of maintaining corporate standards.

Marketers must work to maintain and upgrade the basic marketing system technologies they have put in place. Most offline marketing systems still operate in a batch mode, with weekly, or even monthly, data updates. If users are to be able to react within a relevant window of a perceived need (e.g., a day or two), it is essential that marketing systems be updated on a daily or hourly basis. These systems may also need to analyze transactional data on the fly and have the ability to react almost instantly to insights from the analyses or in response to triggers that are tripped by specific actions. Leveraging this sort of technology requires that organizations have the right decision rules, processes, and organizational capabilities in place. It also requires the interaction of marketing systems with other systems, such as e-commerce, call centers, sales, and retail systems.

Marketing operations or resource management software can offer numerous potential benefits to establishments that are organizationally ready to implement these technologies. These tools have the ability to manage workflow, facilitate teamwork across different functional groups (including outside agencies and other vendors), and help make marketing operations more efficient. Many organizations that suffer from weak operations management have not fully understood or articulated the problems they face. Before purchasing a software "solution," companies need to do the legwork necessary to define the issues and outline the processes and needs that would be addressed by the software.

Although technology alone will not alter the dynamics of a marketing organization, technology lies at the core of a disciplined marketing approach based on increased market intelligence and enhanced customer value. This chapter introduces the reader to the key areas of marketing technology, provides an overview of available technology, and offers guidance on how best to make technology choices. We also examine techniques for building an infrastructure that serves your marketing objectives—delivering information, enabling analysis and measurement, and driving processes to reach strategic goals.

LEVERAGING MARKETING TECHNOLOGY

We have seen many positive advances in recent years with regard to marketing technology. Some members of the marketing profession have embraced technology as a means of understanding customer behavior, reaching out to customers, and reasserting marketing's vital role within customer-focused companies. Those who are behind schedule will no doubt follow as it becomes increasingly obvious that those who do not embrace technology will be at a disadvantage.

The actions of customers, at a detailed level, are no longer a mystery. Where once we pushed products to mass markets of which we had little understanding, we now have the ability to learn the preferences and priorities of our customers and then act on that knowledge. More importantly, it has become a great deal easier for customers to reach out and talk back to companies, through e-mail, call centers, and Web sites. All of these different levels of interaction leads to massive amounts of data.

Organizing, understanding, and acting on this data and information, however, is still a challenge for most organizations. The interaction of marketing and data has been analogous to a dysfunctional personal relationship, in which marketing was accustomed to talking, not listening. Listening is a difficult skill, but is essential to building strong relationships. Data-gathering technology has given companies new eyes and ears, but their organizational ability to process this information and act on it (by truly listening) has yet to catch up.

For the past 15 years, most marketing technology investments have been centered around the following:

- Customer data marts
- Analytic environments for analyzing this customer information
- Campaign management systems for managing direct marketing campaigns
- Reporting systems, usually leveraging some form of business intelligence software

While there are still a great number of companies where these types of systems are nonexistent, many other systems are in place but do not work particularly well. In the latter case, the issue usually lies in one of the following areas:

- The system was designed without adequate time and attention focused on the business requirements or processes it was meant to support.
- The IT department, a software vendor, or the systems integrator was leading the effort, rather than marketing.
- There was inadequate knowledge transfer from the systems integrator to the IT staff (those responsible for maintaining the system).
- Users were not represented on the development team and training was inadequate.
- The system is not dynamic enough to keep up with shifting business requirements.
- There remains an old marketing customer information file that is being kept by a loyal few and users prefer to use it instead of the new system.

Each of the above issues is solvable, and the solutions become progressively easier as one gets down the list.

CREATING MARKET VALUE THROUGH TECHNOLOGY

Considering the changing relationship between companies and their customers, it is more important than ever to leverage technology, providing insight to market and customer data, as well as compelling and seamless connections to our customers. While some use the term "Marketing Automation" to describe these efforts, it is increasingly apparent that such technology goes beyond automating processes, helping us transform and optimize them, as well. In the process, we elevate the marketer's status by providing high-impact, real-world opportunities to create market value.

World-class companies realize that they can *enhance their marketing efforts* significantly if they capitalize on technology to identify market opportunities, improve their campaigns, and strengthen customer relationships. Technology has enabled companies to launch campaigns faster, understand the impact of those campaigns, and make quick adjustments. Organizations also use marketing technology to gain greater market and customer insights through better measurement and feedback, enhancing their interaction with customers.

Technology has enabled companies to *collect customer information and act on it with increasing effectiveness.* Powerful databases store highly detailed insights into customer purchasing and interaction history, credit and payments, needs and interests, as well as customer profitability and potential. The Web has provided marketers with detailed information on browsing behavior, shopping basket activity, checkout (shopping cart abandonment remains an issue for many companies), and reaction to pricing and promotions. Packaged goods companies have always had surprisingly keen insight into the customer's response to price changes, special promotions, and displays, through scanner data analysis. For them, well designed Web sites offer the ability to get in touch directly with their best customers and understand their motivations and intentions.

Here are some examples of ways companies are using technology to leverage customer data as they provide personalized experiences for customers.

- Lands' End's "My Virtual Model" program allows users to customize the fit of everything from jeans to pajamas, dress shirts to T-shirts. This technology offers their customers a custom fit at prices that are far more reasonable than those of a custom tailor. Customers must provide a fair amount of information about themselves, but do so willingly, because they see the enormous benefit.
- Harrah's Entertainment's "Total Rewards" program (discussed in Chapter 7,) uses technology to track individual hotel and casino guests across properties and geographies, recording their needs and interests as well as their level of play and spending. Harrah's uses the data gathered through this program to match products and services with individual customer preferences, and to create offers and specialized packages with an eye toward the customer's overall value to the company.
- Credit Union of Texas, one of the largest credit unions in the country with more than $1.1 billion in assets, has leveraged its marketing software to determine the best locations for profitable new branches and to devise highly targeted marketing campaigns. The use of modeling software demonstrated to the organization that drive time (which can vary significantly from actual distance) is the single most critical variable determining whether a customer would remain loyal. "If a branch was within a 10-minute drive, we had a checking account," explains Jerry Thompson, the credit union's Senior Vice President and CIO.[1] "But if the drive was 10½ minutes, we didn't. It was that stark." Credit Union of Texas also leveraged analysis of prospective customers for its leasing services. These efforts helped boost marketing response rates for direct mail pieces from 1 percent to 4.5 percent, and drove down the cost of customer acquisition from $200 to $44 per new customer.

Yet another powerful benefit that companies have realized through new technology is the ability to more effectively manage channels of interaction and commerce. Customers want to do business in many ways—in person, over the phone, and on the Web. They also expect organizations to be accessible for shopping or answering questions around the clock. Interacting with customers anytime and from anywhere can be an easy part of automating customer relations. The hard part is recognizing the customer across these channels and ensuring that levels of service are comparable, meeting reasonable expectations. ATM customers do not expect service with a smile, but they do expect to receive their money quickly, without being forced to view an ad for a home equity loan.

If companies are to win the loyalty of their customers, they must be able to address them as individuals in every channel of interaction. New investments in multichannel marketing capabilities have enabled General Motors, for instance, to strengthen relationships with its "family market," a group of 7.5 million constituents which is comprised of GM employees, their extended families, and GM retirees. Traditionally, the company would reach out to this market through multiple, fragmented business units, an approach that often lead to overlapping offers. "To avoid defection, we had to look at things from our customers' vantage points," says Lisa Anne Charney, Executive Director of Enterprise Customer Management at General Motors.[2] "We had to enable customers to communicate with us through any channel they wanted, while offering them targeted products and services. We couldn't do that effectively through our traditional, decentralized model."

GM was able to develop a centralized call center approach that allowed agents to actively cross-sell and up-sell GM cars, insurance, and other products to the family market. GM's new customer contact center, dubbed "C3," provides customers with a single point of contact for all needs. It also helps GM sell bundled product and service offerings, and increase customer loyalty. All contact data, such as purchase history and account information, is now universally available to agents on the system and enables them to conduct a seamless dialogue with customers.

"Revenue is up because our ability to manage leads and convert them is better than ever," says Charney. "We are saving on marketing costs by targeting customers for multiple products through coordinated campaigns, rather than bombarding them with eight different direct mail pieces for eight different products. And thanks to the solution's strong analytics, we can now measure how well we are doing with given customer segments and adjust our sales and marketing accordingly."

Similarly, companies have leveraged marketing technology to *generate measurable results and feedback*. Some can now precisely track customer needs and buying patterns using marketing optimization solutions. These companies can run more tests, experience more failures and successes, and use the information they generate in the process to adapt to changing trends, making rapid course corrections.

CRM TECHNOLOGY: LIFTING THE FOG OF DISAPPOINTMENT

Despite such successes, marketers that intend to capitalize on technology must face up to the disappointments of the past that now leave senior management wary of such investments. The technology industry, overall, has not yet recovered the credibility it lost in recent years as buyers began expressing the full measure of their dissatisfaction. According to research conducted in 2001 by the UK-based Standish Group, merely 55 percent of IT projects that cost less than $750,000 came in on time and on budget and have met established expectations.[3] However, Standish could find no projects valued over $10 million in its study that met this definition of success.

This fog of disappointment carries over to the world of CRM. In a study of CRM capabilities such as campaign management and marketing analytics, the market intelligence and advisory firm IDC found that merely 35 percent of executives stated their expectations had been met.[4] And just 20 percent of financial services firms—among the leading implementers of CRM technology—stated that front office technology investments the late 1990s had generated gains in profitability in, according to a study by McKinsey Global Institute.[5]

In the previous chapter of this book, we talked about the much-publicized failure of a CRM implementation at AT&T Wireless. This failure was a major factor in AT&T Wireless losing its lead position in the marketplace and being sold in an auction to a competitor, Cingular. There is a lesson in this for marketers and technology vendors alike. Software vendors tend to overpromise on the current capabilities of their software and employ the overused line "that feature will be included in our next release." Before marketers and their IT partners plunge into the circus of proposals and dog-and-pony presentations with software vendors, they need to find the answers to some critical questions.

- Do we have a clear business case for the purchase of this technology and related services?
- Is our organization truly capable of leveraging this technology to the fullest extent? If not, then what do we need to do in order to prepare ourselves to get maximum mileage out of this software?

- How much of that preparation has to precede the software purchase and how much can be done with and after the purchase?
- What are the true total costs of ownership? (Software purchase and license fees tend to be a significant part of the cost, but are by no means the whole cost.)

The challenge that marketers face lies in establishing a credible foundation for new technology investments based on real business value, as well as improvements in processes and practices. Figure 8.1 shows an approach to this decision that puts the technology acquisition in a business context.

Tool Evaluation and Vendor Selection

Choose technology vendors carefully. Separate the claims from the real functionalities they can offer, and look for viability and support from the vendor. Companies such as our own, Quaero, have a keen understanding of the pros and cons of competing software products, developed from numerous difficult implementations. We also have the added advantage of understanding the business environments, and are able to develop business cases and then match the software more appropriately to true business needs. Here are a few pointers for evaluating and choosing tools and vendors.

- Develop your business case for the relevant solution; identify the criteria for selection and shortlist vendors before you fall in love with a particular vendor or a specific feature offered by one of them. Does it make sense for you to try and stay with software vendors that are already providing other capabilities to your organization or should you go with a specialty vendor? Your existing Enterprise Resource Planning (ERP) and CRM suite vendors may have some marketing operations, campaign management, and analytics capabilities, but they may not be appropriate for your needs, even though IT may be more comfortable with those packages.
- Invite vendors for demos, proofs of concept, and in-depth discussions. Use these events to determine whether they understand your business.

- Talk to references, visit reference sites, and talk to industry analysts that can be excellent sources of information, such as Gartner, IDC, or Forrester. However, be aware that these analyst firms often have lucrative relationships with technology companies and some may be better at insulating their analysts from business pressures than others. Marketing colleagues in other companies who have some experience can often be a source of unsanitized references.
- You may not want every module that is being sold by the vendor. Be selective about what you pay for, but get options on the other modules so you can buy them later if you need them. Your negotiating position will never be as strong as it is during the initial purchase.
- Explore ways that payment can be tied to performance.
- Ensure that the vendor will supply you with relevant support. If you are considering a small vendor, find out how stable and solvent they are. These factors may impact how well you will be supported if you purchase their product/software/solution. (The same may be true even for large businesses, as evidenced by Oracle's purchase of PeopleSoft.)

MARKETING'S TECHNOLOGY IMPERATIVE: TAKING THE LEAD

The successful introduction and application of marketing technology depends on a commitment to leadership. Without executive leadership, technology will wither or fail. Marketing leadership must view technology through three critical perspectives: *the governance perspective, the investment perspective,* and *the enablement perspective.*

The Governance Perspective

The ultimate success of marketing depends on linkages with operations, channels, and other functional units within the enterprise. Therefore, marketing's perspective on technology must encompass the entire span of customer-focused, front-office technology as well as back-office technology necessary to support the customer.

FIGURE 8.1 *Planning and Implementing Marketing Automation Projects*

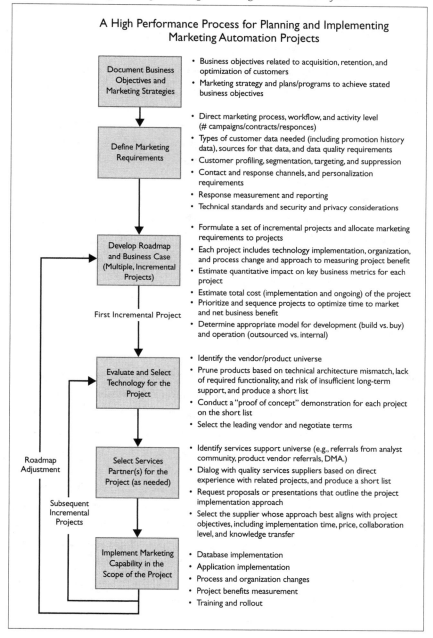

A High Performance Process for Planning and Implementing Marketing Automation Projects

Document Business Objectives and Marketing Strategies
- Business objectives related to acquisition, retention, and optimization of customers
- Marketing strategy and plans/programs to achieve stated business objectives

Define Marketing Requirements
- Direct marketing process, workflow, and activity level (# campaigns/contracts/responces)
- Types of customer data needed (including promotion history data), sources for that data, and data quality requirements
- Customer profiling, segmentation, targeting, and suppression
- Contact and response channels, and personalization requirements
- Response measurement and reporting
- Technical standards and security and privacy considerations

Develop Roadmap and Business Case (Multiple, Incremental Projects)
- Formulate a set of incremental projects and allocate marketing requirements to projects
- Each project includes technology implementation, organization, and process change and approach to measuring project benefit
- Estimate quantitative impact on key business metrics for each project
- Estimate total cost (implementation and ongoing) of the project
- Prioritize and sequence projects to optimize time to market and net business benefit
- Determine appropriate model for development (build vs. buy) and operation (outsourced vs. internal)

First Incremental Project

Evaluate and Select Technology for the Project
- Identify the vendor/product universe
- Prune products based on technical architecture mismatch, lack of required functionality, and risk of insufficient long-term support, and produce a short list
- Conduct a "proof of concept" demonstration for each project on the short list
- Select the leading vendor and negotiate terms

Roadmap Adjustment

Select Services Partner(s) for the Project (as needed)
- Identify services support universe (e.g., referrals from analyst community, product vendor referrals, DMA.)
- Dialog with quality services suppliers based on direct experience with related projects, and produce a short list
- Request proposals or presentations that outline the project implementation approach
- Select the supplier whose approach best aligns with project objectives, including implementation time, price, collaboration level, and knowledge transfer

Subsequent Incremental Projects

Implement Marketing Capability in the Scope of the Project
- Database implementation
- Application implementation
- Process and organization changes
- Project benefits measurement
- Training and rollout

Smart governance depends on prioritization of attention, however, so marketing must first decide what it can immediately impact and what it can indirectly influence. Initially, marketing leaders must focus on marketing technology. Marketing will undermine itself if its involvement in technology becomes too expansive and unfocused. Indeed, this explains much of the failure associated with earlier waves of CRM technology. By focusing on the immediately manageable areas of technology that promise to generate the most impact, marketing can create wins and generate momentum for wider efforts going forward.

Governance also implies responsibility and accountability. In any marketing technology implementation, the danger is that accountability for technology outcomes will be shifted to the IT group. However, IT generally does not have direct insight into the business objectives and processes that are being supported through marketing and other customer-focused technology. Marketing is responsible for the results associated with its initiatives, and must also take a leading role in the management of technologies that enable those initiatives.

The Investment Perspective

Investments must be linked to outcomes and expected outcomes. Marketing leaders must manage a portfolio of different technologies and observe the progress of their investments in relation to objectives. They also must determine a useful method for segmenting and analyzing IT investments. Some organizations judge these investments based on their expected returns or level of criticality. Some look at technology investments through a life cycle (early stage to mature), while others create separate classes for investments that are operational, improvement-oriented, or innovative.

No matter which method it employs, however, marketing must create a rational and analytical way of prioritizing IT investments, or these investments are likely to be made on intuitive, emotional, and political grounds. A portfolio approach, where different technology investments are matched to appropriate short- and long-term marketing objectives, enables leaders to assess technology potential and performance in a relatively sensible and dispassionate way. It matches financial and strategic objectives to technology investments.

Using a portfolio approach also encourages marketing leaders to continuously manage and measure the value of an IT investment. Too often, companies create ROI models merely to justify an initial investment. Once the investment is made, very little rigor goes into analyzing or maximizing the value of the technology. As a result, IT assets depreciate more rapidly and the full degree of value is lost. Quite often, companies can gain substantial benefits by managing technology investments more actively, diligently, and continuously.

"Companies should evolve their processes, skills, and tools for driving quantifiable results from IT by extending current capabilities," contends Dan Merriman, President of Chapin Consulting. The model shown in Figure 8.2, developed by Chapin Consulting, illustrates how strategy, value management, and implementation should be integrated as components of a value management process.[6] Few if any companies have fully developed and integrated each of these components. Companies can use this model as a long-term target to guide the evolution of each component and to develop processes to support the investment perspective of their own organization.

Highlighted in the center of the chart are the steps of the value management process that should be undertaken for each major initiative that will significantly impact the business. The links between this process and corporate/IT strategy planning are shown in the top portion of the chart, in which a "portfolio" of IT initiatives is defined, prioritized, and managed, explains Merriman. The relationship between this

FIGURE 8.2 *Value Management Process*

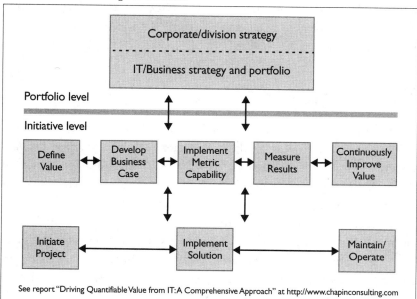

See report "Driving Quantifiable Value from IT: A Comprehensive Approach" at http://www.chapinconsulting.com

process and project initiation, implementation, and operations is shown at the bottom.

Any company should follow these five steps when investing in a marketing technology solution:

- *Define value.* Determine the priority business goals, business value metrics, and key people, process, and technology actions of the initiative.
- *Develop business case.* Develop the financial justification for the initiative and establish accountability for the expected business improvements.
- *Implement metric capability.* Design and implement metrics measurement/analysis process, data, and technical mechanisms.
- *Measure results.* Measure and communicate actual results.
- *Continuously improve value.* Actively improve the results by proactively monitoring effectiveness, analyzing outcomes versus targets, and taking action when necessary.[7]

By pursuing an approach to IT investment that emphasizes "continuous value management," marketing and IT leaders put themselves in a position to truly extend and leverage the value of their technology investments. As the era of "big bang" implementations comes to a close and new, incremental approaches become the norm, leaders maintaining a strong investment perspective become disciplined and diligent investors in marketing technology.

The Enablement Perspective

Marketers must also provide leadership with respect to how technology might and should be applied. Marketers can bring critical domain expertise to particular strategies, workflows, and business processes. In the end, all organizations must remember that technology cannot overcome weak process discipline and poorly designed processes.

In recent years, many companies have allowed technology to dictate, rather than support, processes. In many cases, processes have been frozen in rigid, proprietary applications, making it more difficult than ever for companies to improve and adapt marketing processes in relation to marketplace changes. The rising importance of open, componentized, and Web-based architectures has profound implications for the resolution of such problems. This architectural shift away from monolithic systems allows leaders to concentrate on enhancing business processes and practices, as opposed to simply adapting them to work with the features and functions of new upgraded "versions" of applications. As technology becomes less intimidating and more accessible, it enables marketing leaders to increasingly focus on strategy and process as opposed to the technology itself.

Given the changing dynamics of technology, marketers have an opportunity to capitalize on it in powerful new ways. New marketing processes may be expected to increasingly revolve around interactions as opposed to campaigns, important life events instead of demographic targeting, and customer engagement rather than interruption and annoyance. Paradoxically, this architectural shift elevates the applied value of technology even as it makes it increasingly invisible to the marketing decision maker.

Emerging service-oriented and componentized architecture lays the foundation for a new level of agility and dynamism. "Strategic leverage is shifting to processes that enable an enterprise to sense unanticipated change earlier to enable a proper and timely response," writes Gartner analyst Scott Nelson.[8] "As such, marketing communication processes must shift a mindset of 'pre-packaged waves' of programs to the identification and implementation of life events and interaction-driven marketing strategies and tactics."

MARKETING TECHNOLOGY FRAMEWORK

In order to effectively invest in and monitor the value of marketing technology, it is important to have a coherent framework that puts relevant systems and applications in perspective. Without a wider framework, investments are likely to be ad hoc and undisciplined, failing to provide the value and impact that one seeks.

While there are many possible ways of mapping out one's marketing technology infrastructure, we offer here a clear and accessible model. The Marketing Technology Framework must address the following five key elements of the overall marketing process, as illustrated in Figure 8.3.

FIGURE 8.3 *Elements of the Overall Marketing Process*

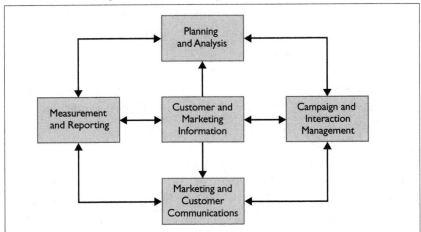

1. Customer and marketing information
2. Planning and analysis
3. Campaign and interaction management
4. Marketing and customer communications
5. Measurement and reporting

As the model suggests, marketing organizations need to begin thinking of technology not merely as a suite of software or a stack of hardware, but rather, components that are designed to support, stream-line, and enhance marketing processes. Toward that end, the framework embeds technology within a set of processes that leverage marketing and customer information.

Compiling Marketing and Customer Information

Some companies will find it most sensible to manage and market to their customers as segments. These market-focused organizations rely on aggregated trend data to develop sophisticated distribution and pro-motional programs. This is particularly true among manufacturers of consumer product goods that sell their products through distributors, resellers, and retailers. However, many more companies are exploring ways to precisely target individual customers with their marketing ef-forts. These customer-focused organizations increasingly rely on "actionable intelligence" to present the perfect offer to the right customer at the right time.

At the heart of all such endeavors lies *marketing and customer information*. Whether it is acquired, integrated and stored in-house, or acquired from third parties (or, most commonly, a combination of approaches), this information is central to all marketing processes. Marketers rely on this information to analyze opportunities, identify relevant markets and customers, and to then produce campaigns and communications. Based on the outcomes of past campaigns and interactions, the marketing database becomes a rich repository of critical marketing knowledge and insight that can guide future efforts.

Increasingly, organizations are consolidating customer and marketing information within a unified data warehouse or marketing data mart environment to facilitate access and action, as illustrated in Figure 8.4. Many companies are wise to outsource the creation and management of their marketing data marts, particularly in the earliest stages of the process. Specialist firms can get a company up and running in far less time than it takes to train an IT department to build and maintain these databases.

Within the data warehouses, companies often maintain separate databases for prospects and customers. (It is beyond the scope of this book, and a somewhat futile exercise, to argue about the use of the term "warehouse" versus "marts," which is why the two terms are used interchangeably and in combination throughout this chapter.) Prospect data tends to be acquired from external vendors in the form of lists, which vary widely in the accuracy of the information they hold.

FIGURE 8.4 *Consolidating Customer and Marketing Information*

Customer data, of course, is often extracted from transaction files in the operational systems, such as billing information, call center inquiries, and so on. There is value in enhancing internal customer data with external information, as well as in linking prospect and customer databases. This type of exchange, however, often conflicts with the organization structure in many companies, where customer acquisition tends to be handled by a group that is independent of customer management, which, in turn, is responsible for cross-selling, enhancing profitability, and retention.

Outsource versus In-house Implementation

There is a great deal of talk surrounding the advantages and disadvantages of outsourcing versus building or buying marketing applications or services. The decision must be made after carefully considering various factors such as speed of implementation, experience of the in-house staff, customer data privacy policies, available resources, budget constraints, and desired amount of control.

Marketing organizations that do not have adequate in-house capabilities or experience sometimes opt for outsourcing, or a combination of outsourced and in-house marketing infrastructure. After gaining experience and skill sets, or when increased budgets or returns on investment justify the move, these organizations tend to bring outsourced services in-house. If your organization is weighing an outsourcing decision, follow the recommendations and reminders in this checklist.

- Make sure you have a viable vendor.
- Ensure your customer data privacy and security policies are enforced.
- Establish that all outsourcing marketing operations are transparent and your teams' needs are relevant and have an appropriate reporting procedure.
- Continue to monitor the outsourced operations as soon as you have decided on the outsourcing method and vendor. Ensure that they reflect your marketing philosophies.
- Make certain that your vendor offers the flexibility necessary for you to move from an outsourced model to the in-house model seamlessly.

Gartner Dataquest estimates that through 2007, compound annual growth in marketing applications investments will exceed 10 percent. When calculating required capital for such an investment, do not forget to incorporate these key elements into the overall contract and project plan: underlying hardware, networking infrastructure, project implementation, process standardization, employee training.

Using Campaign and Interaction Management Tools

Campaign management tools help marketers effectively design and develop campaigns by enabling them to select appropriate customers and prospects. Campaign management tools enable the marketer to segment customers (or markets), design a campaign, execute it, and track it. As the link between planning and execution, these tools form a core element of direct marketing management today. Thanks to such productivity enhancing tools, marketers can now afford to launch greater numbers of more highly focused campaigns, thereby promising a higher return on investment. The leading software tools that specialize in this area are Unica's Affinium Campaign, SAS Marketing Automation, and Chordiant's Marketing Director. Of course, the suite vendors such as Siebel, SAP, and Oracle have modules that perform these functions as well.

A new wave of marketing technology is facilitating *interaction management*, enabling marketers to set parameters and rules as well as generate scripts and offers that will guide interaction within the channel. Such activities can potentially have a powerful impact on customer interactions, making them increasingly personal and compelling. The primary software products in this area are Unica's Affinium Interact, and Epiphany's Interaction Advisor.

These technologies enable a company to react instantaneously to the browsing pattern of a potential or current customer on the Web and present them with offers that are relevant based on their current searching pattern as well as their historic behavior. For instance, a person known to be a Web-window shopper who has not made purchases over the past many sessions receives a very different message than does a first-time browser, even when both individuals display the same browsing behavior.

By recognizing and understanding recent behavioral patterns, these technologies enable call center operators to react to incoming calls or script outbound calls in ways that precisely target the customer's needs at that point in time. Another, relatively mature manifestation of this type of technology is the personalized grocery store receipts that respond to your purchase of Huggies by giving you a checkout coupon for Pampers (assuming Pampers absorbs the cost of this coupon). In this case, the coupon comes regardless of who you are and is based solely on your immediate purchase. The newer technologies provide the added knowledge of past behavior, loyalties, and profitability that can be used before making a promotional offer. Companies such as MarketSoft offer very sophisticated trigger-based marketing capabilities.

Managing Marketing and Customer Communications

Within a company's channels and at its touch points, *marketing and customer communications* programs are executed. This is the point at which a company's campaigns and interaction approaches converge with the actual customer or prospect. Whether the interaction occurs in the form of a presentation of information, an offer, or a service follow-up, the question is what impact it will have on the customer relationship. Will the interaction enhance the value of the relationship or devalue it?

Ensuring that a customer experience is seamless and compelling has become an increasingly difficult challenge in recent years. There are now an array of touch points for customer interaction including the phone, the Web, and the sales force. Prospective customers, in the meantime, may receive messages through still other channels including television, print publications, billboards, online advertisements, e-mail, and direct mail. The challenge lies in managing customer communication and interaction across this multitude of channels, touch points, and technologies.

Increasingly, technology enables us to present messages and offers at a precise moment of opportunity. This capability involves monitoring customer events (transaction and demographic data) to look for changes in the customer situation (change of address, marriage, etc.) or customer interaction with the enterprise. This type of monitoring will require the implementation of event-triggering technology that can actively monitor the customer database for customer events and generate appropriate messages and offers at the right time. All of this function-

FIGURE 8.5 *High Performance Marketing Infrastructure*

Source Systems/ Legacy Data Islands	Data Warehouse	Business Intelligence and Data Mining	Execution, Personalization, and Automation	Message Delivery	Customer Experiences
Internal Data		Planning/ Reporting	Customer Lists	E-mail/ Fax Server	Read E-mail/Fax
Internal Data	Extract, Transform, Load — Data Warehouse	Analysis and Segmentation	Offer, Message Customization	Web Server	View Web Pages
Internal Data		Modeling and Data Mining	Next Message	Production Shop	Read Mail and Brochures
Outside Data		Tracking	Business Rules and Real-Time Differentiation	Sales Force	Interaction w/ Sales Person
				Call Center	Conversation w/ Call Center

Real-Time Data Store

Sales and Transaction Data Session Data Session Data

Feedback Loop

ality can result in a fairly complex customer management and marketing infrastructure, as Figure 8.5 illustrates.

As you follow from left to right in the chart, you will notice that the path of data and information goes through various stages of processing for analytics, decision making, and action, and is explained below.

- Raw data from operational systems and external sources is extracted, transformed, and loaded (ETL) into a data warehouse or mart.
- This data is stored in a data warehouse or mart that is designed specifically for different types of users, including analysts and heavy users, marketing campaign managers, report producers, and so on.
- The information is then used by these various groups for their own purposes, for example, deriving business rules and targeting particular customers for specific messages or offers.
- These campaign messages are then routed through the appropriate channel.
- Once the message is delivered to the customer the response (or lack of it) is captured and fed back to the mart for analysis.

Measuring and Reporting

Finally, technology enables the marketer to measure, assess, and report on the results of marketing activities. This is a central factor in the marketing process that can be facilitated through various performance analyses and reporting technologies, whether in spreadsheets, embedded reporting in various campaign management tools, or more sophisticated "dashboards" and "scorecards."

One breed of technology known as Marketing Resource Management (MRM) applications takes a holistic approach to the marketing process. Starting with high level objectives, these applications help plan, budget, and track marketing activities. As such, they provide the foundation for improved planning, coordination, execution, and measurement of marketing activities. Examples of such applications are Aprimo, and Unica's Affinium Plan. MRM technology is still an emerging field, so these products do differ significantly in their functionality and focus.

It is also important to measure the return on marketing investments to ensure that the results are in line with expectations and that the resulting feedback is used to fine-tune future marketing programs. The ability to produce reports and generate key performance indicators is vital to marketing effectiveness. Ultimately, the process repeats itself as reports and measurements are used to prepare and plan for new campaigns and interactions. At every stage in the cycle, technology can play a valuable, enabling role.

Of course, marketing is not the only process that demands enablement as companies strive to build more powerful and profitable customer relationships. Marketers must explore ways to create the customer-focused technology foundations necessary to build an overall compelling customer experience. This requires marketers to expand their perspective on technology to areas such as sales and service, product development, logistics, and finance. Building such an experience also will require that marketers establish standards and architectures that encompass suppliers and partners, and anyone who contributes to customer-focused processes.

As databases, business processes, and organizational units become increasingly interconnected, marketers must recognize the linkages between marketing technology and the wider infrastructure of customer, enterprise and interenterprise relationships. With that in mind, marketing leaders can play a powerful role in the evolution and development of all customer-related technology within their companies.

CLOSING THE GAP:
REACHING NEW LEVELS

Despite the widespread interest in CRM and marketing automation over the past few years, many marketing organizations still manage multimillion-dollar operations based on spreadsheets and other basic tools. In fact, marketing organizations stand at widely varying levels of maturity in terms of the five marketing technology elements. For example, an enterprise may have invested a great deal in building a comprehensive data warehouse, but may lack the essential tools to segment customers and deliver the lists. Another enterprise may have advanced campaign management software, but have a very scattered customer data infrastructure with poor data quality.

Marketing technology infrastructure can be divided into four levels of maturity—0 being the most primitive infrastructure and 3 having the most advanced and sophisticated technology infrastructure. The tables in Figure 8.6 describe the characteristics of organizations operating at each of these levels of technology infrastructure maturity, in each of four areas:

1. Customer data infrastructure
2. Campaign management
3. Customer communication
4. Measurement and reporting

The information in these tables can be useful for plotting where your own organization's technology infrastructure currently stands and what types of changes it requires in order to fulfill your information and analytic needs in order to achieve key business objectives.

A world-class, level 3 marketing organization might be able to rapidly and proactively shape its strategies to address a dynamic business environment, intense competitive pressures, new customer communication channels, and a changing distribution and product life cycle management dynamics. Companies functioning at this level provide a rich

FIGURE 8.6 *Levels of Maturity*

Levels of Maturity in Customer Data Infrastructure	
Level	**Description**
Level 0	Very primitive. No database is built. A campaign management program directly accesses the source system to extract data. These programs then work on the extracted dataset to create lists. Difficult to get a consistent and complete view of the customer across datasets.
Level 1	Basic. Custom programs use procedural languages to build load programs. Difficult to maintain.
Level 2	Advanced. Robust processes use state-of-the-art technology to support scaleable ETL. Also, Data Quality tools bring consistency and accuracy to the customer data.
Level 3	Very Advanced. Real-time push and pull of information using integration architectures.

Levels of Maturity in Campaign Management: Target Selection Capabilities	
Level	**Description**
Level 0	No tool is used. Ad-hoc programs are run on the operational systems to create the lists.
Level 1	Use of reporting and ad-hoc query tools to create lists.
Level 2	Use of campaign management tool; use of modeling techniques for segmentation.
Level 3	Real-time capabilities, event detection, and triggering.

Levels of Maturity for Customer Communication: Message Delivery Capabilities	
Level	**Description**
Level 0	Use of outsourcing partners for campaign delivery.
Level 1	On-line delivery systems implemented in-house; off-line delivery outsourced.

Level 2	Ability to deliver offers when the customer is most receptive (e.g., store visit, Web visit, contact with call center, etc.). Use of customer profiles and real-time recommendation engines.
Level 3	Ability to constantly monitor customer information and trigger delivery of a campaign based on predefined business rules.

Levels of Maturity for Measurement and Reporting	
Level	Description
Level 0	Use of standard reporting tools for creating and disseminating response metrics.
Level 1	Integrated response tracking and measurement functionality coupled with campaign management applications.
Level 2	More robust analysis with state-of-the-art business intelligence applications.
Level 3	Dedicated measurement dashboard with key performance indicators to proactively monitor performance goals. Marketing operations and resource management infrastructure helps optimize spending and allocation decisions.

and integrated profile of the customer to front-line professionals, while delivering a compelling and seamless experience to their customers.

At the opposite end of the maturity scale, a marketing organization functioning at level 0 has a much less effective marketing technology infrastructure. This level 0 marketing organization—a type which is not uncommon within enterprises today—is at a distinct disadvantage. Because of the scattered or ad-hoc marketing infrastructure, this marketing organization cannot scale to meet growing demands, changing business needs, and competitive pressures.

Marketing technology infrastructures with maturity levels between the most primitive level 0 and the most advanced level 3 have a partial technology infrastructure connecting the five marketing technology dimensions. These infrastructures have custom programs or partially adopted technologies which bring some order to their marketing operations but are still difficult to maintain.

Technology is available to help companies automate processes in the marketing organization and take the marketing technology infrastructure toward advanced level 3 maturity. In order to take steps in this direction, it is necessary to identify areas where technology can drive greater efficiency and effectiveness, reduce costs, or help generate revenue. It is vital to prioritize based on business requirements and objectives, identifying opportunities to build early momentum.

For many marketing organizations, the amount of captured customer data is growing faster than the collective ability to process and mine the data for insights. Transforming the data into insight requires technological investments, employee skill, and capability development to process changes within the enterprise. Time-consuming marketing activities such as planning and budgeting, review, approval processes, creating and developing marketing programs and related assets, and fulfilling and distributing collateral can and should be more constant and automated. Standardizing and streamlining marketing processes will enhance the organization's visibility, accountability, and value. Fortunately, marketing applications are available to implement systemic marketing planning, program management, workflow management, and budget management to produce greater efficiencies of marketing operations. Such applications also can facilitate effective measurement and reporting to all stakeholders.

Key Success Factors for Marketing Project Implementation

- Develop clear goals for a marketing automation initiative.
- Define the areas and marketing tasks where the most potential benefit (i.e., cost reduction or increased revenue) can be gained, and look for the solution that will best achieve those needs.
- Weigh the risks, costs, and requisite benefits of investing in high performance marketing and strive for ROI in 12 to 18 months.
- Break down the project road map to logically phased milestones, which can allow reasonable iterations, and midcourse corrections, enabling progression to the next level of maturity, deliver-

ing clear returns in the shortest possible time. The shorter the time to pay back, the better.

- For complex projects, incorporate three parallel streams of work for every phase, including: 1) scope and design, 2) pilot implementation, and 3) detailed organizational readiness assessment. This approach helps frame the project scale, provides short-term tangible value, and leverages common resources and learnings across all three streams of work.

- Establish a hands-on product review process that defines specific scenarios for all vendors, and requires the vendors agree to use your own data for the evaluation.

- Get the business users to drive the process during the implementation. Watch that the IT team monitors the actual workings of the software behind the scenes. (While it may require more resources than a Request for Proposal, or RFP, this process will result in a more informed decision and will be a better fit overall.)

- Remember that the decision on the implementation partner can and sometimes should be made independently of the software purchase decision. Internal IT groups are typically not the best choice for implementing these specialized solutions, but could, with appropriate training, be qualified to maintain and improve the solutions after they are up and running. The professional services division of the software company tends to be very narrow and specialized on the functions of their own tool, but may lack the ability to provide a broader perspective and go beyond plain implementation.

- Explore the implementation costs associated with a marketing initiative. Place reality checks on vendor claims. While many marketing vendors promise end-to-end delivery (inclusive of the data mart) in three months or less, this is likely only an incremental step, and substantial ongoing effort will be required to mature the customer data foundation over time.

- Ensure that everyone from software administrators to power users to casual users receive adequate training and are supported through the deployment and ongoing maintenance phase. If usage levels are low, be aggressive in understanding the reasons and find solutions for them.

CASE STUDY: CAPITAL ONE'S CUSTOMIZATION STRATEGY

Capital One, which has experienced tremendous growth over the past decade and has been a top-ranking company in the Fortune 500, has made technology central to its overall business strategy. Through the company's proprietary Information-Based Strategy (IBS), it has "mass customized" credit cards and other financial products in powerful new ways.

Dave Jeppesen, Vice President, Direct Marketing Center for Capital One, explains that the company's strategy revolves around three key elements.[9] First, it depends on state-of-the-art technology that is central to the company's business proposition. Second, it thrives on testing analysis. Through a large staff of analysts and world-class infrastructure, the company perpetually tests everything from copy to price points to credit lines. Indeed, it conducted 80,000 tests in 2003. Finally, the company relies on "flexible operations and services" to capitalize on the information it generates. Once new opportunities are identified, the company can act quickly to go into "full production" and "get scale advantage," he says.

The technology underlying these efforts is managed and assessed with tremendous rigor. Explaining his investment strategy, Jeppesen advises other marketers to be crystal clear about business objectives, whether the goal is to increase response rates, reduce costs, or anything that comes to mind. Business goals should guide all decisions. Next, he encourages marketers to "be intentional" about the choices they make. Among the questions he poses is this: Is the technology addressing an immediate challenge or is it designed to provide long-term leverage and competitive advantage? Is it necessary to have "architectural elegance" or is it merely necessary to address a "point" problem?

Jeppesen measures technology investments along what he calls "the ROI curve."[10] Separate from the "technology lifecycle curve," which may or may not align with growth, ROI is concerned with the phases in which financial and strategic returns can be generated from technology. While encouraging companies to map their investments on the curve, he contends that technology should be assessed as an investment portfolio. "Some investments generate high returns; others produce low returns," he says. "Some generate growth, some produce income."

Jeppesen maps investments through birth, growth, and maturity phases. In the birth phase, new technologies are introduced and the goal is to generate a return as quickly as possible. This is analogous to the transformational box in the marketing initiative portfolio in Chapter 3. The growth phase, however, is the most promising. This is where technology can be extended to deliver "massive returns" with minimal investment. This is analogous to the operational box in Chapter 3. Jeppesen describes how his group found new ways to apply data and analytics with a credit decision technology a few years ago—generating a tenfold return on investment. "It's really worth the effort to manage the technology for bigger gains," he remarks.

Ultimately, technology enters a phase of ROI maturity at which point it is necessary to decide whether to reinvent for new growth, invest in maintenance, or allow the technology to phase out. Some companies fail to recognize they have reached this point, and invest precious capital in mature technologies, rather than redirect those funds toward new technology. At this point, the technology becomes "foundational."

Jeppesen explains that the state of investments is measured on a daily, weekly, and quarterly basis and that he is intimately aware of not only the ROI but the NPV (the Net Present Value) of annuity streams that are generated from technology on a discounted basis. "It is very important to be aware and intentional about this curve," he concludes. "It is a portfolio of technology. You have parts of your portfolio that have high return and parts you are investing in for future return and parts that are really at the end of their life cycle in terms of investment."

VIEWING TECHNOLOGY IN THE BIG PICTURE

In this chapter, we have argued that it is critical that technology decisions be made in the context of the business objectives and benefits that they are supposed to drive. We have discussed different frameworks and processes for making technology choices. We also reviewed the overall infrastructural environment for marketing technology. The software world is extremely dynamic and ever changing, so we have refrained from providing detailed descriptions of specific technology companies and their products.

At this point in the book we have discussed in detail each of the six marketing performance dimensions. We now move on to the challenges of bringing all of these dimensions together, weaving a marketing performance culture that is more than just the sum of these parts.

9

THE PERFORMANCE AGENDA

An Action Plan for Disciplined Marketers

"An ounce of performance is worth pounds of promises."

Mae West

In this era of corporate transparency, marketers need to make the value they generate clear and comprehensible. Marketing organizations also must learn to systematically develop, test, and introduce new ways of creating value. Because marketing does not stand alone, strong performance will require the marketing organization to actively embrace the wider goals, objectives, and strategies of the enterprise.

This book has demonstrated how marketers can capitalize on the growing portfolio of capabilities and competencies to accomplish these goals. Having surveyed the various dimensions of marketing performance, we can now explore methods for managing and applying these critical proficiencies in a disciplined and coordinated fashion.

MAKING A TOP-DOWN COMMITMENT TO HIGH PERFORMANCE MARKETING

Many marketing organizations are struggling with measuring marketing effectiveness and improving marketing accountability. This is a particular problem in the areas of mass media advertising but also in areas such as sponsorships (sports, for example), which are significant spending areas for many companies. New product rollouts offer an example of a costly process in need of transparency, discipline, and measurability—all essential components of a high performance marketing culture. Nevertheless, the most rigorous processes and the best measurements will be ineffective unless they are backed up by top management commitment.

New products represent a critical component of growth for companies in most industries. Rolling out new products into the marketplace can be extremely expensive and risky, requiring investments in research and development, new manufacturing or delivery facilities, advertising to the target market, and customer inducements. Despite the enormous amounts of money spent on the new product rollout cycle, however, the majority of new products fail.

In the 1980s, a number of companies such as BBDO, BASES, and Yankelovich developed very sophisticated models, called simulated test markets, to help companies predict the sales of new products before they were introduced to the market. They could also provide detailed diagnostics on what made a new product successful, and whether failures were the result of a product problem or a problem with the marketing plan. Using these models, companies could forecast whether they had a winner or a bomb and make the decision to introduce the product, make modifications to the product or marketing plan, or go back to the drawing board.

Given the tremendous cost of introducing new products in the Consumer Packaged Goods (CPG) industry, businesses within the industry were quick to adopt new forecasting models and approaches. As a result, new product introduction became a much more disciplined and predictable process (relatively speaking) in the CPG sector. These models helped build a performance culture within the new product area of marketing and beyond. They forced a commitment to continual improvement, accountability and results, a process based on learning and change within the organization. This commitment to change is essential, but adopting a sophisticated model is only the first step toward building a performance culture.

In the early 1990s, I was a consultant with a firm that had been hired to help reengineer the new product development and introduction processes in a large packaged goods company. As I interviewed the head of the new product marketing area, I quickly realized he was irritated and skeptical about the project, which had been commissioned by the CEO of the parent company. I asked him why and his response was, "We . . . have a great process [for introducing new products], which we have honed and refined over the years. We currently have a new product in the pipeline. This new product . . . is a pet project of the president of this division. We have done repeated market tests on this concept and the product. It repeatedly earns very low scores. We all know it is a dog, but our president insists on bringing it to market. We are about to spend about $25 million on this launch, and . . . I know we will be withdrawing [the product] from the market in less than a year's time. I am not even sure why we bother doing the testing, if we are not going to heed the test."

In this particular case, we took these concerns anonymously to our client, the CEO, to whom the president of the division reported, and she subsequently made the decision to pull the launch—a decision that paid for our fees several times over. However, this reluctance to formulate sound decisions based on marketing's forecasting results is not an unfamiliar story in many organizations.

Also in the '90s, I was involved with a company that spent more than $200 million on an ad campaign that tested extremely poorly and ultimately failed. This occurred because the CEO decided he did not like the prior advertising campaigns and believed he could do a better job himself. He fired the CMO and worked personally with the head of the ad agency, developing the campaigns, literally, in a smoke-filled room. The Senior Vice President of Advertising became a glorified errand boy in the campaign development process and his authority became diluted. Was he part of the research team at the company, or was he a representative of the ad agency? Was he going to tell the CEO that the ads fared poorly in testing? Not on your life. Would this same CEO have been as bold and cavalier about overriding underwriting risk standards on loans? Probably not, because those were much better established and credible. Marketing, in this case, had not really established its credibility, making it very difficult to stand up to the CEO's arbitrary approach.

Marketing leaders have everything to gain by building and laying out a new performance agenda. They can close the gap that lies between strategy and execution, and in the process, strengthen the linkages that lie between our enterprises and our markets. Still, this new agenda will require marketers to embrace new, often difficult, practices if they are to strengthen their position in the coming years.

PARADIGMS LOST … AND DISCOVERED: RETHINKING STRATEGY, LEADERSHIP, AND LEARNING

This book introduces a new marketing performance framework to explain the key proficiencies necessary to drive its performance. These capabilities and competencies can be thought of as the underappreciated "structural" dimensions of marketing that lie between the strategic and tactical dimensions, long recognized by marketing theorists and practitioners. These strategic dimensions are also referred to as "STP" (strategy, targeting, and positioning). The tactical dimensions are described as "MM," or "market mix," or the "Four Ps" of product, price, place, and promotion.

If marketing's structure is seen through the metaphor of a house, as illustrated in Figure 9.1, the strategic dimensions represent the environment or neighborhood in which the structure exists; its tactical dimensions can be seen as the furnishings and décor that improve the

FIGURE 9.1 *Structural Dimensions of Marketing*

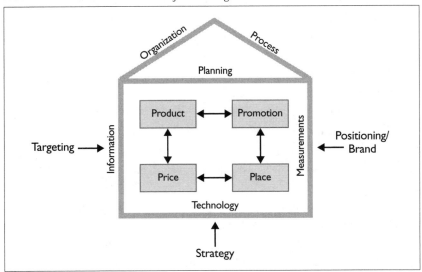

structure's usability. The structure, in other words, serves as a metaphorical connection between the organization's environment and its internal functions; it closes the gap between strategy and execution.

One could argue that STP and MM represent business as seen through the lens of marketing, but this is a constrained view. Furthermore, the proliferation of strategies tends to fragment and divert limited organizational resources. That is why this book focuses on enhancing the existing key business strategies that are driving the enterprise. Disciplined marketing organizations need to broaden their perspective of their marketing structure, applying themselves to the challenge of meeting the objectives and executing the strategies of the business.

Strategy is more than targeting and positioning—it is concerned with the overall goals and objectives of the enterprise. Execution is more than just the Four Ps. It is concerned with channels, interactions, and experiences as well as the value we create and exchange with our customers. An even broader perspective on marketing encourages us to align our business strategies with the goals and priorities of our customers and opportunities in new markets, as depicted in Figure 9.2.

FIGURE 9.2 *Aligning Strategy with Customer Goals and Priorities*

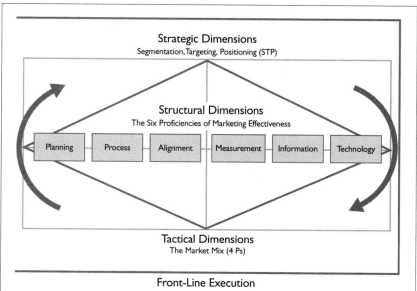

TRANSFORMATIONAL MARKETING LEADERSHIP

Marketing is being challenged in difficult and demanding new ways, and the most significant challenge is to think beyond conventional and departmental perspectives. As we discuss in the concluding chapter of this book, we will increasingly be required to shift our focus from markets as targets to markets as forums, from products to customers, from campaigns to conversations. This is a transformational time for marketing and it will require transformational leadership.

Without disciplined, confident, and consistent leadership, marketing performance initiatives will surely sink back into a state of disarray. These leaders are faced with the challenge of making marketing clear and comprehensible to the balance of the enterprise and with maintaining marketing's firm focus on measurable business results and continual improvement.

The companies that are now performing at world-class levels share a number of common principles and winning practices, as demonstrated below.

- *Ensuring high-level commitment to initiatives.* The challenges discussed in this book require organizations to change the way they function at a very fundamental level. Such a shift in corporate culture and emphasis requires senior-level sponsorship and support. Marketing leaders must use diplomacy to engage their teams in the promotion and rollout of new initiatives and key efforts. Leaders must stick with these efforts despite temporary setbacks or changes in the business environment. In fact, the organization must anticipate and plan for setbacks.
- *Building "dream teams."* Marketing leaders must pay particular attention to the immediate team of people they draw upon to effect change. These are the individuals that will carry the message forward, inspire their people, and frame the opportunities that are before them. The team must be committed to performance and establish new lines of accountability and commitment. An ideal team is comprised of individuals from both the creative and analytical areas of marketing, as well as representatives from fulfillment, sales, service, product development, and other

groups vital to the establishment of a market-driven and, especially, a market-driving organization. Ultimately, marketing performance will rise or fall in relation to this team's competence.

- *Communicating throughout the enterprise.* Objectives must be clear and must be clearly communicated. Processes and practices must be defined to ensure that plans, actions, and outcomes are widely shared. Marketing leaders must engage in a certain amount of evangelism, but more importantly, they must engage in robust dialogue and information exchanges. It is far more powerful to engage the entire organization in a continuing dialogue, than to circumnavigate the enterprise giving PowerPoint presentations and showing media clips. It is also important to consistently update staff on key activities and milestones, whether messages are shared in person, or through e-mail, voice mail, or some other forms of media, meetings, and interpersonal engagement.
- *Training, training, training.* If you expect others to be more concerned of the ability to measure and make decisions based on facts, then they must be trained to acquire and interpret those measurements and facts. We are involved in many engagements at companies where sophisticated reporting and analysis systems are rolled out but never used. This occurs when training is not treated as a priority. There seems to be an implicit assumption in these organizations that smart people will automatically learn and use new processes. After all, it is obvious that this is a better way to do things, correct? Wrong. Some of those with intelligence (especially within organizations that are prone to frequent bursts of enthusiasm for new processes) are just as likely to wait to see if this is a passing fad that will be passed over through benign neglect. Users need to know that this change in culture and methods is not a fad; they need to believe that this approach makes their lives easier, and that it will, in fact, help them advance their careers.
- *Building and sustaining momentum.* Smart leaders recognize that they must constantly build momentum for their initiatives. They must actively promote their successes and build on them. Otherwise, support for the initiative eventually will wither and fade. Many organizations have found that it makes sense to achieve "incremental wins" and ensure they are well discussed and known to all. Based on these successes, the organization gains

momentum for continuing change. At the same time, it is vital to recognize and learn from failure or inadequate performance. Success often lies in turning around a bad situation and using acknowledged weaknesses as a point of departure for improvement. The key issue for marketing leaders is to ensure that there is a continual and steady march toward improvement, so the organization does not lose momentum.

- *Leveraging and repeating successes.* Disciplined marketing encourages us to continuously experiment in order to enhance performance and reach our objectives. Our "experiments," however, may not have a true impact unless they are rolled out on a grander scale. With this in mind, we should look for successful practices and processes that lend themselves to wider application. This principle holds true along all dimensions of marketing performance. Whether we are experimenting with new measurements, new processes, or new technologies, value multiplies as success is extended and leveraged.

Quite clearly, it is a challenge to mobilize marketing organizations and other groups that are critical to the development of customer-focused success. Initiatives are valuable in this effort; they enable us to "package" our goals and objectives within an accessible format. Initiatives are a clear, definable, and measurable set of outcomes around which organizations can rally.

It is important to note, however, that these initiatives must be embedded within a wider organizational and cultural commitment to continual improvement. Transformation is the result of a succession of efforts, activities, and initiatives that are bounded by time. But, marketing leaders must sustain, cultivate, and reinforce performance cultures that underlie these initiatives. Performance culture is a culture of continual learning, adaptation, and improvement. It is a culture of results.

PROMOTING CHANGE THROUGH LEARNING INITIATIVES

Transformational marketing leadership is based on the premise that change must be carefully and thoughtfully facilitated. This kind of leadership does not involve dissolving the organization and starting from the ground level, as revolutionaries of some previous management fads would have it. Instead, it requires a sensible way of managing necessary transitions.

Cultures are remarkably resistant to authoritarian, top-down efforts to drive change because people (particularly skilled and experienced marketing professionals) are resistant to having change forcibly thrust upon them. However, it is untrue that people are naturally resistant to change. To the contrary, most people yearn for new opportunities to advance themselves and perform with greater skill. The question is how to lead the people of the organization through necessary transitions. How do we encourage the marketing organization to adopt, internalize, and apply the critical proficiencies that underlie high performance, without making those proficiencies feel like imposed 'rules?'

How can we transform marketing without burning down the house?

One way some of our clients have approached the challenge of building a more disciplined performance culture is by introducing a more forward-looking, learning initiative.

This initiative provides a context for introducing, cultivating, and embedding the key competencies and capabilities that the organization considers important. There are several aspects of such an initiative that can help build and strengthen a performance culture, thereby perpetually enhancing the organization's ability to effectively learn, adapt, and improve. Among them are the following:

- *Communication and collaboration.* Successful leaders find ways to bring people together so they can share insights, perspectives, and practices. Regularly scheduled meetings, conference calls, brown bag lunches, and off-site events help to build and bind cultures. Some enterprises cultivate "communities of practice" that share certain interests and objectives, many cutting across departmental boundaries. To overcome the barriers of time, geography, and cost, organizations can complement on-site and in-person collaboration with the intelligent use of collaborative technology, including phones, e-mail, groupware, portals, or Web casts.
- *Coaching, mentoring, and professional development* All these can guide the organization's professionals toward excellence in performance. "If people are your most important asset, you ought to develop them," says Steve Kerr, Chief Learning Officer at Gold-

man Sachs. His group, known as Pine Street, develops executives and professionals through a blended approach of role-plays, case-studies, simulations, games, and e-learning.[1] Without such ongoing programs, too much of the organization's process knowledge can be concentrated within a few individuals. Occasionally, at Quaero, we have been asked by clients to return and rebuild data-bases or conduct training programs months after our initial involvement. This is because key individuals left the organization and took with them all institutional memory of the processes we helped establish. When this knowledge is shared throughout the organization, knowledge investments are secured. Furthermore, the ongoing exchange of information and ideas maintains a fresh perspective within the organization, keeping the enterprise poised for improvement.

- *Human capital management.* Research from Towers Perrin demonstrates that professionals gain their highest levels of performance satisfaction when their talents and skills are most productively applied. It is a virtuous cycle. Encourage, enable, and reward high performance and you tend to get more of it. That means it is vital to invest in talent-based performance management, measurement, appraisal, and feedback. As companies gain greater visibility into the result of work-related activities and behaviors, they learn how to enhance and align the performance of individuals, groups and organizations. "That's where the best companies are putting their effort," explains Thomas O. Davenport in his book *Human Capital.*[2]

Ultimately, the most significant contribution of these learning initiatives is their ability to alter the "mental maps" that guide the way marketers and others in the organization think. Companies such as Dell and Wal-Mart have mapped out and delineated the "supply side" of business in ways that have generated tremendous productivity gains.

Today, companies must turn their attention to the "demand side" of business. John Deighton, Professor of Marketing at Harvard Business School and a consultant to many large corporations, informed us that "the difference in performance between the best and the worst in areas like operations and supply chain management has probably narrowed down to a factor of two or three, but the gap between high and low performers in marketing is probably a magnitude of 10 or 15."[3]

Marketers need to rethink the maps and metaphors that have guided their efforts in the past, because those ideas have led the organization astray. In fact, marketing's current maps and metaphors distort our understanding of real-world marketing. They create unnecessary tensions and conflicts, fears, and fragmentations. Marketers must use learning initiatives to help their organization look at the world through new eyes.

CLOSING THE GAP: PERFORMING IN PARALLEL

In the preceding chapters, we have explored the various dimensions of marketing performance—including planning, effective processes, organizational alignment, measurement, information management, and technology—and have outlined their individual power. Now, it is time to speak of the value that these dimensional capabilities and competencies can generate when they are applied in tandem. Through the parallel development and execution of the various marketing proficiencies, organizations enhance their ability to engage markets and learn from experience. This is the course that enterprises must take in order to effectively close the Strategy-Execution Gap.

As we have stated, the dimensions of marketing effectiveness naturally overlap. They may have distinct properties, but their boundaries tend to blur. Planning leads to a clarification of the boundary spanning processes. In order for these processes to be enhanced, they must be tracked and measured. Also, the measurements, if they are to be defensible and credible, require information. Organizational alignment is founded upon central processes that are measured by how well they help execute strategy and attain goals. Information must be collected, housed, analyzed, and distributed through technology. The success of any one dimension, in other words, depends upon the capabilities and competencies that reside within all dimensions.

The portfolio of marketing proficiencies that we have discussed in this book must be managed with care and diligence. While other marketers lose themselves in the contextual concerns of price, promotion, place, and product, disciplined marketers recognize the importance of the structural factors that support strong performance. The Four Ps are indeed important, but their successful application depends on the dimensional proficiencies that are the foundations of all high performing marketing organizations.

Too many marketing organizations expend all their energy optimizing their advertising or marketing communication approaches. Unfortunately they lack a disciplined method to truly maximize these efforts. They may concern themselves with measurement or process, for instance, in a haphazard and inconsistent manner. They may diligently invest in technology or information assets, but their overall marketing efforts plummet because they manage these resources in a virtual vacuum, disconnected from planning processes or unaware of the efforts of other enterprise groups.

All of the dimensions in the marketing portfolio must be managed in parallel if they are to drive performance improvements and breakthroughs. With this in mind, let us return to the three phases of the Marketing Performance Improvement Cycle: *assessing, developing,* and *leveraging.* Having discussed how to apply the improvement cycle to the dimensions individually in previous chapters, we can now discuss how to apply it to the overall marketing portfolio.

Assessing the Marketing Effectiveness Portfolio

Marketing performance improvement begins with a wide ranging assessment of the various proficiencies within each marketing dimension. One must set a baseline before performance can be enhanced. With that baseline established, marketing leaders can begin to monitor the overall portfolio by assessing and reassessing it at regular intervals.

Of course, there may be trade-offs associated with the frequency and degree of measuring, tracking, and monitoring that takes place. Resources are required to monitor and assess the state of the portfolio. Therefore, the cost of monitoring at a certain frequency must be considered in relation to the benefit to be gained.

The key to success in this effort is to establish a defined and consistent assessment process. Whether the assessment occurs on an annual, quarterly, monthly, or even weekly basis, the assessment process must deepen the organization's understanding of the marketing effectiveness portfolio's current state in relation to its desired state. The more effectively the portfolio is monitored, the more one can influence its value and impact on marketing and its focused activity overall.

The objective of the assessment effort for the overall portfolio should be to determine that all dimensions are being appropriately supported. By carefully mapping the performance of all dimensions, marketers can identify—at a high level—where the progress of each dimension stands relative to that of the others. While perfect alignment is not the goal, the organization must ensure that marketing's proficiencies are not neglected. Ongoing and regular assessment should ensure that continuous progress is made in each dimension, and the entire portfolio is moving the organization from the current to the desired state. Assessing and charting its progress is essential to ensuring this improvement.

Developing the Marketing Effectiveness Portfolio

Building on our assessments of the portfolio's current state, we can determine where our investments are most necessary. As the portfolio metaphor suggests, we are managing a set of "assets" whose value will rise and fall, contributing to or detracting from the value of the whole. In this phase of the Marketing Performance Improvement Cycle, we should be considering how we can develop the dimensional capabilities and competencies that deserve the most attention or how we can develop all of them in unison.

Development most likely will require a new investment in building or buying the skills, knowledge, and resources necessary to meet objectives. In some cases, the skills and resources necessary to perform at desired levels may be available, but have not have been adequately marshaled and managed. Recent studies of global productivity suggest that active management is the most profound factor influencing productivity levels. While some have attributed productivity differentials to varying investments in technology, the latest research convincingly suggests that careful attention to goal-setting, incentives, process, and talent are more critical to the overall outcome. Such studies have profound implications for marketing effectiveness. They suggest that performance must be managed with much greater discipline and diligence if companies are to realize the outcomes they seek.

From the perspective of marketing, the development of key proficiencies is the path to performance. Marketing leaders must actively develop the portfolio of dimensional proficiencies through investment, support, and attentiveness. The sheer act of managing performance—of encouraging and applying incentives—tends to drive it to new and higher levels.

Leveraging the Marketing Effectiveness Portfolio

The value of our endeavors to enhance marketing performance must ultimately be demonstrated in measurable results. That is why it is not enough to merely assess or develop marketing proficiencies. Organizations have to actively apply these proficiencies in order to benefit from them. Marketing leaders must constantly seek opportunities to apply these key capabilities and competencies, developing them further through application. After all, we "learn by doing."

With this in mind, it makes sense to establish a "marketing effectiveness council" that is charged with managing and leveraging the key proficiencies. Different individuals within the council may have responsibility over different dimensional proficiencies. Nevertheless, it is vital that these "proficiency managers" collaborate as a team to ensure that their efforts and investments are maximized. And yes, it would be beneficial for them to report back on a regular basis, describing their efforts to leverage the capabilities and competencies that the organization has developed.

Of course, it is not merely the responsibility of these proficiency managers, "champions," or "owners" to identify opportunities to apply these growing strengths. Marketing leaders must promote this view of proficiency within the marketing organization and beyond. In such an environment, managers will not only have responsibility for achieving their key metrics, they also will be accountable for ensuring that they do so efficiently (using the right processes) and effectively (with an aligned organization). Measures of productivity and throughput become as critical as numbers of customers acquired, cost of acquisition, products sold, and other final metrics. Through such efforts, leaders can make it clear that finding new approaches to marketing effectiveness is part of "everyone's job" as much as the management of quality became a pervasive responsibility in organizations in year's past.

Delivering Results through Marketing Proficiencies

As important as the marketing effectiveness portfolio is to the organization, marketing leaders cannot allow it to become a new hammer, with the balance of the organization as a potential nail. The portfolio is not an end in itself. It is a structural or foundational framework designed to help marketing organizations perform more effectively. As such, the dimensional proficiencies within it should be applied appropriately.

Indeed, there are limits to this framework's sensible application. It is possible to measure too many activities, for instance, creating an overwhelming mix of metrics and indicators. It also is possible to spend an excessive amount of time mapping and implementing processes. In all of the dimensions, considerations of value and utility must be weighed against cost. It is important to keep the objective in mind: to enable the marketing organization to enhance the linkage between strategy and execution and free up time for creative idea generation, thereby generating greater value.

In order to perform in parallel, marketing must learn to assess, develop, and leverage all of its core proficiencies in a consistent and continuous fashion. Such parallelism, in fact, is critical to the enhancement of marketing performance and the closing of the Strategy-Execution Gap. It is all too typical for a marketing organization to focus on strategy or tactics, but fail to effectively align these activities, much less align itself with the rest of the enterprise or the true priorities of the customer.

As we focus on the structural dimensions of marketing, we discover the key proficiencies that were always necessary to perform at optimal levels. Some world-class companies have explicitly recognized these dimensions, while others have developed and applied them more intuitively. The rest of us, however, cannot rely merely on intuition. The challenge facing the next generation of marketing leaders revolves around ensuring that these proficiencies are consistently recognized, managed, and applied to deliver impressive results.

10

DISCIPLINE AND DYNAMISM

Reconciling the "Art" and "Science" of Marketing

"I believe the intellectual life of the whole of western society is increasingly being split into two polar groups. When I say the intellectual life, I mean to include also a large part of our practical life, because I should be the last person to suggest the two can at the deepest level be distinguished."

C.P. Snow, *The Two Cultures*, 1959

Marketing is in danger of being undermined by its own hackneyed and exhausted metaphors. Over the years, we have spoken of marketing as science and marketing as art, and we have drifted back and forth between these perspectives.

In the coming years, we must find a way of reconciling these views of the marketing world. World-class companies already understand the importance of this reconciliation, and they realize that these views are not fundamentally incompatible or in conflict. To the contrary, consistent, measurable results will always be impossible to achieve without compelling, creative endeavors and initiatives. The emotional power of "charismatic" brands and "engaging" experiences becomes even more important as customer choices proliferate and the pace of life quickens.

Still, one cannot perform at the highest level of one's creative powers without discipline. Creative and innovative thinking does not simply emerge out of chaos. In fact, good processes, measurements, and organizational alignment result in smoother execution and fewer arguments, and they free up time for creative development and innovation. Ultimately, the creative aspects of marketing must be managed in a disciplined and systematic way. Investments in these aspects of marketing require due diligence and attention to prior outcomes and results.

When we move beyond the long running and pointless debate of marketing as science or art, we can advance into an era of marketing in which discipline drives dynamism. This flexibility to adapt marketing strategy to rapidly competitive landscapes and evolving customer needs is an essential force in the continuing success of great companies. Dynamism is the energy, excitement, and compelling value we bring to the market. It is the gravitational pull that draws our customers close and deepens our connection to them.

DECONSTRUCTING THE ART-SCIENCE ARGUMENT

In the wake of an economic downturn, unsavory business scandals, and the lingering perception of past marketing excesses, the "scientific marketing" camp is once again on the rise. Senior marketing executives are informing interviewers that their emphasis now rests on rigor, diligence, and accountability. Large consulting firms are rolling out new practices touting "marketing as management science." One market research firm has even produced a celebrated report on the rise of "left brain marketing."[1] In order to sell their story, advocates of the scientific approach suggest that, under the influence of creatives, marketing has always lacked discipline and structure and that only now are these necessary elements being introduced. Unfortunately, such activities tend to distort our understanding of the contemporary marketing field.

Today's focus on scientific principles isn't an entirely new phenomenon. The historical truth is more complicated and interesting. Over the past century, the direction of marketing in the United States has swung back and forth like a pendulum between the "scientists" and the "artists." Whether one considers the inspirational impact of revolutionary pamphleteers, the persuasive power of traveling showmen and salesmen of the 19th century, or the impressive rise of Madison Avenue image-makers in the 20th century, it's clear that the country has a long history of vigorous, creative marketing.

But while the first half of the twentieth century may have been dominated by the rise of advertising and marketing as an undisciplined art, the post-war period saw the rise of more scientific perspectives. Research-driven advertising firms, ones eager to demonstrate the rational foundations of their work, became increasingly powerful as the American economy boomed after the Second World War. Emboldened by America's operational and logistical triumphs and the rise of science-driven industries such as pharmaceuticals and chemicals, managers embraced the concept of "planning and control." As *Fortune Magazine's* Geoffrey Colvin writes, "Managers planned and controlled pretty much everything.[2] They believed they could make people buy things with new tools like 'motivational research' ...They could plan revenues with newly developed market projections—50 years out!"

A backlash against this grey-suited, "organization-man" occurred in the late 1950s and early 1960s. Madison Avenue visionaries such as Bill Bernbach, Leo Burnett, and David Ogilvy launched the so-called Creative Revolution.[3] It was a movement that rejected a heavy reliance on market research in favor of intuition and inspiration. Collaborative teams of copywriters and art directors flourished in creative work environments. Organizations encouraged these teams to design campaigns based on simple, honest, and straightforward messages, and customer-leading creativity was more fully unleashed. "I consider research the major culprit in the advertising picture," Bernbach said. "It has done more to perpetuate creative mediocrity than any other factor."

Simultaneously, however, Theodore Levitt, Philip Kotler, and others continued to build the "rational" foundations of marketing. This new school of theorists believed that companies' traditional orientation on production or sales should shift to focus on customer satisfaction. "Management must think of itself not as producing products but as providing customer-creating value satisfactions," wrote Levitt in his highly influential essay "Marketing Myopia," which was published in 1960 in the *Harvard Business Review*.[4] "Otherwise the company will be merely a series of pigeonholed parts, with no consolidating sense of purpose or direction."

The concept of customer focus, as we know it, has endured and flourished. Customers have become central to our marketing frameworks. Indeed, Levitt's legacy finds itself sitting comfortably among today's relationship marketers, even as much of Madison Avenue remains inspired by the creative legacy of Bernbach, Burnett, and Ogilvy. I personally witnessed this struggle and evolution in my first job at BBDO in the late 1980s. That agency, which had been very heavily market research and science driven in the late '70s and early '80s, transitioned into a creative powerhouse under the leadership of Phil Dusenberry while retaining its traditional strength in customer analytics.

The embarrassing setbacks and failures that followed the boom economy of the 1990s have led us to a much more cautious, risk-averse era. Hence, we are witnessing the reemergence of self-styled marketing scientists. Image marketers, however, shouldn't take the fall for the recent excesses of marketing. After all, much of the current scientific positioning is merely appeasement—a defensive act to cover up ineptitude with fancy figuring and incomprehensible models. One might expect to see many of today's fashionable ROI marketers dismissed by their colleagues as statistical charlatans and myopic bean-counters when fashions change again.

DISCIPLINED MARKETING: RIGOR AND VIGOR

High performance marketing requires that we define and articulate marketing in terms of the *cultures* we wish to build. What qualities will those cultures embody? What types of customers do we wish to attract? It is a premise underlying this book that high performance marketing cultures must be infused with both *rigor* and *vigor*. Disciplined marketing recognizes the dynamic interplay of these two qualities. To be rigorous, one must be analytical, quantitative, diligent, and logical. To be vigorous, one must be creative, engaging, empathetic, intuitive, and full of life.

The rigor of the marketing organization is essentially reflected in its marketing effectiveness, particularly in the very rational dimensions of planning, process, and measurement. However, companies are not simply evaluated by their customers on rational terms. The customer's impressions, experience, and level of trust can be far more powerful. Brand, design, and aesthetic appeal may even become more important in an era of information overload and scarce available time.

"[M]ore people in more aspects of life are drawing pleasure and meaning from the way their persons, places, and things look and feel," writes Virginia Postrel, author of *The Substance of Style*.[5] "Whenever we have the chance, we're adding sensory, emotional appeal to ordinary function. Which computer? Which cell phone? Which trash can or toilet brush or pair of sneakers? Aesthetics has become the deciding factor in almost every product that we once considered primarily functional."

Citing brand titans such as Starbucks and Recreational Equipment, Inc., James H. Gilmore and B. Joseph Pine II argue that the "experience *is* the marketing."[6] They encourage companies to create a rich array of experiences in physical and virtual space, deepening the emotional connections that their customers have with them. Whether it's a "flagship venue" or an engaging Web site, Gilmore and Pine urge companies to market experiences in order to attract and retain valuable customers. "People have become relatively immune to messages targeted *at* them," they contend. "The way to reach your customers is to create an experience *within* them." (The case studies at the end of this chapter illustrate the truth of this statement.)

So the demand for creative, emotional, and aesthetically pleasing offerings has probably never been higher. But creative heroism is not the path to enduring success. The dot-com years were full of imaginative ideas and passionately presented visions. But where was the discipline to channel all the capital that these stars attracted? Much like supernovas, these often highly creative organizations burned brightest just before they went dark. Similarly, rigid adherence to rigorous process can be stifling. The history of business is replete with companies that grew dull, boring, and oppressively rule-bound; companies that embraced the myth of "scientific management" and quietly began to die.

In his compelling book *The Whiz Kids*, John Byrne tells the story of a group of veterans of the Army Air Force's Statistical Control Command, who were hired as a unit in 1946 to revivify the struggling empire of Ford Motor Company and, ultimately, failed.[7] The group included Tex Thornton, who later went on to found the conglomerate Litton Industries; Jack Reith, who was responsible for Ford's epic disasters, the 1957 Mercury Turnpike Cruiser and the Edsel, and later committed suicide; and Robert McNamara, who served briefly as Ford's President before becoming the United States Secretary of Defense during the Vietnam War.

While their statistical and financial engineering techniques proved quite effective in controlling costs, the members of this team tended to confine and diminish the innovative strengths of the organizations they led. As Byrnes describes it, these men were emblematic of an era in which decisions were based on "hard numbers and cold facts," where creative thought, experience, and contextual knowledge were heavily devalued. "They persuaded themselves and others that a professional manager can and must control everything without knowing anything about the products the company produces."

Disciplined marketing is not an exercise in control and micromanagement. Rather, it enables us to manage creative even innovative endeavors in a smart and sensible fashion. In successful marketing organizations, discipline and creativity are treated as mutually compatible and are even mutually dependent. The best and most enduring artists, after all, are highly disciplined individuals. Similarly, the investments we make in creative marketing endeavors also must be managed with discipline.

Extending Creativity from a Foundation of Discipline

While returns on marketing investments should be diligently assessed and measured, patience also is a virtue of the successful organization, particularly with regard to promising, yet unproven, initiatives. Disciplined marketing groups can be sensible about riskier, creative investments because they are fully aware of the limitations of trying to rigorously quantify them upfront.

Lending Tree, an Internet-based lending and reality services company, represents an example of an organization that extends its creative reach from a base of discipline. The company rigorously manages its marketing investments. "Marketing here is operations," Lending Tree President Tom Reddin told us in an interview, adding that he and his Chief Marketing Officer are "hyperfocused on the P&L."[8] This discipline enables the organization to procure Web-based advertising, radio, and television placements in a diligent fashion. Yet, it is the creative flair of the company's branding and advertising campaigns (lenders and retailers descend in droves on suburban homeowners to beg for the business), that define the company in the minds of prospective customers. Indeed, branding research suggests the company has awareness levels exceeding 70 percent among American consumers. The company's tagline, "When banks compete, you win," certainly resonates with consumers and demonstrates the potential of striking creative work to cut through in a crowded and noisy marketplace.

Similarly, Pfizer has taken a disciplined approach toward turning its market research into creative marketing and branding campaigns. "We use research to uncover customer insight and drive the next level of innovation," explains Lauri Kien Kotcher, Head of Global Brand Management for Pfizer's consumer business.[9] Diligent research provides ideas, perspectives, and findings that feed into the company's concept streams and lay the groundwork for both new products and new campaigns as part of a rigorous process.

While Pfizer's consumer business relies heavily on advertising worldwide, it also has begun to tap into more innovative marketing tactics such as launching viral campaigns which emphasize word-of-mouth referrals—a very powerful marketing approach particularly in specific segments such as urban and teen markets. Such "guerilla marketing" efforts have contributed heavily to the success of some new products such as Listerine Pocket Packs.

Discipline, as we have stated, invites and enables dynamism. It provides the foundation for a high performance marketing culture, one that is both engaged and engaging, connected and compelling, aware and alive. Disciplined marketing stops the pendulum's swing from art to science and from science to art by placing the creative aspects of it within a disciplined and comprehensive portfolio of investment options. It applies discipline to creative investments, ensuring we receive a higher, more impressive return on them.

This is not an either/or, but rather, a both/and proposition. As one highly creative and highly successful computer company has put it. "*Think different.*" Left needs right. The analyst needs the aesthete. Marketing needs rigor *and* vigor.

THE PORTFOLIO AND THE PENDULUM

Let us abandon the pendulum and return to the *portfolio* metaphor as we consider the challenge of managing creative marketing. A well-balanced portfolio tends to have a mix of investments that present different risk-reward profiles. From this perspective, we can think about investments in creative (often immeasurable or unproven) marketing endeavors as aggressive investments. Proven, quantifiable investments may fall into a more conservative, yet dependable, category.

Tomorrow's leading marketers will be those who recognize that creative, unproven marketing often needs to be assessed with different criteria than those used to assess clearly measurable investments. The results of television advertising, for example, are far less measurable than those of direct marketing campaigns. The success of these methods must be assessed according to the objectives the organization is pursuing. After all, advertisements may provide awareness or interest among a wide audience (some call it "air cover"). Direct marketing may prove to be a powerful way of generating transactions among a much smaller, targeted group. Nor are these two approaches necessarily distinct and unrelated. Companies such as Capital One and Bank of America have learned that advertising can significantly improve the lift or performance of their direct marketing efforts.

While the current frenzy of interest in ROI-driven marketing might encourage a senior executive to simply pull the plug on all marketing investments that cannot be rigorously quantified, it may instead make sense to merely rebalance the portfolio of investments.

The challenge is to manage creative investments within a disciplined portfolio, much as we have discussed in earlier chapters. Within our Marketing Initiative Portfolio framework, marketing investments can be spread around.

As discussed in Chapter 3, experimental or transformational investments may prove more difficult to measure in quantifiable terms than activities that are more familiar and recognized. Endeavors in these areas may be considered creative or potentially innovative. They may represent a higher risk, but also a higher reward than other types of investments. Furthermore, not all creative, difficult to measure investments fall into these categories. Companies may consider many of their branding and advertising activities which are often difficult to quantify, to be operational or foundational, because these activities are considered necessary to the running of the business.

With this in mind, we may decide to look at our investments through a different portfolio perspective, as shown in Figure 10.1. The Customer Engagement Cycle, that we have previously identified, offers us one vehicle for determining how to balance our portfolio of invest-

FIGURE 10.1 *The Customer Engagement Cycle*

	Awareness	Consideration	Inquiry	Purchase	Expansion
Business Objective	Breakthrough and recognition	Relevance and inclusion in decision set	Differentiate and inform through two-way sharing	Move to desired action; shared commitment	Ongoing engagement and development
Event Description	Presentation of messages and/or an initiation of contact designed to generate customer awareness of product, brand, or service	Presentation of messages and/or an initiation of contact designed to encourage prospective buyer to demonstrate interest in product, brand, or service	Exchange of information in a two-way dialogue or targeted information request	Actions designed to encourage purchase, loyalty, etc.,—leading to an exchange of value	Actions designed to encourage additional exchange of value and deepening commitment

ments. For instance, we can spread our investments out with regard to such objectives as customer *awareness, consideration, inquiry, purchase,* and *expansion.*

What one may find is that there is a high correlation between creative and hard-to-measure investments in the awareness stage, but that investments become highly quantifiable as one enters the purchase and expansion stages. Remember, one may have never reached the later stages without investing in marketing activities at the early ones.

Smart marketing investment decisions are not simply a matter of choosing the most proven and quantifiable options. Instead, they often require us to step back and develop a comprehensive understanding of investment and return, actions and outcomes. By taking a wider, more comprehensive perspective, we learn to intelligently compare alternative investment options, prioritize our initiatives in an informed way, and allocate our resources for maximum returns. The portfolio perspective provides us with a smarter, more promising way to invest in marketing.

Enhancing Creativity through Discipline

Unsurprisingly, one can expect resistance against one's efforts to infuse discipline in a creative environment, particularly when many creative groups prefer to "thrive on chaos." The myth of the "lone inventor" or the "creative genius" runs deep. Such figures always seem to be challenging the system or breaking the rules. It is rare in American culture, at least, to come across stories that celebrate the triumphant power of structure, process, and organization.

The point of disciplined creativity is not to shackle exceptional people and render them incapable of extraordinary work. Instead, the objective is to systematize creative processes, actions, and activities to realize the best possible outcome.

In his book *Jamming*, management theorist John Kao contends that managers can enhance and leverage creativity by actively supporting practices and processes that allow it to flourish.[10] "[T]he minds of gifted people are what truly distinguish one organization from another," Kao explains. "But minds alone, however prolific with fresh ideas, are nothing without processes specifically designed to translate these fresh ideas into value to products and services."

That said, one cannot assume that creativity typically takes place in a chaotic environment. To the contrary, creative marketing groups often develop very sophisticated processes to produce their work effectively. The challenge may lie in the linkages between the creative groups and the rest of the marketing organization, just as marketing often struggles to collaborate with other operational groups within the enterprise.

Organizations need a disciplined approach to ensure creative efforts are well integrated into the processes of the marketing organization and the business overall.

This approach begins with a recognition that creative marketing endeavors, whether focused on advertising and marcom or sales support or product design and development, must be managed in a systematic manner. Marketers must apply process discipline to these creative endeavors, defining and mapping out the action steps of the processes to be used, clearly delineating linkages between groups. The more visible the process, the more predictable and repeatable it becomes. Marketing leaders also must ensure that creative marketing initiatives are rigorously assessed and evaluated. This helps to guarantee that objectives are met and resources are efficiently and effectively deployed. Finally, the marketing organization must align creative efforts across the enterprise, to benefit from collaboration with others who have a stake in the outcome, including sales, product development, and partners.

Testing the Market Validity of Creative Efforts

One key way to apply disciplined thinking to creative marketing initiatives is through validation. Consider the product development process, a creative endeavor that stands to benefit greatly from the creative input of marketing. The Marketing Leadership Council has found in its research that companies where marketers possess "high levels of proficiency in the front end of the new product development process—identifying and evaluating market opportunities—outperform their peers in revenue, profit, and market share increases."[11]

Interestingly, many creative and design professionals reflexively resist efforts to "listen to the market." There is a deep strain of valid arguments that discounts customer opinions prior to a product introduction. Customers, according to this school of thought, must be led, not followed, because they don't fully understand the possibilities. As Henry Ford once said, "If we had asked the public what they wanted, they would have said 'faster horses.'" Ford's point should be duly noted. Companies should not think of themselves as merely "customer driven." To a great extent, they must be "customer driving." This is a *dynamic tension* that companies should recognize and accept. It is dangerous to be overly solicitous of one's customers just as it is perilous to ignore them altogether.

Despite concerns about the limitations of research, it is sensible to test, analyze, and validate marketing activities whenever possible. Analytically driven, direct marketers are familiar with testing campaigns to evaluate their impact. This type of diligence, however, has a place in all creative marketing activities. One cannot assume that a particular marketing message or campaign will be as well received by customers as it was by the managers and executives who signed on.

With this in mind, marketers must bring a certain level of disciplined validation to the creative endeavors themselves. It makes sense to test advertising, branding, and other creative marketing approaches in particular markets and with particular focus groups before rolling them out on a wider scale. It is impossible to know with exact precision how customers will react to a new campaign, process, or product roll-out. Companies should resist the fashionable temptation to avoid testing for fear of becoming backward-looking. The objective of testing is to assemble and assess enough solid feedback to make the next set of decisions necessary to move forward, as did the simulated test marketing models developed by companies such as BASES in the 1980s.

At times we have had to counsel clients who question the cost of testing, not just the financial outlays but also the opportunity costs of holding out markets or segments from being marketed to, as control groups. This is a very short sighted approach. Conversely, companies also should avoid overtesting, which can drain resources unnecessarily. Many companies spend vast sums on market research projects generating insights that are superfluous or could have been derived through smaller tests.

Research on creativity and innovation also suggests that many companies often fail to engage in collaborative prototyping and iteration. Too often, creative deliverables are thrown over a wall between an advertising agency and a line of business. Little effort goes into ensuring that the campaigns created are well aligned with the objectives of the business and the dynamics of targeted markets. Such collaboration will become increasingly critical in the coming years if marketing is to ensure it is maximizing the return on its investments.

Leveraging Creativity through Process Discipline

To move beyond the self-limiting view that creativity only takes place in creative departments, it is critical to recognize the imaginative and breakthrough thinking can be found throughout the marketing organization and beyond. Creativity, in other words, is everywhere, waiting to be cultivated and channeled. This creativity actually can be more fully leveraged through discipline, structure, and process.

"The opportunity to improvise and develop unique ways of working may seem like a freedom, but it is really a burden," writes management theorist Michael Hammer.[12] "It dooms people to constant turmoil over who is supposed to do what and when. Lack of process actually subverts creative work. By contrast, discipline and structure channel and leverage creative energy."

Not only does discipline liberate creatives to focus on much higher tasks, it awakens the creative potential of the organization as a whole. "Beyond the direct performance improvements, more subtle benefits accrue from introducing discipline and structure into previously chaotic environments," adds Hammer.[13] "One [such benefit] is that the work becomes more reproducible, more predictable, and less dependent on luck, heroics, and extraordinary talent."

Discipline puts creative work within a manageable frame. It enables managers to more intelligently direct resources to activities that might deliver breakthrough results. Discipline doesn't leave these possibilities to mere chance. It enables companies to manage, measure, and improve their work processes. In fact, smart managers will actively encourage their people to seek out those improvements that lie beyond current ways of thinking. In chaotic environments, resources are spread chaotically. In disciplined environments, they can be more precisely targeted to creative acts, enhancements, and even breakthroughs.

Such thinking, however, may require difficult transitions as well as new attitudes and behaviors. Individuals who have adapted to more chaotic and undisciplined environments may actively resist these transitions. Therefore, leadership becomes critical. Leaders must actively promote and reinforce the changes they hope to bring to the table. Marketing organizations will look to their leaders for clear messages of what is at stake and what level of seriousness the approach is being given. Many people are familiar with the perpetual embrace and abandonment of trendy management initiatives within their organization. Deep commitment, which no doubt should be reflected in performance appraisals, compensation arrangements, and professional development activities, will be necessary if an organization is to introduce an enduring approach to managing creativity that defies previous cultural norms.

Michael Schrage, author of the book *Serious Play*, suggests that the alignment of incentives will require new structures and performance management approaches.[14] "You cannot say, 'We want collaboration,' and then reward people based on individual job reviews," he contends, noting that it is vital to assure individuals that they are encouraged to work and perform in a collaborative manner if one wants optimal results.[15] "I have seen many of these 'collaborative issues' rapidly diminish in organizations that have instituted 360-degree job reviews." The *dynamism*—the life and spirit, character, and culture—of an enterprise will be reflected in both its most public activities and its quieter, more personal interactions. Creativity can be found in a far-reaching branding initiative or a global advertising campaign. But it also can be found in a brief, one-on-one conversation with a salesperson or a call center representative. The key is to have the necessary foundations in place to ensure that creative acts are encouraged and supported in a disciplined fashion, toward the goal of amplifying and extending the creative capacities of the enterprise. This is particularly necessary in marketing, which oversees activities such as branding, campaigns, public relations, and influences an array of other customer-facing activities.

THE DYNAMIC ENTERPRISE: ENGAGED AND ENGAGING

Marketing is now challenged to move beyond the stable and enclosed models of its conventional boundaries. For decades, the profession has been trained to *analyze, plan, implement,* and *control* its own programs. This approach promotes the notion that marketing operates semiautonomously, separate from the rest of the enterprise. At the same time, marketing mix models have long portrayed communication with the customer (and prospect) as a unidirectional act. In these models, the customer is at the end of the sender-message-receiver communication chain, and the assumption is that the advertising message will drive action on its own.

These organizational and communication models are inappropriate for our interactive, collaborative, and boundary blurring era. High performance marketing requires that we incorporate feedback and collaboration into our models, thinking, and action. While relationship marketers have had a profound impact on marketing practice over the past few decades, most have yet to *engage* their markets and customers on a truly dynamic, personal, and compelling level.

With companies having made numerous advancements on the supply side of business in recent decades, they now need to address the opportunities for "demand innovation," as Mercer consultant Adrian Slywotzky exlains.[16] According to Slywotzky, companies now can generate new growth "by expanding the market's boundaries." The opportunity to create a more *engaging* customer experience, one that is based on knowledge of the customer's present and potential value, is certainly enormous. Similarly, Slywotzky believes companies can actively leverage their product positions "as a starting point from which to do new things for customers that solve their biggest problems and improve their overall performance."

But leadership is the essential catalyst for this change. Marketing is in a powerful position to help drive these initiatives and activities, but can do so only through effective communication and collaboration with the rest of the enterprise. Marketing must align itself with senior leadership and other operational groups and facilitate the enterprise's alignment with its markets and customers.

The dynamic enterprise, one that is perceived as truly extraordinary by its customers, will have closed the Strategy-Execution Gap. On a foundation of disciplined leadership, such an organization actively learns and acts, is engaged and engaging. Marketing, for many reasons, has a central part to play in this endeavor. In the role of catalyst, marketing can energize, invigorate, and elevate the enterprise. It can reconcile discipline and dynamism.

CASE STUDY: STARBUCKS' CUSTOMER EXPERIENCE MANAGEMENT

Starbucks Coffee is an excellent example of a company that has developed highly effective marketing without following the conventional wisdom. It redefined, and some would say reinvented, the entire market for coffee in the United States and in other countries. It has a fanatically loyal group of customers who go out of their way to get their caffeine dose at Starbucks—and pay handsomely for the privilege.

At this point, I would like to make two disclosures. Firstly, I am one of those loyal customers. Secondly, Starbucks is not a Quaero client, so most of this narrative is told from the point of view of a customer, not a consultant or a marketing expert.

In the Best Global Brands by Value listing for 2004 (published by Business Week and Interbrand) Starbucks is listed as No. 98 among the most valuable brands internationally and its value is computed at $2.4 billion. Without discussing in detail the methodology of how Interbrand computes this value, we can all agree that Starbucks has become the dominant brand in coffee, with a premium image for great coffee and related drinks and products. This fact is particularly remarkable given that Starbucks does not advertise. Most people have never seen an ad for Starbucks, and the company certainly won't be found in Ad Age's list of the top 100 advertisers. Imagine that—building a great global brand without any advertising support.

Even though I have a Starbucks card and always make my purchases at Starbucks using my card (more for the convenience than for any other benefit), Starbucks does not know I exist, because they have never asked me for any personal information. The benefits I gain by registering my card on their Web site is the replacement of the lost cash value if I were to ever lose my card and the ability to automatically recharge it when the stored cash value dips below the level I specify. They collect so little data about me, yet they are able to keep me as a loyal customer, one who is an advocate and provides free word-of-mouth advertising to boot!

Imagine that: valuable customer relationships without spending a zillion dollars on CRM technology. How does Starbucks do it?

First, the brand: Starbucks has understood, better than almost any other company, the importance of *customer experience management*. This is a relatively new buzz phrase. When you walk into a Starbucks, you just don't get a cup coffee, you step into a different world. The Starbucks experience has its own language, its own currency, its own food and drink, and merchandise "souvenirs." Starbucks' willingness to invest in an ambience that is welcoming and encourages patrons to stay and linger may have been expensive, especially in places like Manhattan, but has been richly rewarded by customer loyalty and repeat business.

Marketing has been a very integral part of Starbucks' strategy to attract, retain, and grow a particular segment of customers. It is extremely careful about its image and has communicated that very strongly to its customer base. The company has linked its image brilliantly to a retail strategy and distribution in their choice of locations, of music they sell in their stores, the causes they support, the newspapers they sell, and, of course, the coffee they brew. No wonder Starbucks is recognized as a global brand leader, despite the lack of spending on formal media advertising. This outcome has been achieved in a very deliberate, effective, and sustainable fashion.

The second area where Starbucks has excelled is in customer loyalty which, in this case, is inextricably linked to the brand image. How did they achieve this without actually knowing much about their customers? Again, they realized early on that the main conduit to customers' hearts, wallets, and loyalty was through the people who served them, by the *baristas*, in Starbuckspeak.

Starbucks can serve a cup of coffee in more than 19,000 ways, offers five types of milk to place in it, and five different kinds of sweeteners. Starbucks is extremely disciplined about hiring, training, and retaining the baristas who must make those 19,000 combinations of coffee. In my own case, the baristas at my local Starbucks will often have my drink ready for me before I reach the counter. They spot me out in the line, know what I usually order and just need to swipe my card when I get up to them.

All of this adds up to a great customer experience and a willingness to pay $4 or more for a cup of coffee. More importantly, it leads to customer advocacy and word-of-mouth advertising that is worth a great deal more than any Super Bowl ad. This kind of advertisement occurs thousands of times a day at the right time and place across hundreds of communities across the world.

Starbucks' customer loyalty could be threatened, however, if changes in the job market or other competitive pressures weakened the company's ability to hold on to its baristas. Starbucks could arm itself against such threats by mining information about the coffee choices and other preferences of their frequent customers who use their card. Gathering this data is a fairly straightforward process that requires relatively minimal investment. Adding this effort to its currently successful marketing efforts could help insure Starbuck's success through a changing competitive climate.

Starbucks is an example of a company that has excelled in the art of marketing and has been highly disciplined in the execution of that art, but could probably perform even better by incorporating a bit more science as it moves forward and continues to grow.

THE MARRIAGE OF SCIENCE AND ART, DISCIPLINE, AND DYNAMISM

Marketing, by its very nature, requires constant renewal. Ideas, whether they are products or messages, become stale through repetition. When is the right time to move over to a new message? What essence of the brand must be maintained as a constant thread through the new messaging or in new products? These and other questions can be answered through the marriage of the science and art of marketing, leading to a very disciplined and dynamic marketing culture. In this book's conclusion, after summing up these and other issues detailed throughout this book, we look at some evolving trends that can be expected to have an important impact on marketing.

MARKETING FRONTIERS

The Future Is Now

Marketing, as we have seen, is under severe pressure to reinvent itself. As the marketing leadership of several world-class companies shows, this reinvention is indeed happening. Today's marketing organizations are being called on to clearly and consistently deliver results.

While there is a great deal of attention being focused on the *accountability* of marketing at present, it is important to recognize that such efforts are just a start. It is not enough for marketing to merely account for its activities, and then report its findings up the chain. What shareholders, board members, and senior executives truly want is *performance*. But performance will not be elevated without new thinking and new action. If marketing is to enhance its credibility throughout the enterprise, then it must take a series of challenging steps and embrace entirely new levels of discipline. It must build certain capabilities and competencies, and then actively leverage them to meet key objectives.

The central role of marketing, as underscored here, is to execute and enhance the strategies of the business. That is what it means to close the Strategy-Execution Gap that lies between top business objectives and front-line execution. Marketing has a powerful opportunity to step

245

into the breech, deepen the connections between company and customer, and ensure that resources are invested for maximum impact.

Enduring growth depends on the vigorous interplay of strategy and execution as detailed in—the Strategy-Execution Cycle. Marketing can ensure this cycle is continuously improved and accelerated, generating a steady flow of impressive performance gains. Its performance, as we have seen, draws on more than the strategic factors of segmentation, targeting, and positioning, or the tactical factors of product, place, promotion, and price. It also depends on the fundamental structural factors of *dynamic planning, effective processes, organizational alignment, appropriate measures, information assets,* and *enabling technologies.* Whether explicitly acknowledged or applied in an ad hoc, intuitive fashion, these structural factors have always been critical levers of marketing success. This book contends that companies have much to gain by leveraging these competencies with much greater force and consistency.

HIGH PERFORMANCE MARKETING AT WORK IN THE REAL WORLD

In the case studies presented throughout *High Performance Marketing*, you have witnessed how world-class marketers such as Harrah's, Capital One, Royal Bank of Canada, Bank of America, Procter & Gamble, Gillette, and Starbucks have grasped these new realities of marketing. These companies do not pride themselves on radical moves, expensive ad campaigns, or mysterious methods. Rather, these successful marketers bring a remarkable level of clarity, rigor, and diligence to their marketing endeavors, and they perpetually and consistently enhance performance levels. In other words, they close the Strategy-Execution Gap by leveraging the six fundamental structural factors of high performance marketing you have learned in this book.

They rely on dynamic planning approaches by setting clear goals and objectives, all the while encouraging adaptation that reflects new learning and changing market realities. Planning is a key vehicle for guiding and driving action. It enables marketers to set expectations, establish commitments, and clarify how resources can be most effectively invested. As Gillette demonstrated, planning also can be a powerful factor in a turnaround and a solid platform for continual improvement. Some marketing leaders have even begun to think of marketing investments in terms of marketing portfolios. This approach enables them to carefully prioritize investments; fully funding the initiatives that are vital and proven, while ensuring promising new initiatives also receive backing.

In addition, world-class marketers focus on visible and effective processes. Whereas many activities have been performed in an inconsistent and ad hoc fashion in the past, disciplined marketers realize that smart process provides repeatability, predictability, and leverage. Companies such as Bank of America, Dow Corning, and General Electric have relied on process discipline to ensure visibility and consistency in their marketing initiatives. Increased process visibility also brings marketing out of its solitary compartments and departments.

Rather than focusing on individual marketing tasks and subprocesses, today's organizations are emphasizing wider, cross-functional processes. Customer-facing processes transcend the immediate authority of the marketing organization, but marketing must influence these methods to realize intended results. Disciplined marketers, therefore, are taking steps to ensure that such processes are successfully designed, managed, and enhanced.

Through organizational alignment efforts, marketing spans boundaries and elevates itself within the enterprise. Marketers are forced to step outside of the rigid box that it has become in many companies, one that increasingly limits marketing initiatives to marketing communications, promotions and discounts. It strengthens its credibility by actively aligning its actions with the strategic imperatives of the CEO and the CFO, as well as the executional responsibilities of organizational groups such as sales, service, product development, manufacturing, and logistics. As our case studies have demonstrated, KeyBank's marketing organization built momentum for its marketing efforts by partnering with the CFO; SunTrust has enhanced customer profitability by more closely collaboration between marketing and call center operations; Procter & Gamble has rolled out an initiative it calls "connect and develop" that links marketers with product designers and technical specialists. Market and customer insight, a key asset that marketing is best situated to develop and marshal, is the coin of the realm in many of these alignment initiatives.

Measurement, of course, also has been a critical factor in the equation of leading performers. It is through key metrics and indicators that it defines its impact on the enterprise and drive performance improvements. While performance can be measured in both quantitative and qualitative ways, it is clear that marketers must have a measurement model to guide their actions. Moreover, they must be able to link actions and outcomes in a credible fashion. Royal Bank of Canada is a tremendous example of a company that has moved beyond merely measuring product sales to measuring the value of its various customer segments and has enhanced the profitability of its customer portfolio in the process. Disciplined marketers have embraced the opportunity to measure their own activities, vividly demonstrating to the rest of the enterprise that they are generating impressive returns.

As customer and market intelligence become increasingly vital to performance, we find world-class marketers investing in the capabilities and competencies necessary to leverage these assets and realize their full value. These marketing organizations have stressed the value of analysis and models, databases, and customer profiles. Harrah's Entertainment manages and mines its customer databases to provide a personalized experience to its individual guests, recognizing and rewarding their unique value. Companies such as Harrah's are addressing the cultural, strategic, motivational, and infrastructural challenges associated with capitalizing on their information assets. But they also make certain that the information within these assets is effectively operationalized by front-line groups such as sales and service.

Finally, we observe among disciplined marketers a sensible and sober approach toward information technology. These marketers know technology is not a magic bullet that will solve problems on its own, but they have not recoiled from employing it either. Capital One has developed a powerful "ROI Curve" that enables it to closely observe the value delivered by particular technologies and invest appropriately. Companies such as Capital One realize that marketing technology enables them to enhance the precision of their analysis, the productivity of their campaigns and the quality of customer interactions and experiences. As marketers apply the same investment and management discipline to technology investments that they are applying to marketing overall, they learn to extend and capitalize on technology's value as an enabling force.

Disciplined marketers know that they will not reach their ambitions merely by manipulating their segmentation and positioning efforts. They understand that to realize necessary levels of proficiency on this front, it is necessary to *assess, develop,* and *leverage* all of the six fundamental factors of performance. Not all marketing organizations can expect to be equally proficient across all dimensions. In fact, some factors may prove to be distinctly more important to performance within a given organization than others. Through a continuing cycle of improvement, marketing organizations identify the areas that require development as well as those that represent particular strengths. They determine where they must invest to gain the levels of proficiency they seek, and they take the steps necessary to capitalize on the strengths they have built.

Having laid the foundations for disciplined marketing, it then becomes vital to look at what it takes to be truly remarkable in the eyes of its customers. We recognize that the art and science of marketing must be reconciled to obtain this goal. Customers largely are drawn to companies based on an emotional connection and an aesthetic appeal. Companies, therefore, must demonstrate energy and vigor, creativity, and passion if they wish to thrive the coming years. As this book contends, they must be *dynamic.*

Brand titans such as Starbucks and Apple certainly embody these characteristics. One has reinvented the coffee house and extended its value as a part of its customers' social lives; one had the courage to "think different." It has not only given personality to personal computers by introducing a new look, feel, and appearance, but is now busily transforming the recorded music industry. To companies such as these, the offering–the product or the service or the experience–*is* marketing. They have breathed new life into established industries and triumphed through shared consumer enthusiasm. But these were not merely creative, right-brain endeavors. They married discipline and dynamism, bringing rigor and focus to the creation of extraordinary new products, services, and business models.

IMPORTANT SHIFTS ON THE MARKETING FRONTIER

As we look ahead, we see a number of trends playing out that can be expected to have an important impact on marketing. This book has emphasized the power of marketing to assert itself within the enterprise, playing the role of catalyst in transformative initiatives. With this in mind, it is also clear that many of these transformative efforts can be, and are, accelerated through vigorous marketing leadership. Here are some of the key "shifts" now visible on the marketing frontier.

From Markets as Targets to Markets as Forums

Whether one looks at the active customer engagement made possible by eBay or the intense customer evangelism associated with Apple, it is clear that customers increasingly are playing a vigorous role in the value creation process. Traditionally, customers were viewed as being outside the "value chain." Not anymore. Customers now actively provide advice to companies and they even promote products to their friends and colleagues. Such trends blur the traditional distinctions between company and customer, partner and supplier. "In the emerging concept of a market," write C.K Prahalad and Venkat Ramaswamy,[1] "the roles of the company and the consumer converge."

The marketing organization has a unique and privileged perspective within these emerging forums. Senior leaders look to marketing to provide insight on customer demand and behaviors. Marketing is in a powerful position to listen to the customer and enable the company to learn more effectively. Marketing should be able to facilitate the "cocreation" process. The balance of the organization, in the meantime, should be able to look to marketing to provide insight with respect to trends, patterns, opportunities, and challenges as they concern the current customer and the customer of the future.

From Product-Focus to Customer-Focus

In the coming years, many companies will struggle to find new sources of differentiation, profitability, and shareholder value. Over the past few decades, many of these gains have been discovered through operational excellence, process discipline, and quality improvements. Companies such as Dell, Wal-Mart, and General Electric have reflected the powerful efficiencies and improvements to be gained by rigorously managing the supply side of business. Now, the opportunities for improvement and innovation are greatest on the demand side of business.

But if companies are to capitalize on this underlying trend, they must increasingly organize around their customers as opposed to their products. They must be able to tell which customer segments are creating wealth and which ones are destroying it. Some farsighted thinkers suggest that companies must increasingly organize around segments and manage "customer portfolios," much as they have managed product portfolios in the past. Royal Bank of Canada, for instance, has subdivided its key segments to reflect customer needs and profitability. This enables the company to invest its resources for maximum precision and impact, ensuring that managers are dedicated to skillfully growing various customer segments.

While companies that have a direct connection to their customers (such as those in financial services, telecom, and retail) may be faster to move in this direction than companies that go to market in a more indirect fashion (such as consumer-packaged goods firms), we are likely to see movement in this direction across the board.

From Campaigns to Conversations

There's a growing sense of "resistance" among consumers, forcing marketers to rethink the traditional paradigm that relies on interruption. "Consumers today are less responsive to traditional media. They are embracing new technologies that empower them with more control over how and when they are marketed to," said Jim Stengel, Procter & Gamble's Global Marketing Officer, in a recent speech.[2] "They are making more purchase decisions in environments where marketers have less direct influence," he added, pointing to in-store, word-of-mouth, and professional recommendations as examples.

Given these circumstances, it is clear that marketing must continue to innovate and improve if it is to remain a relevant force in the enterprise. What seems clear is that organizations will increasingly redirect marketing resources from outbound, enterprise-initiated marketing campaigns to the management of inbound, customer-initiated interaction ones. By leveraging sophisticated customer databases and profiles, companies will be able to offer ever more precise care and guidance, and generate personalized offers that reflect individual preferences and priorities. As firms become more intelligent with regard to their individual customers, they can recognize particular life events, such as upcoming weddings or relocations, and engage in conversations that are appropriate to the given context and circumstances.

Such efforts promise to transcend one-to-one interactions, reaching into the community of influencers in which a prospective customer might be found. As the viral marketing of movies such as the Oscar-winning *Crouching Tiger, Hidden Dragon* and hot products like Apple's iPod suggests, there are hidden networks of potential buyers for marketers to reach and "tipping points" to be crossed if they are to realize outstanding success.

Innovative marketing, however, will depend on a disciplined approach to marketing investment. By managing marketing resources, capabilities, and competencies with intelligence and precision, marketers can open up greater opportunities to truly capitalize on these trends. They can anticipate and act, not merely sense and respond. They can drive the development of new markets as opposed to merely being market-driven.

The next era of marketing will demand greater intensity and assertiveness from the marketing organization. It will demand that marketing step out of the veiled realm of mystique and demonstrate clear performance in the full light of day. The relevance, credibility, and impact of marketing depend on embracing this disciplined perspective, and actively reporting it to the remainder of the enterprise. But it can't stop there. Marketing also must become a powerful force in the enticement and engagement of customers. It must reflect the life and excitement of the company it represents. It must open new territory on the frontiers of market dynamism.

Chapter 1

1. *Second Annual Guide to Advertising and Marketing, Fact Pack 2004 Edition, Ad Age*, 15.

2. Based on Quaero, McKinsey & Co., *Ad Age*, Marketing Leadership Council estimates.

3. Marketing Leadership Council, 2003 Marketing Investment Benchmarks, September 2003 (Washington, D.C.; Corporate Executive Board, 2003), 5.

4. Devin Leonard, "Nightmare on Madison Avenue," *Fortune*, June 28, 2004, 92-108.

5. Jim Stengel, Global Marketing Officer, The Procter & Gamble Co., "The Future of Marketing," presentation to the AAAA Media Conference, February 12, 2004.

6. Gary Singer and Chris Halsall, McKinsey & Co. white paper, "Restructuring Marketing Spending to Do More with Less," March 2002, 1.

7. In-Stat/MDR, "Segment Churn: Impact of Local Number Portability on Churn for Wireless Voice Services by Provider and Market Segment," report released Sept. 17, 2003.

8. Accenture white paper, "Marketing: Underrated, Undervalued, and Unimportant?" 4-5.

9. Forrester Consulting, "2004 Benchmark Survey of Senior Marketers." Commissioned by Unica Corp., March 2004.

10. "E-Commerce Takes Off," *Economist*, May 13, 2004, http://www.economist.com/printedition/displayStory.cfm?Story_ID=2668033.

11. Yankelovich, Inc., "2004 Marketing Resistance Survey," April 15, 2004, 4.

12. Ibid.

13. Paul F. Nunes and Frank V. Cespedes, "The Customer Has Escaped," *Harvard Business Review*, November 2003.

14. Philip Kotler, *Kotler on Marketing: How to Create, Win and Dominate Markets*, (New York: The Free Press, 1999).

15. Steve Silver, "Bring on the Super-CMO," *Strategy & Business*, Issue 31, Summer 2003.

16. Nicholas Varchaver, "Scanning the Globe," *Fortune*, May 31, 2004, 144-156.

17. Drawn from a phone interview with Andrew Abela, June 17, 2004.

18. IBM Business Consulting Services research study, "Doing CRM Right: What It Takes to be Successful with CRM," 2004, 1.

19. Manuel Ebner, Arthur Hu, Daniel Levitt, and Jim McCrory, "How to Rescue CRM," *McKinsey Quarterly*, (Copyright: McKinsey & Company, Inc., 2002 Special Edition: Technology), 50.

20. IBM Business Consulting Services research study, "Doing CRM Right: What It Takes to be Successful with CRM," 2004, 11.

21. Gary Loveman, "Diamonds in the Data Mine," *Harvard Business Review*, May 2003.

22. Britton Manasco, "Winning the 'Moneyball' Game," *1 to1 Magazine*, March 2004, 21-24.

23. Bob Woodward, *Maestro: Greenspan's Fed and the American Boom* (New York: Simon & Schuster, 2001).

24. David Dell, "The CEO Challenge: Top Marketplace and Management Issues—2002," The Conference Board Research Report (New York: The Conference Board, 2002).

25. Jennifer Pellet, "Conference Report: The Global Growth Imperative," *Chief Executive*, February 2004, Vol. 195, http://www.chiefexecutive.net/depts/conf_report/195.htm.

26. Nirmalya Kumar, *Marketing as Strategy: Understanding the CEO's Agenda for Growth and Innovation* (Boston: Harvard Business School Press, 2004), 5.

27. Drawn from an interview with Cathy Bessant, Bank of America, Charlotte, North Carolina, June 3, 2004.

28. David O. Becker, "Gambling on Customers," *McKinsey Quarterly* (McKinsey & Company, Inc., 2003, Number 2), 46-59.

Chapter 3

1. Marketing Leadership Council, 2003 Marketing Investment Benchmarks, September 2003, 5.

2. Spencer Stuart, "CMO Tenure: Slowing Down the Revolving Door," white paper, July 2004.

3. Clive Humby, Terry Hunt, and Tim Phillips, *Scoring Points: How Tesco Is Winning Customer Loyalty* (London: Kogan Page, 2003), 36-37.

4. Patricia Sellers, "Inside Procter & Gamble's Innovation Machine," *Fortune*, May 31, 2004, 166-180.

5. David O.Becker, "Gambling on Customers," *McKinsey Quarterly* (Copyright: McKinsey & Company, Inc., 2003 Number 2), 46-59.

6. Spencer Stuart, ibid.

7. Amir Hartman, *Ruthless Execution: What Business Leaders Do When Their Companies Hit the Wall* (Upper Saddle River, New Jersey: FT Prentice Hall, 2004), 41.

8. Marcel Corstjens, and Jeffrey Merrihue, "Optimal Marketing," *Harvard Business Review*, October 2003.

9. Drawn from a phone interview with Peter Klein, Gillette, August 31, 2004.

10. Rosabeth Moss Kanter, *Confidence: How Winning Streaks and Losing Streaks Begin and End* (New York: Crown Business, 2004), 86, 165-66.

11. Drawn from Gillette press release, July 29, 2004.

Chapter 4

1. Forrester Consulting, "2004 Benchmark Survey of Senior Marketers," commissioned by Unica Corp., March 2004.

2. CMO Council, "Measures and Metrics: The Marketing Performance Measurement Audit," June 9, 2004.

3. Marketing Leadership Council, 2003 Marketing Investment Benchmarks, September 2003.

4. Stephen Brown, *Marketings–The Retro Revolution* (London: Sage Publications, 2001), 39-54.

5. CMO Council, ibid.

6. Drawn from an interview with Cathy Bessant, Bank of America, Charlotte, North Carolina, June 3, 2004.

7. Drawn from a phone interview with William Moult, Sequent Partners, May 7. 2004.

8. Eric Bonabeau, "Don't Trust Your Gut," *Harvard Business Review*, May 2003.

9. Richard H Levey, "Reichheld Reconsiders," *Direct Magazine*, February 1, 2004.

10. Ibid.

11. Drawn from a phone interview with Trish Mathe, KeyBank, June 10, 2004.

12. CMO Council, ibid.

13. Christopher D. Ittner and David F. Larcker, "Coming Up Short on Nonfinancial Performance Measurement," *Harvard Business Review*, November 2003.

14. Drawn from a phone interview with Andrew Abela, Marketing Leadership Council, June 17, 2004.

15. Drawn from a phone interview with Dipak Jain, Kellogg Business School, Northwestern University, May 22, 2004.

16. Frederick F. Reichheld, "The One Number You Need to Grow," *Harvard Business Review*, December 2003.

17. Guy Powell, *Return on Marketing Investment* (RPI Press, 2002), 6.

18. Elaine M.Cummings, "Metrics Revolution," *CMO Magazine*, September 2004.

19. Stuart Agres, Stefan Daiberl, Bill Moult, and Jim Spaeth, "Maximizing Shareholder Value by Bridging the Metrics of Finance and Marketing," an unreleased white paper, 2004.

20. Pat LaPointe, "Interview: Tim Ambler of London School of Business," *MarketingNPV*, Volume 1, Issue 4, 2004, 15.

21. Robert C. Blattberg, Gary Getz, and Jacquelyn S. Thomas, *Customer Equity: Building and Managing Relationships as Valuable Assets* (Boston: Harvard Business School Press, 2001), 10.

22. Blattberg, ibid.

23. Don Peppers and Martha Rogers, PhD, *The One to One Future: Building Relationships One Customer at a Time* (New York: Currency Doubleday, 1993).

24. Don Peppers and Martha Rogers, PhD, "The New Accountability: An Open Letter to Stock Market Analysts," *1 to1 Magazine*, May/June 2004, 49-50.

25. Larry Seldin and Geoffrey Colvin, *Angel Customers & Demon Customers: Discover Which Is Which and Turbo-Charge Your Stock* (New York: Portfolio, 2003), 5.

26. Gary Loveman, "Diamonds in the Data Mine," *Harvard Business Review*, May 2003.

27. Britton Manasco, William S. Hopkins, and Carter J. Lusher, "CRM Redefined: Beyond the Front Office and out to the Customer," Knowledge Capital Group research report, Summer 2000.

28. V.C. Narayanan, "Customer Profitability and Customer Relationship Management at RBC Financial Group," Harvard Business School case study, March 25, 2002.

29. Ibid.

Chapter 5

1. Yankelovich Inc., "2004 Marketing Resistance Survey," April 15, 2004.

2. Jim Stengel, Global Marketing Officer, The Procter & Gamble Co., "The Future of Marketing," presentation to the AAAA Media Conference, February 12, 2004.

3. Drawn from an interview with Cathy Bessant, Bank of America, Charlotte, North Carolina, June 3, 2004.

4. Presented at the CRM Association of Chicago, Quarterly meeting, March 10, 2005.

5. Pat LaPointe, "ServiceMaster: Voice of the Customer Says, 'It's OK to Raise Prices,'" *MarketingNPV*, Volume 1, Issue 4, 2004.

6. Pat LaPointe, "Making Six Sigma Work for Marketing," *MarketingNPV*, Volume 1, Issue 4, 2004.

7. Drawn from an interview with Rose Corvo, Bank of America, Charlotte, North Carolina, June 22, 2004.

8. Pat LaPointe, "Interview with Scott Fuson, Dow Corning," *MarketingNPV*, Volume 1, Issue 4, 2004.

Chapter 6

1. CMAT, "State of the Nation II: 2002," an ongoing global study of how companies manage their customers.

2. Mohanbir S. Sawhney, "A Manifesto for Marketing," *CMO Magazine*, Summer 2004.

3. Jerry Noonan, "Marketing Leadership—Good to Great," Spencer Stuart Web site, http://www.spencerstuart.com/ArticleViewer.aspx?PageID=10096&ArtID=4074647.

4. Drawn from an interview with Meheriar Hasan, Wells Fargo, San Francisco, California, June 23, 2004.

5. William Thompson, "Market the Marketing Department," *CMO Magazine*, Summer 2004.

6. Drawn from a phone interview with Andrew Abela, June 17, 2004.

7. Forrester Research, Inc., Anderson/Ragsdale, "Why Marketing Should Own the Contact Center," April 9, 2004.

8. Drawn from an interview with Karen R. Haefling, KeyBank, Cleveland, Ohio, July 21, 2004.

9. Drawn from an interview with Greg Holzwarth, SunTrust Bank, Atlanta, Georgia, May 18, 2004.

Chapter 7

1. Marketing Leadership Council, "Boosting Returns on Customer Data Investments," November 2002, 6.

2. Drawn from an interview with Tom Graham, Mutual of Omaha, Omaha Nebraska, June 7, 2004.

3. Britton Manasco, "Winning the 'Moneyball' Game," *1 to1 Magazine*, March 2004, 21-24.

4. Ibid.

5. Yankelovich Inc., "2004 Marketing Resistance Survey," April 15, 2004.

6. Gary Loveman, "Diamonds in the Data Mine," *Harvard Business Review*, May 2003.

7. David O. Becker, "Gambling on Customers," *McKinsey Quarterly* (Copyright: McKinsey & Company, Inc., 2003, Number 2), 46-59.

8. Drawn from a phone interview with Peter Klein, Gillette, August 31, 2004.

9. Bob Thompson, "Tesco Shines at Loyalty," *CRM Guru*, April 1, 2004.

10. Clive Humby, Terry Hunt, and Tim Phillips, *Scoring Points: How Tesco Is Winning Customer Loyalty* (London: Kogan Page, 2003), 4.

11. Britton Manasco, "Winning the 'Moneyball' Game," *1 to1 Magazine*, March 2004, 21-24.

12. Ibid.

13. Eric K. Clemons and Matt E. Thatcher, "CapitalOne: Exploiting Information-Based Strategy," *Proceedings of the 31st Hawaii International Conference on System Sciences (HICSS '98)*, published by the IEEE Computer Society, 1998.

14. Martha Rogers, PhD, "CMO vs. CIO: Who Wins the Budget Battle?," *INSIDE 1 to1*, May 24, 2004.

15. Ibid.

16. Aelera Corp research report, 2003 Marketing and IT Executive Survey, June 17, 2003.

17. Ibid.

18. Drawn from a phone interview with Trish Mathe, KeyBank, June 10, 2004.

19. Christopher Koch, "AT&T Wireless Self Destructs," *CIO Magazine*, April 15, 2004, http://www.cio.com/archive/041504/wireless.html.

20. Ibid.

Chapter 8

1. Otis Port, "Virtual Prospecting," *Business Week*, March 23, 2001.

2. Britton Manasco, "New Technology Helps Marketers Engage Customers and Build Profitable Relationships," *CRM Project, Volume 3*, October 30, 2002.

3. James J. Jiang, "Software Project Risks and Development Focus," Project Management Journal, March 2001, Volume 32, Issue 1.

4. Barney Beal, "Forget the Failures, IDC Says CRM Delivers," *SearchCRM.com*, February 3, 2004, http://searchcrm.techtarget.com/originalContent/0,289142,sid11_gci948330,00.html.

5. Manuel Ebner, Arthur Hu, Daniel Levitt, and Jim McCrory, "How to Rescue CRM, *McKinsey Quarterly* (Copyright: McKinsey & Company, Inc., 2002 Special Edition: Technology), 50.

6. Dan Merriman, "Driving Quantifiable Value from IT: A Comprehensive Approach," a white paper from Chapin Consulting, 2004.

7. Ibid.

8. Scott Nelson, VP Distinguished Arafat, Gartner, Inc., "The Nine Ways in Which CRM Will Change," January 15, 2004.

9. Drawn from transcripts of the National Center for Database Marketing Winter Conference in Orlando, Florida, December 4-5, 2003.

10. Ray Schultz, "Capital One's High Tech ROI Curve," *Direct Magazine,* January 1, 2001.

Chapter 9

1. Kellye Whitney, "Steve Kerr: Managing the Business of Learning," *Chief Learning Officer Magazine.* August 2004, 34-37.

2. Thomas O. Davenport, *Human Capital: What It Is and Why People Invest in It* (San Francisco: Jossey-Bass, Inc., 1999).

3. Drawn from an interview with John Deighton, Harvard Business School, Durhan, North Carolina, May 11, 2004.

Chapter 10

1. Eric Schmitt, "Left Brain Marketing," Forrester Research, April 6, 2004.

2. Geoffrey Colvin, "A Concise History of Management Hooey" *Fortune Magazine,* June 28, 2004, 166-176. © Time, Inc. All rights reserved.

3. Stephen Brown, "Marketing—The Retro Revolution," London: Sage Publications, 2001, 31-32.

4. Theodore Levitt, "Marketing Myopia," Harvard Business Review, 38 (4), 1960.

5. Virginia Postrel, "Why Buy What You Don't Need?" *Innovation Magazine,* Spring 2004, 31-36.

6. James H. Gilmore and B. Joseph Pine II, "The Experience *Is* the Marketing," white paper produced by Strategic Horizons LLP, 2002.

7. John Byrne, *The Whiz Kids: The Founding Fathers of American Business—And the Legacy They Left Us* (New York: Doubleday, 1993).

8. Drawn from an interview with Tom Reddin, Lending Tree, Charlotte, North Carolina, August 19, 2004.

9. Drawn from an interview with Lauri Kien Kotcher, Pfizer, Morris Plains, New Jersey, June 1, 2004.

10. John Kao, *Jamming: The Art and Discipline of Corporate Creativity* (New York: Harper Business, 1997), 1.

11. Marketing Leadership Council, 2004 Marketing Investment Benchmarks, September 2003, 34.

12. Michael Hammer, *The Agenda: What Every Business Must Do to Dominate the Decade* (New York: Crown Business, 2001), 96.

13. Ibid, 97.

14. Michael Schrage, *Serious Play: How the World's Best Companies Simulate to Innovate* (Boston: Harvard Business School Press, 2000).

15. Michael Schrage, "The Ethology of Innovation," *Reveries Magazine*, March 2001, http://reveries.com/reverb/marketing_strategy/schrage/index.html.

16. Adrian Slywotzky and Richard Wise with Karl Weber, *How to Grow When Markets Don't* (New York: Warner Books, 2003), 15-16.

Conclusion

1. C.K. Prahalad, and Venkat Ramaswamy, *The Future of Competition: Co-creating Unique Value with Customers* (Boston: Harvard Business School Press, 2004).

2. Jim Stengel, Global Marketing Officer, The Procter & Gamble Co., "The Future of Marketing," presentation to the AAAA Media Conference, February 12, 2004.

Share the message!

Bulk discounts
Discounts start at only 10 copies and range from 30% to 55% off retail price based on quantity.

Custom publishing
Private label a cover with your organization's name and logo. Or, tailor information to your needs with a custom pamphlet that highlights specific chapters.

Ancillaries
Workshop outlines, videos, and other products are available on select titles.

Dynamic speakers
Engaging authors are available to share their expertise and insight at your event.

Call Dearborn Trade Special Sales at 1-800-621-9621, ext. 4444, or e-mail trade@dearborn.com.

Dearborn™
Trade Publishing
A **Kaplan Professional** Company